D1561681

The American Discovery
of Europe

The American

Discovery of Europe

JACK D. FORBES

UNIVERSITY OF ILLINOIS PRESS · URBANA AND CHICAGO

Library of Congress
Cataloging-in-Publication Data
Forbes, Jack D.
The American discovery of Europe /
Jack D. Forbes.
p. cm.
Includes bibliographical references and index.
ISBN-13: 978-0-252-03152-6 (cloth : alk. paper)
ISBN-10: 0-252-03152-0 (cloth : alk. paper)
1. Indians of North America—Transatlantic
influences. 2. Indians of North America—First
contact with Europeans. 3. Indians of North
America—Migrations. 4. Europe—Discovery
and exploration. 5. North America—Discovery
and exploration. I. Title.
E98.T73F67   2007
917.04'11—dc22   2006015295

Dedicated to

Grandson

Jonathan Patrick "Jack" O'Hearn

Contents

Acknowledgments

I began collecting material relating to this book almost two decades ago, especially in connection with my research on African-Native American historic relations. I am indebted to many great libraries, such as the Bodleian of Oxford, the British Library, the Royal Dutch Library, the University of Leiden Library, the Portuguese National Library, the National Library of France, and many others in the United States. I also have corresponded with, or visited, numerous individuals in many museums and universities, especially in England, Cornwall, Wales, Ireland, Scotland, Denmark, Norway, Iceland, Canada, the Azores, Spain, the Faeroes, France, and the Netherlands.

I wish to express my deep gratitude to each and every curator, scholar, and museum worker who responded to my requests for advice, information, or assistance. Their names will largely be found in the bibliography. I also wish to thank the numerous librarians who have assisted my search for obscure sources, and especially the staff in the Interlibrary Loan Office at the University of California, Davis.

My work has also been assisted by several colleagues who have helped check out my translations from Latin, especially Professor David Traill, and others who assisted me with translating Elizabethan English script, especially Professor Winfried Schleiner; however, any errors are mine.

I am sure that I have incurred many other debts that I hereby acknowledge with grateful thanks. I need to especially thank my Native American Studies colleagues and students at the Davis and Berkeley campuses of the University of California for listening to me speak many times about "the American discovery of Europe." I especially wish to thank my wife, Carolyn L. Forbes, for her constant support and helpful criticism.

My thanks also go to those who have assisted my research as student assistants, and especially Joachim Roschmann and Anita Green. Those helping me with word processing deserve mention also, including Jane Foster and The Secretariat of Davis, California.

The American Discovery
of Europe

Introduction

PICTURE GIANT TURTLES from the Caribbean following the Gulf Stream to the coasts of Cornwall and other parts of Europe, diving occasionally to feed upon jellyfish as they make their epic journeys. Picture also Ancient American mariners, perhaps from the Caribbean or the east coast of North America, also following the Gulf Stream in dugout boats, large and small, reaching places as diverse as Ireland, Holland, and Iberia. Visualize the surprise of Christopher Columbus when he actually met two such Americans, a man and a woman, at Galway, Ireland, some fifteen years before making his famous voyage of 1492.

The story of Ancient Americans as seafarers, mariners, and navigators is, for me, a fascinating although often overlooked aspect of history. Evidence presented here will show that American Indians were builders of great boats, up to almost one hundred feet in length in the Caribbean, and were outstanding students of the ocean's currents, storms, winds, and resources. The epic story of American seafaring includes maritime cultures of northeastern North America, fishing at sea for challenging prey such as swordfish, developing advanced toggling harpoons as early as 7,500 years ago, and evolving the "Red Earth" culture that may have spread as far as Europe.

The story of ancient seafaring also includes the daring voyages of Eskimo (Inuit) groups from Greenland and Labrador using ingeniously designed kayaks and larger umiaks, voyages that took them along the coasts of Greenland, sometimes passing underneath huge ice mountains arching over the coastline and always facing terrible obstacles from storms and drifting ice. Unbelievably perhaps, intrepid Inuit kayakers show up in the waters of England, Scotland, and elsewhere, whether arriving directly from America or escaping from European whaling vessels.

Along the coasts of South America, too, our story includes seafaring by nations such as the Caribs and Tupi-Guarani, with large dugouts of their own and with ocean rafts also being utilized. And our story would be incomplete without reference to the impressive freight-rafts used along the Pacific Coast and their counterparts in the Caribbean and Atlantic. Sails were often used both on rafts and in canoes (*canoas*) and pirogues (*piraguas*). Early sails seem to have been made of palm matting (or other fibrous material on Lake Titicaca) fixed to a pole mast with tough cording made from plant fibers.

Foreign visitors were incredibly impressed with American maritime ability and technology, whether in the waters of Greenland in the north, or south to the Caribbean and South America. In the latter areas huge trees with durable wood made it possible to manufacture boats of incredible size and flexibility, boats whose finished width was far greater than that of the original tree, since gradual pressure carefully applied allowed the hull to be expanded outward. Similarly, planking was often used to increase the height of the vessels. The Spaniards counted up to almost one hundred oarsmen in some vessels and remarked upon the protection given to the boats when beached by means of onshore shelters especially erected for that purpose.

We can assume, I believe, that boat building of that type extended back many centuries or even millennia. In the far north also it would appear that watercraft were being manufactured several thousands of years ago. Thus there is a long time period available for voyages both within American waters as well as across the Atlantic.

Our story also includes an examination of ancient migrations, theories of human origins, and evidence relating to the beginnings of human life in the American hemisphere. These fascinating topics must be dealt with in part because some scholars have argued for a great antiquity for Homo sapiens (modern humans) in America and even that migrations took place to Europe from America tens of thousands of years ago. Since our topic is the American discovery of Europe, we are compelled to look at such theories, however unpopular they may be in current anthropological circles.

In telling the story of American travel, one must touch also upon the activities of Europeans, since such activities often result in Native Americans arriving in Europe, usually as captives but sometimes as ambassadors, guests, entertainers, and curious visitors. In this connection our story includes evidence relating to possible Norse activity in carrying at least some Americans to Europe up to five centuries before 1492. Possible ancient contacts from Europe are also examined, such as alleged Solutrean-period spear-point-makers crossing the Atlantic in the Pleistocene, as well as later Roman, Irish, and other possible visitors from east to west.

Another fascinating possibility resulting from contacts across the oceans has been the spread of diseases. In this context, the story must include the theory that early Norse encounters spread disease epidemics to the Dorset people of Labrador and Newfoundland. The apparently sudden disappearance of Dorset culture, the later decline and abandonment of great American cities such as Cahokia, Illinois, and similar events in Mesoamerica suggest that diseases may have been introduced by pre-1492 European or other contacts, or by Americans returning from across the oceans. It is difficult to explain the wholesale disappearance of cultures, cities, and peoples without considering the likelihood of diseases carried in both directions (as may have been true in the case of syphilis).

The spread of plants from one region to another has also been considered possible evidence for early inter-continental contacts. The story of America's acquisition of many plants of possible Southeast Asian or African origin is beyond the scope of this work, but references will be made to the movement of flora and foods from America to Europe and the Mediterranean region.

One of the great mysteries of the North Atlantic has been the question of what happened to the Norse colonies in Greenland. The European settlers seem to have disappeared between the 1400s and 1700s and several theories have been developed to attempt an explanation, including climatic deterioration, cultural stagnation, and pirate raids. Our story will shed light upon the dramatic disappearance of the Norse, showing that some became Americanized, intermixing with Inuits and Beothuk people of Newfoundland, but with a number of their descendants ending their lives as slaves in Europe and even South America.

After 1492 the majority of Americans arriving in Europe, the Canary Islands, and the Mediterranean came as captives. In spite of some records that shed light upon their existence in cities such as Sevilla and Valencia, we actually know very little of their fate. They must have had a decided genetic impact upon the populations of Iberia and doubtless many were sold, by the Portuguese especially, to other parts of Europe. We know also that some reached North Africa (as well as West Africa) and Britain, but as of yet, little is known about possible Portuguese and Spanish sales of slaves to Germany and the Baltic.

Taken together, the pre- and post-1492 periods offer the possibility that many Europeans have a trace of American ancestry, enough to complicate, perhaps, the work of geneticists seeking to trace human history by means of blood markers and DNA characteristics. I think, however, that the heart of our story must consist in the skill, courage, and adventurousness of these Americans who set sail on the high seas in kayaks of skin, dugouts of wood, great rafts, dugouts joined together, and even, on the coast of California, in the *tomol* boats of sewn-together planks. These Ancient Americans were sailors and explorers, even in the coldest and most dangerous of seas. Neither the frigid climate of northern Greenland nor the hurricane-stirred waters of the Caribbean succeeded in blocking their setting out to sea for food, trade, and love of adventure.

Francis Bacon, in his "New Atlantis" (ca. 1623), has a spokesperson for the mythical Pacific island of Bensalem relate the story of how the ancient Americans had very large fleets sailing the seas.

> About 3,000 years ago, or somewhat more, the navigation of the world (especially for remote voyages) was greater than at this day . . . and the great Atlantis (that you call America) which have now but junks and canoes, abounded then in tall ships . . . that the said country of Atlantis, as well that of Peru, then called Coya, as that of Mexico, then named Tyrambel, were mighty and proud kingdoms in arms, shipping and riches: so mighty, as at one time . . . they both made two great expeditions; they of Tyrambel through the Atlantic to the Mediterranean Sea; and they of Coya through the South Sea upon this our island.

Allegedly, none of the Mexicans were able to return to America from that expedition, and about a century later Atlantis-America was largely destroyed by great inundations. "So you see, by this main accident of time, we lost our traffic with the Americans, with whom of all others . . . we had most commerce."[1]

As we shall learn, Bacon's fable was not so wildly improbable as some might have supposed!

I.

Americans across the Atlantic: Galway and the Certainty behind Columbus's Voyage

SOMETIME DURING THE 1470S a group of Native Americans followed the Gulf Stream from the Americas to Ireland. We don't know if they were from the Caribbean region or from North America. We don't know if their journey was intentional or if they were driven eastward by a storm. What we do know is that two or more Americans, at least a man and a woman, reached Galway Bay, Ireland, and were there seen by Christoforo Colomb (Columbus) long prior to his famous voyage of 1492.[1]

This momentous event, largely ignored by white historians, marks a beginning of the modern age, since it is precisely because of this experience that Columbus possessed the *absolute certainty* that he could sail westward to Cathay (Katayo or China) and India.

It is true, of course, that Columbus later learned of many arguments favoring the possibility of being able to sail directly westward from Europe to Asia. Most of these arguments were based upon logic, though, and not upon actual, concrete evidence. They were arguments derived from books that Columbus studied and annotated or from conversations and correspondence.

It is significant that all of the "hard" evidence Columbus had learned about originated with the actions of Americans or of the American environment itself. That is, the most concrete evidence that a land lay directly to the west of Europe and the offshore islands (such as the Azores) was derived from the drifting of American seacraft to the Azores, from the discovery of American bodies washed ashore, and from the arrival of carved wood and natural objects (driftwood, logs, seeds, reeds, and debris) driven by currents and winds from the west. Columbus learned of them second hand. He did not see them himself, but learned of them from other persons.

Columbus also read books, such as *Historia rerum ubique gestarum* of Aeneas Sylvius Piccolomini (Pius II), that "Indians" had been driven by storms to Europe. This was important evidence to him. He wrote in the margins of his copy of *Historia rerum,* opposite the reference to Indian vessels reaching Germany with people and merchandise: "Si esset maximam distanciam non potuissent venire cum fortunam sed aprobat esse prope." Translated: "If it was an extremely great distance [between India and Germany] the vessels could not pass without ill fortune; but this proves it is near at hand."

This remark shows that Columbus was carefully studying Aeneas's *Historia* as part of his examination of the feasibility of sailing westward to Asia. It also proves that Columbus was quite interested in the evidence that Indians could sail to the coasts of Europe; but what a difference between reading of that in a book and actually seeing Indians in the flesh with one's own eyes!

Columbus wrote also in the margins of Piccolomini's *Historia rerum* the following incredibly significant comment: "Homines de catayo versus oriens venierunt. Nos vidimimus multa notabilia et specialiter in galuei ibernie virum et uxorem in duabus lignis areptis ex mirabili persona."[2] All of Columbus's notes in Piccolomini's *Historia rerum* were written in a very late Latin with terms that are not always clear, but the first part of the preceding note reads unmistakably: "People from Katayo came towards the east. We saw many notable things and specifically in Galway, Ireland, a man and wife." The note then goes on to use late Latin terms that are presented in almost shorthand manner and that have been interpreted variously. One author translates "in duabus lignis areptis ex mirabili persona" as "deux personnes accrochíes à deux épanes, un homme et une femme, une superbe créature"; that is, "two persons hung on two wrecks, a man and a woman, a superb creature."[3]

Another author translates the same phrase quite differently as "un homme et une femme de grande taille dans des barques en dérive," or "a man and a woman of great stature [or well-built] in boats adrift."[4] Samuel Eliot Morison presents us with still a different interpretation, as "a man and a woman taken in two small boats, of wonderous aspect."[5]

A fourth translator states "Hombres de Catayo vinieron al Oriente. Nosotros hemos visto muchas cosas notables y sobre todo en Galway, en Irlanda, un hombre y una mujer en unos leños arrestados por la tempestad de forma admirable." [People from Katayo came to the east. We have seen many notable things and especially in Galway, in Ireland, a man and a woman on some wood dragged by the storm, of admirable form.][6]

The problem with Columbus's Latin is that *duabus lignis* means literally "with two woods" or "with two timbers or logs." *Lignis* does not specifically mean either boat or wreck. The most logical conclusion is that *lignis* was used to refer to two dugout logs, to Native American–style *piraguas* or *canoas* as found from South America northward to Virginia and Massachusetts. Europeans would have lacked a word, other than log, to describe a solid wood boat. (Columbus later used the Arab term *almadía* for such craft.) Incidentally, this use of *lignis* confirms that the people of Katayo were indeed from America and not "flat-faced Finns or Lapps," as Morison suggests. People from the north would not have been going in an easterly direction and they would not have had log boats. Moreover, they would not have been drifting on logs either, since the currents of that area came from America to Galway and would have carried any Sami or Finnish drifters to the far north of Norway, not to Ireland.

Americans in various stages of manufacturing a dugout boat. "Der Landschafft Virginia," in Theodor De Bry, *America 1590* (Munich: Verlag Konrad Kolbl, 1970), plate XI.

A complete translation has to also deal with the term *areptis,* which might be related to *repto* (to creep or crawl) or is the equivalent of Spanish *arrastrar* (to drag), but which more likely is related to *arreptum,* to get into one's possession. Thus the complete text of Columbus should read: "People from Catayo towards the east they came. We saw many notable things and especially in Galway, Ireland, of a man and wife with two dugout logs in their possession, of marvelous form."[7]

This, then, is perhaps the most exciting piece of writing ever composed by Columbus and one of the most significant paragraphs in the history of the Atlantic world. With this we have solid, indisputable evidence that Columbus and others had seen Native Americans at Galway on the west coast of Ireland and that the Americans had arrived from the west going towards the east. Columbus probably saw the Americans in 1477 and it seems very likely that this was the event that compelled him, a few years later, to begin actively preparing for a voyage to the west.

The visit, then, of the Americans to Galway in the 1470s was no mere isolated incident. It forms part of a chain of causation leading directly

The pre-European use of rafts and sails along the Panama and South American coasts. From Girolamo Benzoni, *History of the New World* (London: Hakluyt, 1857), 6.

to the 1492 Columbus voyage and, indeed, forms one of the most important links in that chain *because it was Columbus's only firsthand experience of America prior to 1492.*

But, of course, Columbus referred to the people he saw at Galway as being from Katayo (Cathay). He did not call them "Indians," although from the location of his note in the *Historia rerum* it is clear that he was thinking of Indians when he wrote about people from Katayo (since he had been discussing the earlier arrival of Indians in Germany immediately before).

Let us now proceed to examine what Columbus meant by Katayo, as well as determine when he made his visit to Galway and when he wrote his comments in the margin of the *Historia rerum.*

It has generally been supposed that Columbus visited Galway in 1477 because he himself states that he sailed northwards to the vicinity of Thule (Iceland?) in February of that year. Segundo de Ispizúa supposes that the Galway visit occurred in 1472, but this is unlikely as Colombo is witness to a will in Italy on March 20, 1472, and on August 26 he contracted with

Mode of navigating in the Northern (Caribbean) Sea. From Girolamo Benzoni, *History of the New World* (London: Hakluyt, 1857), 6.

a wool merchant there. Almost a year later we again learn of him join-
ing with his family in the sale of a horse. There are gaps from the fall of
1470 through early March 1472, but he would have been only nineteen to
twenty-one years old and very possibly was learning the weaver's trade
rather than that of a sailor.[8]

It is much more likely that Colombo sailed to northern waters only after
being shipwrecked in Portugal in the summer of 1476, since the Portuguese had a well-established trade with Galway. Moreover, the Genoese
do not seem to have traded directly with Galway and their shipping was
at risk due to the same kind of naval battle that had resulted in Colón's
swimming to the Portuguese coast. Morison asserts that "there is no reason to doubt that Columbus made a voyage to Galway and Iceland in the
winter of 1476–1477 . . . and returned to Lisbon by spring."[9]

Columbus was probably only a common seaman in early 1476 and, most
likely, went to Galway and Thule in the same capacity. In 1478 he was
placed in charge of a shipment of sugar to the Madeira Islands, indicating
perhaps some literacy. In later years he learned to read and write in Latin
and Castilian, but we can be reasonably certain that he took no written
notes at Galway and that he depended upon memory for the note he
made probably four years later.[10]

It seems likely that Colombo became interested in exploration and
cosmography after his visit to Galway and Thule, and after living in the
Madeira Islands and Lisbon between 1478 and the early 1480s. But it was
probably after he moved to Lisbon that he began to acquire books and to
make notes in their margins. According to Morison, he was ready to make
his first proposals to the king of Portugal in 1484 and 1485. By 1486 he
was ready to present his arguments to Spanish officialdom. Of course, he
continued to do research until January 1492, when the Spanish sovereigns
finally accepted his plan, as well as later.[11]

Our first solid evidence of Colombo's investigations occurs in relation
to his engaging in correspondence with Paolo dal Pozzo Toscanelli, an
Italian physician and cosmographer who accepted the reports of Marco
Polo to the effect that Asia extended eastwards for a far greater distance
than had been previously believed. Columbus was able to obtain an introduction to Toscanelli and the latter sent him a copy of his letter of 1474
to Fernâo Martins, the contents of which relate directly to Colombo's
later ideas about Katayo and Cipango (Japan). Morison states that the
correspondence with Toscanelli had to have been concluded before May
1482, when the latter died.[12]

It is significant that Colombo's annotations make frequent reference to the Great Khan (the ruler of the Mongol Empire that included all of China and surrounding regions) and to "Cataio." For example, there are at least eighteen specific marginal notes on the Great Khan. Thus the reports of Marco Polo, partly as interpreted by Toscanelli, were apparently in Colombo's mind when he made his margin notes.

The most important books written in by Colombo were Pierre d'Ailly's *Ymago Mundi* and Aeneas Sylvius Piccolomini's *Historia rerum ubique gestarum*. Piccolomini's work was first published in Venice in 1477, and Columbus's copy was of that first edition. Pierre d'Ailly's *Ymago Mundi* was probably first printed in 1480–83, although written in 1410–14 and available in manuscript copies at libraries before 1480. Colombo's copy had no date of publication, but one annotation within refers to "this year of 1488," which leads one to affirm that the copy was obtained at least by that year. Because Columbus had the reputation of being a bookseller we might assume that he obtained his *Ymago Mundi* as soon as it was printed, between 1480 and 1483.[13]

It seems quite likely that Colombo wrote most or all of his marginal notes in Piccolomini prior to about 1485, while his copy of d'Ailly was still being written in up to 1488 and even 1491 in one case. All notes in these books precede his voyage of 1492, although certain other books were being written in after his voyages to the Caribbean.

I believe that the note on Galway was written before he had an opportunity to study the Toscanelli letter of 1474 (received, presumably, by 1482). This is because it can be argued that Colombo's thinking about "the Indies" (a term already used in 1375 on the famous Catalan map) went through two major phases: (1) a Great Khan-Katayo phase; and (2) a Great Khan-Katayo-Cipango phase.

The Catalan map of 1375 gives great prominence to "Catayo" and makes it the most important feature of east Asia. Cipango is not shown. Colombo's notes in both Piccolomini and d'Ailly refer to the Great Khan (eighteen times in Piccolomini) to "Kataium" and "Cataio," to Seres (a synonym for Katayo or China), to India and to India's geographical relationship to Spain, and to other parts of Asia; but Cipango (Japan) is not a feature of any of the notes for these two books, even though d'Ailly does make a reference to the island of Cyampagu. This then constitutes Colombo's first phase, when he was interested primarily in Katayo and India.[14]

It is known that Colombo was studying his copy of Piccolomini in 1481, when he wrote that year as a current date in the margin. I believe that it is at that time also that he wrote the note about Galway because presumably by 1482 he had received a copy of the Toscanelli letter to Martins. A copy of the letter in Colombo's handwriting was found in his copy of Piccolomini's *Historia rerum* and both are now located in the Biblioteca Colombina of Sevilla, as are his other books.

In the letter, Toscanelli refers to a chart that he had drawn showing Zaiton as a major port (as did the Catalan map of 1375) in the region of the Great Khan. "His seat and residence is for the most part in the province of Katay." He goes on to state:

> From the city of Lisbon westward in a straight line to the very noble city of Quinsay [Hangchow] 26 spaces are indicated on the chart. . . . This city is in the province of *Mangi,* evidently in the vicinity of the province of Katay, in which is the royal residence of the country.
>
> But from the island of Antilia [a mythical island], known to you, to the far-famed island of *Cippangu* [Japan], there are 10 spaces. That island is very rich in gold, pearls, and gems; they roof the temples and royal houses with solid gold. So there is not a great space to be traversed over unknown waters.[15]

The Toscanelli-Martins letter probably led Colón into his second phase, one where Cipango became almost as important as Katayo as an objective and where provinces and cities such as Mangi, Zayton, and Quinsay were frequently on his mind. This was the phase he was in during his voyages from 1492 to 1504.

I believe that Colón stated that the Americans whom he met in Galway in 1477 were from Katayo because, at the time the note was written, he was thinking of Katayo as being the most prominent place directly to the west of Ireland and Spain. After 1482 one could argue that he might well have referred to the Americans as being from Cipango because that island, which was supposed to have been very large, was located by Toscanelli as being much closer to Europe. The Martin Behaim globe of 1492, for example, shows a large Cipangu island due west of the Madeira, Canary, and Cabo Verde islands and about 25 percent closer to Africa than is Zaitan, Mangi, and the Asian mainland.

Drifters from the west arriving in Ireland, from the Toscanelli-Behaim perspective, could well have come from Cipangu, although Behaim's map does place "Cathaia" (Katayo) exactly due west of Ireland, but at a greater distance to the west.[16]

My belief, then, is that Colón gave the Americans the origin place of Katayo or China because he was writing that note in 1481 (or earlier) and before he had seen the Toscanelli letter with its information about Japan. The only other possibility is that the Americans had stated that they were from a place called Kat-ai (or some similar sound was uttered), and that name was seized upon by Colón or others to mean the "Katai" of Marco Polo and the Great Khan. The word "Kit," "Kait," or "Ke'it" is very common in Algonkian languages, meaning "great," so there are a number of interesting possibilities that could be explored. For example, "Kait-hikan" is a term for the ocean.

In any case, Colón believed that the Americans had come from China in the Indies or Upper India, a place where he very much wanted to go. Now let us see more precisely what Colón believed about Katayo, Cipango, and the Indies, beginning with a review of his margin notes in d'Ailly.

One note that he repeats at several points (due to d'Ailly's text) is to the effect that Spain and Portugal (Hispania) were very close to the eastern end of India, separated only by a small sea. For example, he wrote that "India est prope Hispania" (India is near to Spain) and that "from the extremity of Spain to the commencement of India is not of great distance." Also, that "ambit brachium maris inter indiam et ispaniam" (an arm of the sea extends between India and Iberia). Still further, he notes that Aristotle states that between the end of Iberia and the beginning of India is an easily navigable sea. (This idea is repeated.)

Other notes relate to the fact that India is "immensely large," embracing 44 nations, 118 peoples, and "one third part of the habitable world."

Colón wrote also: "ad ultimum indie ulterioris pro oriente debet dici oriens, ad ultimum hispanie pro occidente debet dici occidens": that "the Orient" is at the extremity of India and that "the west" is properly seen as being at the extremity of Iberia, or put another way, that India and Iberia are opposite each other.

Information about Katayo was also found in d'Ailly. Colón wrote that "the kingdom of Tarshis is at the end of the Orient, in the end of *Katay*. It was in this country, at the place called Ophir, that Solomon and Jehoshaphat sent ships." Thus Colón confounded Ophir with *Katayo,* although after 1492 he confused it with Haiti (which he supposed was Cipango). He also regarded Katayo as being at the end of the Orient, thus being that part of India (or the Indias) that was closest to Europe.[17]

Colón's notes in Piccolomini's *Historia rerum* include one that seems to reflect his knowledge of d'Ailly's *Ymago Mundi:* one note in which he states that "hoc est in principum indie scilicet in fronte hispanie et hibernie in septentrionem." In short, it is seen that the commencement of India is opposite to Iberia and Ireland to the north. He also repeats the idea that Strabo and Pliny taught that India was the "third part of the world," that is, an extremely extended part of the globe.

Katayo is also referred to in several of Colón's notes in Piccolomini, in addition to his reference to the people from Katayo seen at Galway. The most significant is one in which he says: "Kataium non est tam ad septentrionem ut pitura demonstrat," that Katayo is not as far northward as its location (on a map) is presented. He also states that the emperor "magnus can" (Great Khan) "de cataio" rules over a multitude of provinces.

The "Seres" (Chinese), he continues, "ad orientum quibus ad ortum terram incognitam." The Seres are of the eastern edge; to the east is unknown land. "Hic incipit Asie pars partium atingere." Here begins a region of Asia to reach; that is, China or Katayo is as far as known Asia reaches. Also noted is the idea that Asia in its northern part extends up to be opposite to Thule (Iceland) and that the east is without an end (terminis).

Colón also wrote a note to the effect that the empire of the Great Khan extended to the Iaxartes River, to the Bactrians, and to other peoples "as far as India."[18] But most significant of all is Colón's marginal note in which Piccolomini refers to Indians reaching Germany in the Middle Ages. There he writes, after noting Piccolomini's statement that the northern ocean in its entirety is navigable: "Auctor docet prout in germaniam fuit inventum naves indorum cum homines et merces" (the author tells of the discovery in Germany of the Indian ships with people and merchandise). Then Colón proceeds to write the note that I translated at the beginning of this chapter, to the effect that the distance was not great between India and Europe. Following that he referred to his encounter with the people of Katayo at Galway.

Taken together, the preceding evidence clearly shows Colón believed the Indians of Piccolomini had crossed from Asia directly to Europe, going eastward across a combined Pacific-Atlantic ocean, and the distance involved was not great because India and Europe faced each other across a relatively small body of water. In the same manner, he believed the Americans of Galway were people from a part of Asia called Katayo and Katayo was also directly across from Europe. In this, he was confirmed by their arrival from the west, the only direction in which people can come if they are drifting to the west coast of Ireland.

It seems clear that Colón took Piccolomini's *Historia rerum* very seriously indeed. One of Colón's extremely important notes, wherein he stated that India was opposite Iberia and Ireland (and which includes his drawing of a pointing hand) is immediately preceded by this telling information: that on the route to the Chinese (Seres) one would encounter "the antrophagos . . . a people rude and barbarous and an impenetrable land," near a mountain called Tabin that dominates the sea. "Beyond, very far from the coast of Seres, one finds the people very peaceful." Thus Colón already knew that both peaceful and human-eating peoples could be found near China *before* he ever reached the Caribbean. Little wonder, then, that he invented the "timid" Arawaks and "cannibal" Caribs on his very first journey.[19]

Perhaps by now the reader will have begun to share Colón's picture of the world as he studied the writings of d'Ailly and Piccolomini, a world in which the existence of the Americas and of the immense breadth of the Pacific were both unknown to European thinkers (and where the size of the oceans was made smaller by Colón's miscalculation of the circumference of the globe). To fully comprehend Colón's ideas about Katayo we must, however, proceed to examine the evidence of his own 1492 diary (as copied by some unknown person and then presented by Bartolome de las Casas) and letters.

First, let us begin by documenting Colón's use of the terms "India" and "Indias," along with "indio" for the inhabitants thereof. As has already been noted, the term "the Indies" had already appeared on the Catalan map of 1375, a usage made appropriate by the concept that several Indias, or parts of India, existed (such as "India Superior," "India Meridional," "India extra gangem," etc.). As noted previously, India embraced many nations and peoples lying to the east of the River Indus (Indos).

At the beginning of his journal Colón wrote to the king and queen of Castilla that "you thought of sending me, Christóbal Colón, to the said regions of India . . . by the route to the West, by which route we do not know for certain that anyone previously has passed. So, after having expelled all the Jews . . . Your Highness commanded me to go . . . to the said regions of India. . . . and I took the route to Your Highnesses' Canary Islands, in order from there to take my course and sail so far that I would reach the Indies." It is conceivable that this language may have been subsequently altered by Las Casas, but we can reserve judgment until after examining other references.

On October 12, 1492, Las Casas states: "They reached an islet of the Lucayas, which was called Guanahani in the language of Indians [lengua de yndios]. Soon they saw naked people." Clearly this was written later by Las Casas, since Colón could not have known such information on his first day of arrival. But on October 17 Colón's own words are seemingly presented when he makes reference to "todos estos yndios que traygo" (meaning "all these Indians whom I bring," having kidnapped some) and "a tres destos yndios" ("three of these Indians" whom he had placed on board the ship *Pinta*). Thereafter Colón makes frequent use of the term "yndio."

Thus the first clear use of the term "indio" by Colón to refer to Americans arises in connection with his having forcibly kidnapped "seven that I caused to be taken in order to carry them away." The use of the term "yndio" by Colón indicates, of course, that he believed the islands they had reached were part of India.

Shortly thereafter, Colón makes reference to "estas yndias" or "these Indias," which is his first use of the plural form after the introduction to the journal cited above. On November 12, he writes of having kidnapped "siete cabezas de mugeres" (seven head of women) and three children, "and also these women will teach much to our men [or "ours"] their language, which is all one in all these Islands of yndia." A few days later Colón saw "large rats of those of yndia also," and made another reference to "estas yndias."

Finally, near the conclusion of the voyage Colón remarks that "these Indies are very near the Canary Islands." Thus he certainly believed that he had reached a region that he could refer to as either India or Indias and that the people contacted were *indios*.[20]

As Colón approached the Azores in February 1493, he wrote two letters. The first, to Luís de Santangel (counselor to the king and queen), states that "I have passed to the yndias with the fleet . . . where I have found many islands populated by people without number. . . . The first island . . . the yndios called Guanahani. . . . The fifth island [I called] Juana [Cuba] . . . and I found it so large that I thought that it would be firm land [a continent], the province of Catayo." He then sent two men by land to see if a king or great city could be found but none was seen so Colón concluded that Cuba was an island as the "yndios" had been telling him. Later he referred to how, when he first arrived "a las yndias," he captured by force some native people, and how the Americans of an island at the entrance of "las yndias" were "ferocious" (the Caribs of the Lesser Antilles) and used canoes to rob "all the islands of yndia." Essentially the same information was repeated in a letter to Gabriel Sánchez (which was soon published in Rome in Latin before the end of 1493, giving the first printed news about "the Indies" in Europe).[21]

Thus Colón confirmed his usage from the diary, asserting that he had reached "islands of India" or "the Indias" and that the people were *indios*. He also stated in his letter that he believed initially that Cuba was part of the province of Katayo. Let us follow up on this detail by reviewing what his journal has to say about Katayo and Cipango.

On October 6, being far out in the Atlantic following a westerly course, Colón was advised by Martín Alonso Pinzón to steer southwest by west. Las Casas writes that to Colón it seemed that Pinzón said this "because of the island of Cipango and the Admiral saw that if they missed it they would not be able to strike land so quickly and that it was better to go at once to the mainland and afterward to the islands." Colón continued west for another day but on the ninth he veered to the southwest and west-southwest for several days. Thus it is not clear if he decided to try to reach Cipango or to go on to the continent of Asia itself.

After reaching the Lucayo (Bahama) islands, Colón states: "I want to go to see if I can find the island of Cipango." A few days later he writes: "And afterwards I will leave for another very large island that I believe must be Cipango . . . and which they call Colba [Cuba]. In it they say there are many and very large ships and many traders. And from this island [I will go to] another which they call Bofío [Bohío or Haiti]. . . . But I have already decided to go to the mainland and to the city of quisay [Quinsay] and to give the letters of Your Highnesses to the Grand Can [Khan]." Thus Colón initially thought that Cuba was Cipango and that he could go on from there to Asia, where the city of Quinsay and the Great Khan of Katayo could be found. Thus he believed that he had entered the Indies to the north of Cipango.

On October 23 Colón wrote: "I should like to leave today for the island of cuba, which I believe ought to be Cipango." Later he said that "I believe that . . . according to signs that all the Indians of these islands . . . make . . . that it [Cuba] is the island of Cipango." And in Las Casas's words, "the Indians that he brought said that from the islands to Cuba was a journey of a day and a half in their *almadías* [boats]. . . . He left there for Cuba, because from the signs that the Indians gave him of its size and of its gold and pearls he thought it must be . . . Cipango." When the Spaniards reached Cuba, Las Casas noted that "the Admiral understood that large ships from the Grand Khan came there and that from there to *tierra firme* was a journey of ten days." After being in Cuba for a time, the captain of the *Pinta* (Martín Alonso Pinzón) learned that there was a city called Cuba four days away, "and that that land was mainland of great extent and that the king of that land used to have war with the great Khan whom they call cami and his land or ciudad Faba [Habana]."

The admiral then decided to send emissaries with a letter to the king of the land (already referred to in Colón's letter to Santangel). Las Casas adds: "And he [Colón] says that he must strive to go to the Grand Khan, whom he thought was somewhere around there, or to the city of Cathay [Kat-ay] which is of the Great Khan; which he says is very large according [to] what he was told before he left Spain."

To summarize, Colón initially believed that Cuba was Cipango, but he became increasingly confused over the information that Cuba extended to, or was part of, a very large land mass, instead of being ten days' travel away from one. He probably had learned of the existence of Florida and North America but he wasn't sure if Cuba was an island or connected to that continent. If Cuba was an island it could be Cipango, but if it was "firm land," then it had to be part of Katayo or Asia. As we shall see, Colón soon transformed Haiti into Cipango because of his uncertainties about Cuba and because of the gold acquired from the Americans of Haiti.

In any case, Colón convinced himself that the native Cubans he had contacted were at war with the Great Khan's people and that "this is *tierra firme* and that I am, he says, off Zayto and Quisay one hundred leagues more or less from the one and from the other." Again Colón sent out messengers to try to locate a local king. Las Casas stated that, in spite of the failure of that mission, he (Colón) still "affirms that that island [of Cuba] is *tierra firme*." Colón had many wild ideas, including one of utilizing the Americans' cotton: "I think that it would sell very well here without taking it to Spain but to the big cities belonging to the Grand Khan, which doubtless will be discovered." Colón subsequently sailed to Haiti (Bohío), noting again his belief that the Great Khan was waging war on the Americans of the region. Las Casas pointed out that Colón continued "up until then" to believe that Cuba was part of the mainland.

Native Americans allegedly told Colón that "the island of Bohío was larger than Juana, which they call Cuba, and that it is not surrounded by water. And they appear to mean that here behind this Hispaniola, which they call Caritaba, there is a landmass of exceedingly large size."

Thus once again Colón learned of the North American continent, and he also continued to believe for some unexplained reason that the Great Khan was to blame for every report of warfare in the region.

By December 24 Colón was beginning to relocate Cipango to Bohío-Haiti, both because of evidence of gold and because of a region on the island called Cybao. Thus Cipango, instead of being a very large island, was reduced to a province on an island, at least for a period of time.[22]

At the conclusion of his 1492–93 voyage, then, Colón believed Cuba should be (sería) mainland and part of "the province of Catayo," and Bohío-Haiti was Cipango and "a place more convenient and a better place for the mines of gold and for all trade as with the mainland of there as with that of the Great Can."[23] Our evidence, thus, is that for Colón, Katayo consisted in the vicinity of Cuba or the adjacent North American mainland, whereas Cipango correctly had to lay "off shore" to the east. One might suggest then that the Americans whom Colón met at Galway fifteen years before were Cubans or other nearby Native People (Arawak-Taíno people of the islands or nearby Floridians or Caribs). This, however, presumes that Colón saw some concrete similarity with their features or watercraft, and it also ignores the Algonkian etymology of "kait," as already discussed.

On subsequent voyages Colón was gradually forced to move Katayo westward to the Central American mainland while retaining Haiti as Cipango. Nonetheless, on his second voyage he still believed that Cuba was "mainland," although he often was confused by touching upon different sections along the south coast. "Then sailing NW in order to find Cathay according to the opinion of the Lord Admiral we found that this was a gulf." On June 12, Colón had most of his crew sign a statement that Cuba was not an island.[24] Sometime after the second voyage, Colón wrote a marginal note in Pliny, whose work he had begun finally to study at first hand, to the effect that "the island of Feyti [Haiti] or Ophir or Cipango to which I gave the name of Spagnola . . ." Thus he was still convinced that Haiti was Cipango, although virtually no subsequent mapmakers were to agree with him.[25]

During his fourth voyage, Colón wrote: "On 13 May I reached the province of Mago, which borders upon the province of Cathay."[26] This is a reference to his arrival along the coast of Central America, where he also noted, "They tell me that more inland toward Cathay they have them interwoven with gold," with reference to the cotton cloth. He also believed that the Ganges River of India was only ten days' travel away, on the other side of Central America.[27]

Colón's beliefs, as modified by the ten years of exploration, are reflected by two maps attributed to his brother Bartolomé Colón, maps that seem to have accompanied a letter sent from Jamaica on July 7, 1503. In these maps the coast of Central America from Panama to roughly Honduras and

Belize is shown as being part of the east coast of Asia, from Malaysia to China. The two versions are drawn slightly differently, one having a more or less north-to-south coastline, whereas the other has a large landmass or peninsula jutting out eastward in the vicinity of Yucatan. The placenames on the Caribbean side of this part of "Asia" are largely those used by Colón on his fourth voyage, although some are misspelled (beragnia for Veragua, banassa for Banacca island, Manaua for Maraca perhaps, etc.).

The version with the large peninsula facing east has on the left (inland) the "Serici" or Chinese Mountains, beyond that is "Serica," "Sinar magnus," and "Sinarum Situs," repeated just to the left of the coast, while a very prominent "India Extra Gangem" binds the region together with the Malay region, Southeast Asia, and the Ganges River of India. "India Intra Gangem" lies to the left, north of Tap[ro]bana or Ceylon.

The two maps incorporated Colón's revised idea that Katayo or China was located just inland from the Caribbean coast of Nicaragua and Honduras. Interestingly, neither map depicts Cuba at all, thus implying that perhaps Cuba somehow still might connect with a landmass. Cipango is not shown either, but "Spagnola" (Haiti) is depicted somewhat inaccurately in relation to "Jamaicha." The map was apparently prepared by an Italian, judging from these latter two spellings.[28]

The maps serve to tell us that Colón believed Katayo was still located in the middle region of America, somewhere between Cuba and western Mesoamerica. For Colón this area continued to be part of "India Beyond the Ganges." In 1504, for example, he referred to the island of Jamaica as being "en la India." A few mapmakers continued for a time to show the American mainland as being part of Asia, almost precisely as Colón envisioned it. The globe of Orencio Fineo (1531), for instance, shows Cathay as being exactly in the location of Mexico in relation to North America and Florida (to which it is connected). To the south Cathay adjoins Central America. South America alone is called America.[29]

Other mapmakers shifted "Catay" back to a separate Asia, as did Leonardo da Vinci (ca. 1515) with Zipugna (Cipango), Terra Florida, Haiti, and so on, as islands located to the north of a large island-continent of South America (labeled "America"). A very similar map by Lenox (ca. 1512) shows "India Superior" in the area of China, but otherwise is quite similar to da Vinci's. Essentially, "Catay" or "India Superior" were opposite Ireland and Europe (although at quite some distance). Other mapmakers, such as Roselli (1506) also had the "Provincia Kathay" located in northern Asia, while placing Zipangu, Cuba, Haiti, and so on, as islands out in the middle of the Ocean Sea.

An interesting map by Sebastian Munster (sixteenth century) follows the above pattern but places "India Superior" to the northeast of "Cathay" and "Quinsay" and far north of the island "Zipangni" (Cipango). Thus the notion is set forth that upper India includes all of east Asia. Justifiably, then, the Chinese and Japanese as well as the Indonesians ("Indo"-nesians) could all be considered Indians, and were called thus by the Spaniards and others.[30]

The American natives were, of course, seen by most mapmakers as being completely separated from India. But Spain, following the tradition of Colón, refused to refer to the Native People of the "New World" or "America" as Americans or Novomundenses (New Worlders). It was left to the Dutch, French, and other northern Europeans to call the Native People "Americans" (along with using "Indian" and such repulsive terms as "savages" and "wildmen").

Interestingly, Giovanni da Verrazano's objective when making his voyage of 1523 was "to reach Cathay, on the extreme coast of Asia" by finding a passage between the troublesome "islands" of the North American landmass. Needless to state, Colón's idea of Katayo was very, very different from any of these, since to the time of his death he seems never to have conceived of the vast distance lying between his American Katayo and the real Katayo on the Asian mainland.[31]

The Americans whom Colón met in Galway in circa 1477 were said by him to have come from Katayo. We now know what Colón meant by Katayo and how it remained one of his major objectives through all of his voyages. It is of great interest that Colón never returned to that page of Piccolomini's *Historia rerum* to alter his original entry. The Americans of Galway always remained from Katayo and Katayo always remained just beyond Colón's port of call in Caribbean America.

2.

The Gulf Stream
and Galway:
Ocean Currents
and American Visitors

IT REALLY ISN'T very surprising that Colón met Americans at Galway circa 1477 for two reasons: first, because Galway is directly reached by the great North Atlantic Ocean currents and winds coming from the Americas; and second, because Galway has for ages been a natural bay and port, having direct communication with the Mediterranean world, Spain, and Portugal.

Ocean currents, rivers in the sea, have played important roles in history, especially in terms of the migration of plants, animals, and humans. The currents are also vital parts of the knowledge of any seagoing people, since the currents and prevailing winds that usually accompany them are exceedingly important factors in determining who goes where, and who gets to return alive, when the sea is the highway of travel. In essence, modern European navigation in the Atlantic and European expansion had to wait for the Portuguese to learn how to utilize the winds and currents of the Atlantic to their advantage. This knowledge enabled the Portuguese to sail to the Azores and Newfoundland, to India and to Brazil, and, when transferred, it enabled the Spanish, French, English, and Dutch to follow a path of trans-Atlantic trade and empire-building.[1]

I think that we can make a very good case that Native American navigators were very familiar with the crucial significance of currents and winds, since there is virtually no better place to learn about them than in the Caribbean region. Moreover, knowledge of currents and winds would have been expected of most eastern seaboard Native Americans as well as Inuits of Greenland and Newfoundland people. Before analyzing the navigational knowledge of Americans, however, let us examine the "rivers" of the Atlantic.

What we see at first glance are two great circular rivers in the Atlantic Ocean: the northern circle running in a clockwise direction from its southern equatorial edge and the southern circle flowing in a counter-clockwise direction, with a smaller counter-equatorial current in between, running easterly towards Africa. In reality these great "rivers" sometimes swirl off into eddies and "meanders," nonetheless maintaining a steady "push" in the dominant direction when considered overall. The trade winds provide the initiating thrust for the system of currents in the North and South Atlantic. They drive the water between the tropical regions from Africa toward America, producing the "Equatorial Current." This westward drift shifts from north to south with the seasons of the year. Between the areas of the northern and southern trade winds there is a region of "equatorial calms," and in this area there is a "counter-current . . . that runs eastward, sometimes with considerable velocity, towards the Bight of Biafra." Although it is possible to argue that the western-moving Equatorial Current "begins" off of Africa, in fact, the current connects directly with currents flowing southward from the North Atlantic (the "end" of the northern clockwise circle) and northward from the South Atlantic (the "end" of the counter-clockwise southern circle). The Equatorial Current moves straight across the Atlantic toward the Antilles islands and the South American coast, but the greater force of the southern Equatorial Current is deflected northward by the coast of Brazil, since it hits the coast north of Cape St. Roque, so that the part of the current going along the Guiana coast (which by then also includes Amazon River water) eventually squeezes between Trinidad and Tobago and gradually joins with the northern Equatorial Current, which has passed through the Antilles. The current along the Guiana coast (called the Guiana Current)

> acquires a greatly augmented rate, running ordinarily at the rate of from thirty to fifty miles, and occasionally at a rate of 80 miles in the 24 hours. Entering the Caribbean Sea, it is reinforced by the portion of the Equatorial Current which flows in between the Lesser Antilles; and it then passes westwards along the northern coast of South America until it is deflected northwards by the coastline of Central America, and driven between the peninsula of Yucatan and the western extremity of Cuba into the Gulf of Mexico, at the rate of from 30 to 60 miles per day.

The current then divides into two streams, both of which converge along the northern coast of Cuba, where they also combine with part of the northern Equatorial Current that has run northwesterly to the north coast of Cuba. Thus combined, the "Gulf Stream" (or Florida Current) then shoots northward along the coast of Florida, through the Florida Channel, sometimes reaching speeds of four to seven nautical miles per hour but averaging overall about forty-eight miles per day. On average, a mass of water equal to twenty-five times as much water as all the rivers of the world carry is forced through the Narrows of Bimini at a rate of ten cubic miles per hour. The Gulf Stream then runs along the eastern seaboard of North America as far as Cape Hatteras, being separated from the coast by a band of cold water that has a north to south current. At Cape Hatteras the stream turns gradually eastward "in the form of a fan, its three warm bands spreading out over the Atlantic surface to an aggregate breadth of 167 miles whilst two cold bands of an aggregate breadth of 52 miles are interposed between them. The innermost warm band is the one which exhibits the highest temperatures and greatest rate of flow, its velocity being greatest where it is pressed on laterally by the Arctic Current, so that a rate of four miles per hour is occasionally observed."[2]

The southern portions of the above currents were discussed by Pedro Martir as early as 1515, having first been described by Native Americans to Spanish visitors and then encountered by various captains and pilots from the mid-1490s onward. Benjamin Franklin was much interested in the Gulf Stream as it passed along the North American coast, near Nantucket. A Captain Timothy Folger told him (ca. 1786): "We are well acquainted with the stream because in our pursuit of whales, which keep to the sides of it but are not met within it, we run along the side and frequently cross it to change our side, and in crossing it have sometimes met and spoke with those packets [ships] who were in the middle and stemming it. We have informed them that they were stemming a current that was against them to the value of three miles an hour and advised them to cross it, but they were too wise to be councelled by simple American fishermen."[3] The Gulf Stream is sometimes called the North Atlantic Current east of Sandy Hook and south of the Grand Banks of Newfoundland, where it turns due eastward across the Atlantic. According to some observers, the Stream "loses all its special attributes, as to be no longer recognizable to the east of the meridian of 30° W. long. — there degenerating into the general easterly drift of that region of the Atlantic which is kept up by the prevalence of westerly winds. . . . Where the Florida Current or true

Gulf Stream can last be recognized . . . it is there flowing *almost due east,* at a rate which would require about 100 days to bring it to the Lands' End [England]." The same author argues that the "transport of trunks of trees, drift-timber, fruits, shells, etc., to the Western Hebrides, the Orkney, Shetland, and Faroe Islands, and the coast of Norway may be fairly set down to the surface-drift sustained by the prevalence of S.W. winds."[4]

Another authority notes that the Stream continues on across the North Atlantic at a one- or two-knot speed: "The force of the current diminishes as we go east across the Atlantic and on reaching Europe the more diffuse stream splits. Part must follow the wheel-like circulation of the whole North Atlantic body of water, while a segment reaches up to trail around Scotland, finally to die out around the approaches to Spitsbergen. On the way this latter stream of warmish water gives solace to the northwest Scottish coast, providing palm trees at Ullapool and pleasant warmth at Oban."[5] The author then goes on to discuss seeds, plants, and animal life carried by the "Gulf Stream" to the west coast of Ireland and elsewhere, which we will discuss below in connection with other evidence of the impact of the Gulf Stream–North Atlantic Current on communication.

A very well-informed authority, Henry Stommel, states that the North Atlantic Current "which appears to be made up of a number of separate streams, eddies, or branches (exactly which we do not yet know) is often obscured by a shallow, wind-driven surface movement called the *North Atlantic Drift,* which varies from time to time, depending upon the winds."[6] This, then, may be the reason that some other writers are not certain about the nature of the Gulf Stream's extension eastward. For our purposes, however, it is only necessary to stress that the winds from the west and the current *both* flow in an eastward direction, thus taking drifting boats or other floating objects directly towards Ireland and Europe, sometimes at great speed, as we shall see.

Not all objects drift northwards to Ireland and Scotland, however, since part of the North Atlantic Current or Drift swings in a southeasterly direction towards the shores of France, Spain, and Portugal, and beyond to the Madeira, Canary Islands, Cabo Verde Islands, and eventually, as the North Equatorial Current, back to the Antilles and Caribbean.

One has to visualize the route of the Gulf Stream–North Atlantic Current system as a faster-moving rim around a hub of more slowly rotating warm water of the central North Atlantic known as the Sargasso Sea in its southwestern sector. This huge water mass "is the North Atlantic Central Water . . . [and] it occupies the upper 1000 m. of the central regions of

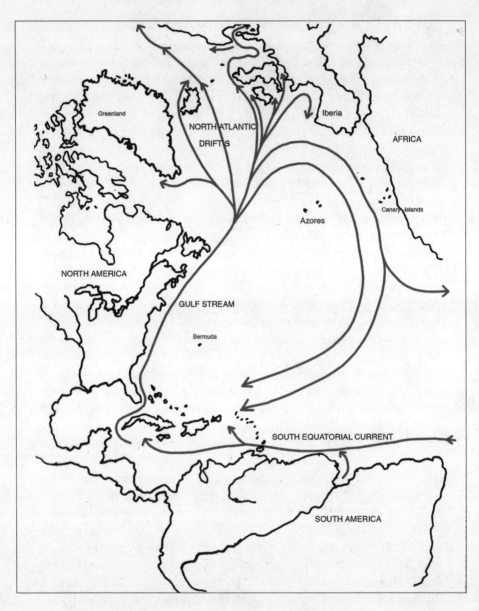

Currents of the North Atlantic (simplified). Map by Jack D. Forbes.

the North Atlantic and takes part in the wind-driven surface circulation which gives rise to the Gulf Stream." Later, Stommel states that "the central North Atlantic Ocean is covered to a depth of about 700 m. with a layer of warm water, slowly drifting toward the southwest [from Europe] under the combined influence of the stress of the wind and the earth's rotation. [It] is bounded . . . by the Gulf Stream [to the west]—a narrow, intense, northeastward-flowing current which returns to the north again the southward-driven Sargasso Sea water that has passed through the Caribbean and has turned [north] through the Florida Straits." The Gulf Stream, as it turns towards the east near the Grand Banks, acts as a kind of "dynamic barrier, or dam" that forces the warm, slower-moving water to its south, pursuing a clockwise rotation by preventing it from "overflowing" the colder water to the north of the Stream.[7]

The significance of this, for our purposes, is that Americans caught up in a storm might well end up in the Azores Islands if they became caught up in one of the more inner eddies of the Stream, or they might reach the west coast of Spain or Portugal, missing in both cases Ireland and southwest England. There is evidence that both scenarios took place, as we shall see later on.

The Gulf Stream, after it leaves the Caribbean at least, is not a rich feeding ground for most fish or whales (as noted by Franklin). It "is too warm to encourage the kind of fish which are the main catch of North Atlantic waters . . . [and] as Piccard noted during his submarine voyage in the Gulf Stream . . . there was an unexpected dearth of animal life," at least from Florida to Cape Hatteras. On the other hand, some tropical species, such as flying fish, are brought northwards (along with a mass of seaweed) by the Stream, including jellyfish. It also plays a critical role in the migration of young eels from the eel breeding grounds in the Sargasso Sea to the east of Bermuda, taking them to the rivers and freshwater ponds of Ireland and other parts of Europe. It is thought that the eels reaching eastern North America are one-year-olds, those reaching Ireland are three-year-olds, while those reaching Scandinavia and the Mediterranean are five-year-olds.

United States Navy observers, flying five hundred feet above the Gulf Stream, reported: "Repeatedly we have noticed large schools of fish swimming just inside the wall in the warm water, including tuna and blues. . . . One time we spotted a herd of some 200 sea turtles swimming south—again just inside the warm water layer. Along this interface, one also finds thousands of birds. . . . And lumber: on just one flight we must

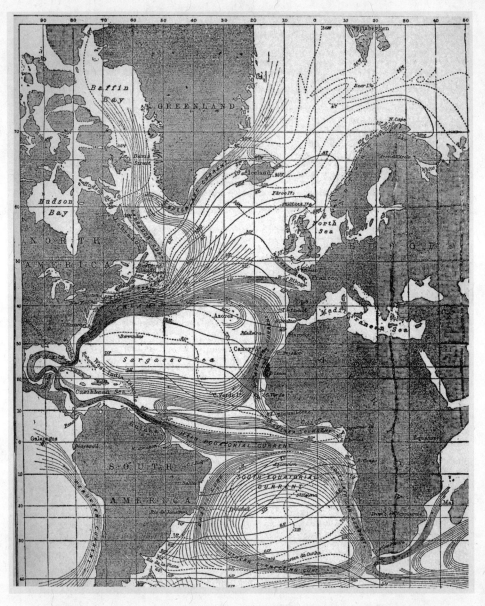

Detailed currents of the Atlantic Ocean. From William B. Carpenter, "The Atlantic Ocean," *Werner Encyclopaedia* (Akron: Werner, 1909), vol. 3, plate 1.

have spotted enough lumber to build a couple of skyscrapers. . . . every stick of it caught just at the interface."[8] This is very significant, because human travelers, especially those who were used to following fish schools and studying the patterns of the sea, could have maintained both good speed and adequate food by following the interface zone along the west and north edges of the Stream.

Now let us examine some of the evidence relating to the carrying of objects from America to Europe, and even on to Africa.

One contemporary author, William H. MacLeish, visited the vicinity of Galway Bay to find that viable American seeds had arrived in that area, including ones responsible for a variety of orchid and the Pipewort. "But what brought the American pipewort? Close by Dog's Bay. . . . in one pool, grew unimposing stems with primitive heads poking above the surface, a few inches of miracle. Pipewort does not belong here, yet it grows here. . . . I walked Dog's Bay Beach where [one] . . . finds sea hearts and other visitors from the west after equinoctial storms."[9] Another writer, T. F. Gaskell, tells us about the "beans" that arrive on the west coasts of Ireland and Scotland, derived from Jamaica (more about which later). These "seabeans" were noted on the Norwegian coast as early as 1751 by Erich Pontoppidan, who wrote: "It is of the size of a chestnut, obicular, yet flat, or as it were compressed on both sides. Its colour is a dark brown yet in the middle, at the junction of the shells, it is variegated with a circle of shining-black, and close by that another of a lively red, which have a very pretty effect." Pontoppidan thought the beans could be from a sea plant or from "an Indian vegetable of the tribe called *Pediculus elephantinus.* . . . As to bringing this vegetable from the opposite coasts of America, whence wood and the like are known to be driven towards Iceland, this is so long a voyage, that the beans would infallibly putrefy." He was wrong, of course.

James Wallace, writing of the Orkney Islands in the early 1690s, described the beans as "these pretty Nutts ["Molluca Beans"] of which they use to make Snuff Boxes." He also noted that "Sometimes are cast in by the sea, pieces of Trees and sometimes Hogsheads of Wine and Brandie."

The American "beans" have played an important role in Hebridean life for centuries. A visitor to the region around 1700 wrote: "There is a variety of Nuts called *Molluka* Beans, some of which are used as Amulets against Witchcraft, or an Evil Eye, particularly the white one, and upon this account they are wore about Children's Necks, and if any Evil is intended to them, they say, the Nut changes into a black colour." This could possibly indicate that the use of the beans may extend back to at least circa 500 CE (AD) prior to the conversion of the Hebrideans to Christianity. Certainly they were still being valued for their "good luck" as recently as 1948, especially the white variety called "Virgin Mary's beans." A man named Pennant, visiting Islay, Scotland, in 1772, wrote about the

> Molucca beans, which are frequently found on the western shores of this and others of the Hebrides. They are the seeds of the *Dolichos wrens, Guilamdina Bonduc, G. Bonducetta,* and *mimosa scandens* of *Linnaeus,* natives of *Jamaica.* . . . I was for resolving this phenomenon into ship wrecks . . . but this solution of mine is absolutely denied, from the frequency and regularity of the appearance of these seeds. *American* tortoises, or turtles, have more than once been taken alive on these coasts, tempest-driven from their warm seas; and part of the mast of the *Tilbury* man of war, burnt at *Jamaica,* was taken up on the Western coast of Scotland.

These facts give probability to the beans arriving by currents and winds. Some of these "sea beans" have been found fossilized in a bog in south Sweden, thus indicating antiquity.[10]

The arrival of Jamaican beans in the Hebrides, Orkneys, and on the Norway coast serves only as one example of the significant American impact upon the British-Irish region. Gaskell tells us that living passengers from the Americas to Ireland include "blue snails," the Portuguese man-of-war, and living plants. "Some of the indigenous wild flowers of the west Ireland coastal fringe have origins in America, and almost certainly have been transplanted with the favour of the Gulf Stream. For example, the American water plant, the 'slender naiad,' is found near Roundstone and Slyne Head." American ingredients in the Irish flora include an orchid found only in southwest Ireland and nowhere else in Europe, and another allied orchid found only in the Lough Neagh basin and in one place in west Scotland, the Pipewort, spread from Cork to Donegal, found also in west Scotland, and Canadian Blue-eyed grass (an iris, actually), widespread in the west of Ireland. There is also a freshwater sponge, widespread in Ireland and found in west Scotland, which otherwise belongs only to America.[11] Could human beings have carried some of these species to Ireland, unintentionally perhaps, providing them with an environment free of continuous exposure to salt water?

Another item of great importance in the North Atlantic Drift is timber. Significantly, Lindsay Scott tells us that charcoal from a site dated in the first century BC, or AD, on the island of Barra in the Hebrides of Scotland has been identified as spruce. It was used as a timber in the roof of an aisled roundhouse farmstead. "Import of wood from Norway at that date is very improbable, even if the formidable task could have been faced of towing timber in the North Atlantic astern of ships then available; and it is not much more likely that the wood came from a Norse ship wrecked on Barra. Enquiries were therefore made into the probability that the spruce was drift-timber from America, and Dr. J. B. Tart of the Maine Laboratory, Aberdeen, considers that the probability is high." Even earlier than the wreck on Barra, archaeological work in the Shetlands has revealed post-holes of a large building that contained remains of posts up to 10 inches in diameter that have been identified as spruce, along with sherds from the beaker culture. (The beaker folk appear about six thousand years ago in Europe.) Scott goes on to note that there are still immense quantities of spruce in Newfoundland and Labrador, and that the spruce should be able to survive the Atlantic passage quite well. "There is thus ample reason to suppose this unrequited American export capable of constituting a substantial factor in the economy of those western coastlands of the British Isles that lacked good building timber."

Scott continues by asserting that the "quantity of drift timber coming ashore is still significant, at least on the coast of Skye and the Outer Hebrides."[12] The arrival of wood in the west of Ireland and at Galway will be noted separately below.

Alexander von Humboldt, the German naturalist, took a great interest in the Gulf Stream, of which he wrote in the 1830s: "Before the warm current reaches the Western Azores, it separates into two branches, one of which turns at certain seasons . . . towards Ireland and Norway, while the other flows in the direction of the Canary Islands and the western coast of Northern Africa." He noted that "stems of the South American and West Indian *dicotyledons* have been found on the coasts of the Canary Islands. . . . Shortly before my arrival at Teneriffe a stem of South American cedar-wood (*Cedrela odnata*) thickly covered with lichens, was cast ashore near the harbor of Santa Cruz." This illustrates the possibility that Americans might have drifted to the Canary Islands, something that could explain similarities sometimes observed between the indigenous Canarios and Native Americans.

The Madeira Islands, just north of the Canaries, also are known to receive *Fava do mar* (sea beans) from the Americas, as do the Azores farther to the northwest. Von Humboldt took note of the examples of materials reaching the Azores Islands in the fifteenth century, including "bamboos, artificially cut pieces of wood, trunks of an unknown species of pine from Mexico or the West Indies, and corpses of men of a peculiar race, having very broad faces." Von Humboldt also reports that Colón had heard from a settler in the Azores "that persons in sailing westward had met with covered barks, which were managed by men of foreign appearance, and appeared to be constructed in such a manner that they could not sink, *almadias con casa movediza que nunca se hunden*" [italics in original]. The great naturalist here refers to information gathered by Colón during his pre-1492 studies of the Atlantic. We shall review the latter again when discussing American voyages of the Middle Ages and Late Middle Ages.

Samuel Eliot Morison noted that in 1939–40 "large driftwood rarely comes ashore on the outer Azores, but an old gentleman recalled that after the great storm of 1869 he saw cast up on the beaches of Sâo Miguel a number of tree trunks, 'bluish, horizontally striped with black.' These are easily identified as the Cuipo tree (*Cavanillesia platanifolia*) which grows in Central America; the wood is superlatively light so that it floats high and catches the wind." Von Humboldt also believed that the Gulf Stream sometimes reached as far as Iceland, where its sea coasts "like those of the Faroe Isles, receive a large number of trunks of trees, driven thither from America; and this drift-wood, which formerly came in greater abundance, was used for the purposes of building, and cut into boards and laths. The fruits of tropical plants collected on the Icelandic shores, especially between Raufarhaven and Vapnafiord, show that the movement of the water is from a southerly direction."[13] The significance of American timbers drifting southward in the Labrador Current or northwards in the Gulf Stream, and then being picked up by the North Atlantic Current, may not have been lost upon American fishing folk and navigators from Greenland, Newfoundland, and the Nova Scotia coast southwards.

Other evidence of the rapid movement of objects from the Caribbean to Scotland is provided by the example of the

> mainmast of the English ship of war, the Tilbury, which was destroyed by fire in the seven years' war on the coasts of Saint Domingo, was carried by the Gulf Stream to the northern coasts of Scotland; and casks filled with palm oil, the remains of the cargo of an English ship wrecked off Cape Lopez in Africa, [which] were in like manner carried to Scotland, after having twice traversed the Atlantic, once from east to west between 2° and 12°

north lat., following the course of the equinoctal current, and ones from west to east between 45° and 55° north lat. by help of the Gulf Stream.

Reference was also made to a bottle with a written paper in it that was thrown from a ship in 38°52' north latitude and 63°58' west longitude on January 20, 1819, and that arrived on June 2, 1820, at the Rosses near the Island of Aran at the entrance to Galway Bay.

Many other bottles have also been set out by the Newfoundland fisheries department near the Grand Banks and northwards to Labrador, designed to float just beneath the sea surface so as to not be directly affected by winds. Twenty bottles were "retrieved at points stretching from the Azores to Norway, with concentrations of six on the Irish coast and six on the west coasts of Scotland, including the Orkneys and Shetlands. The period varied from 11 to 17 months." Bottles set out in the region of latitude 60° N, longitude 20° W (some two hundred miles south of Iceland) have usually reached the coasts of the Outer Hebrides or on those of the Orkneys, Shetlands, or Norway.[14]

During the last century and a half such items as Caribbean shells, coconuts, bamboos, "confirmed turtle," and pumice have continued to reach the west coast of Scotland. Pumice of possible Caribbean origin is also common in west Scottish archaeology sites, some of non-Mediterranean type being found in a chamber tomb on the Island of Skye for example.[15]

Jean Merrien (a.k.a Freminville), a French authority on the sea, tells us that valuable hardwood from "the rivers of Mexico" was also carried by the Stream to be washed ashore on the coasts of Ireland and Wales. This was an extremely important source of rare tropical woods for the people of that region.

Merrien, a student of navigational history, also states that "the first attempt—the first success [of crossing the Atlantic]—could only come from the American side . . . because the crossing is much less difficult in that direction. A French writer has said (justly, in all probability) that if America had been the Old World its inhabitants would have discovered Europe long before we did, in fact, discover America." Of course this may, indeed, be what happened, that Americans reached Europe long before any Europeans reached America.

Merrien tells us also that one can sail in a "straight line" from Boston via Newfoundland to Ireland and Cornwall "with almost the certainty of fair winds." The other direction requires "twice the distance, thrice the time, and four times the sweat." In the 1860s a 48–foot sloop, *Alice,* was sailed from North America to the Isle of Wight in less than twenty days with very favorable winds; and in recent times a wooden raft was propelled from Canada to northern Europe by means of the North Atlantic Current. Stephen C. Jett cites the sixty-eight-day passage of one William Verity from Florida to Ireland in a 12–foot sloop, as well as the crossing by two men from New York to the Scilly Islands in fifty-five days in a 17–foot dory powered *only by oars.*[16]

More recently (1980), a French boatman, Gerald d'Aboville, completed a three-thousand-mile journey across the Atlantic from Massachusetts to Brittany in seventy-one days *solely by rowing.* (In 1991 he also rowed across the Pacific in a 26–foot kayak.)[17]

Early evidence of successful voyages across the North Atlantic includes the crossing by a Norseman, Porhallr, with eight companions, from New-foundland in a *bateau,* going directly from America to Ireland, according to Merrien. This is probably the same voyage as that carried out by a small group of Norsemen about the year 1010 in a small boat treated with seal blubber after their main ship became rotten. Only half of them were able to get into the small boat and in that they traveled, by sail or oars is not clear, from the Greenland Sea to Dublin, Ireland.[18]

In 1347 a group of seventeen or eighteen Greenlanders in a very small boat with no anchor were blown by a storm from the coast of Markland (probably Labrador) all the way to Iceland.[19] Thus, it is absolutely certain that small boats, some without sails, have easily traversed the North Atlantic *from America to Europe.*

The reverse, however, is not true except with the large Norwegian vessels of the 800s and later, *after* the Norse learned how to take advantage of currents and winds (the East Greenland Current, for example) existing at high latitudes and leading towards Greenland, or with other Europeans sailing at equatorial latitudes west of the Canary and Cabo Verde islands.

Samuel Eliot Morison, certainly a noted scholar of the Atlantic, tells us in emphatic terms: "it is impossible for a vessel to be 'blown across' the North Atlantic from east to west: I challenge anyone to produce a single instance."[20] Jimmy Cornell, in his *World Cruising Routes,* also tells us that it is difficult to sail directly from Europe to North America: "the great circle route from the English Channel . . . is probably the most difficult as there is a battle with headwinds all the way across." A sailing vessel can detour to the north, departing as from the north of Scotland, in the hope of picking up an easterly wind, but: "all of these routes . . . are affected by fog and ice and their timing is therefore crucial." The reason for going to the north of Britain "is to stay north of the lows that move across the Atlantic from west to east and produce easterly winds in higher latitudes. These may attain gale force, but at least their direction is favourable." Because of fog and ice they can only be attempted "later in the summer." Attempting to select a route south of about latitude 37°N, so as to avoid the Gulf Stream, "can be counterproductive as this brings the possibility of straying into the Azores high."

The northerly alternative is dangerous because "violent storms . . . often occur in the eastern Atlantic after the middle of August." Thus only a brief window of opportunity is open for east to west journeys north of Britain.

The North America to Europe direction is "a cold, wet and foggy route at the best of time, at least it has the advantage of both favourable winds and current. . . . The most difficult part of the voyage is the first few hundred miles . . . the winds should be westerly around 15 knots. . . . The favourable effect of the Gulf Stream becomes less noticeable from about longitude 40°W where it changes its name to the North Atlantic Current." It should be noted that in earlier time periods, such as the Late Pleistocene, the northerly route from east to west would not have been available to boats. During that period the North Atlantic would have been very dangerous, with strong westerly winds and currents clashing directly with sea ice. While an America to Europe crossing might have been possible, via the Gulf Stream, an east to west voyage would have certainly been inconceivable.

Added to the difficulties of the above is the fact that the northbound route from, say, Iberia along the French coast, is very difficult even today. "The prevailing northerly winds of summer, the Portuguese trades, which provide excellent sailing conditions for southbound passage, make the task of reaching northern destinations very difficult throughout the summer months." Moreover, crossing the Bay of Biscay is dangerous due to southwest gales: "it is wise to make some westing and not follow a rhumb line across the Bay. As a rule, a SSE or SE track should be avoided. . . . Because of the relatively shallow water, seas can become extremely rough in a moderate storm."[21] The reason for mentioning the above is that some anthropologists have advocated an ancient voyage from southwestern Europe to America, a voyage from the Iberian or Biscayan region northward and then across the Atlantic *against* the winds and Gulf Stream.

In any case, those investigators who are interested in "evidence" for Phoenician, Jewish, and European visitors to pre-1492 mainland North America perhaps should be looking in the other direction, that is, for evidence of American influences in Europe.

It should be noted that farther south there are currents that could have carried Americans directly to central and southern Africa, in addition to currents that could carry Africans to the Caribbean or Brazil. Since it is not our purpose here to examine early contacts with Africa, we will not pursue this line of exploration.

We might also mention the currents of the Pacific, if only to refer to the many instances of human beings surviving after drifting on them for long periods of time. For example, there are a number of records of Japanese being carried by the Japan Current to the west coast of America. "All the European residents [of ca. 1870] in Yokohama know the Japanese interpreter, Joseph Hico, who once, when out fishing with some members of his family, was driven out to sea by a gust of wind, and caught by the great equatorial current. . . . The unfortunate fishermen were carried far into the Pacific in a northeasterly direction, but they fortunately met an American vessel, which rescued them, and landed them at San Francisco."

In the century after 1770, as many as sixty drifting Asiatic craft reached the Pacific coast. Among these craft, Japanese junks with survivors are known to have reached Santa Barbara and Sitka during the early 1800s.[22]

Now let us turn to look specifically at Galway and the adjacent west coast of Ireland. Galway Bay and the Aran Islands at its mouth are ideally located to be the arrival point for drift objects from the North Atlantic Current. The Irish coast juts out westward just north of Galway Bay, making the latter a sort of catch basin for current-carried debris driven still further towards shore by westerly winds.

A major interest of the Aran Islanders has long been the gathering of timber and wreckage from the sea. According to one resident, "Many of the older houses of the islands have rafters cut from beams washed ashore and carried off and hidden before the coastguards or the landlords' agent got wind of them, and even today islanders keep an eye out for such prizes, as I do myself. Recently an elderly and, as I had thought, frail couple, neighbours of ours in the west of the island, managed to drag a thick tree trunk eighteen feet long up a steep shinglebank." Another bay on the island's coast was "always well known for the flotsam that accumulated in it, and its name, Poll na Briocarnach, refers to fragments of wreckage. In the last century there was a winch on the clifftop for hoisting up timbers, and I am told that the O'Malleys . . . kept a man stationed here to claim anything of value that came ashore." Even the inner shore of the largest island was a good place to look for driftwood. A place called "Poll na Loinge," Inlet of the Ship, was where "bodies and cargo" from a wrecked sailing vessel had come ashore "long ago."

Dead persons often washed into Aran. "Strangers washed up on the shore, of whome no one could tell if they had been [Catholic] believers or not, were also buried here . . . [at] a place not consecrated by the Church."[23] Not surprisingly, Galway was very early known to the Mediterranean world and was a major port for the Portuguese and Spaniards during Colón's lifetime. Tacitus wrote that Ireland was in constant communication with Spain, a fact that is not at all surprising in that the last conquerors of Ireland, the Gaels, arrived from Galicia in northwest Iberia. According to James Hardiman, Galway lay "particularly convenient" to contact with Spain.

"Modern" Galway began its existence in the Middle Ages as a port where merchants gathered, many of them from Wales, England, and elsewhere. Then Galway came under the control of the Norman kings of England and in 1380 Richard II authorized Portuguese merchants from Lisbon to come regularly to Ireland and Galway to trade. The "route from Lisbon, and the northern parts of Spain especially, to Galway became a notable highway of commerce." By 1493 commerce with Spain was "regular and friendly" and a Galway merchant went to Cadiz. Trade was also long-established with Italy and Flanders.[24]

Maps of this period, including the Upsal map of 1450, show "Galuei" prominently on the west coast. Colón should have known of Galway not only from maps, however. As early as 1160 the Irish had a hospital at Genoa and thereafter indirect commerce occurred with Genoese merchants. Nonetheless, Colón would probably not have reached Galway if he had not taken up a sailor's life with the Portuguese.[25]

In Galway itself there are strong traditions of Colón's visit to the city. In particular, St. Nicholas Church, founded in 1320, is thought to have been the place where Colón worshiped. A postcard currently published by the church states: "Tradition has it that Christopher Columbus prayed here before crossing the Atlantic." A brochure issued by the church states that "the most famous sailor traditionally associated with this church is Christopher Columbus, who buried a crewman and took on a Galwegian as a replacement before sailing westwards. St. Nicholas's is therefore believed to be the last building in which he worshiped before discovering the New World."[26] This is "pure malarkey" as one might say, since Colón departed from the Canary Islands in 1492 and came nowhere near to Galway. It does, however, tie in with another tradition that one "Guliermo Ires natural de Galuy en Irlanda" sailed with Colón in 1492. Thomas Johnson Westropp wrote in 1912 that Colón "was in touch with Galway, the centre of Irish lore of Hy Brasil [a mythic island in the North Atlantic], for he included among his sailors in 1492 William Irez, of Galway, in Ireland."[27] This tradition was also referred to in 1942 to the effect "that a Galway man made voyages to the American continent previous to Columbus, and that he eventually accompanied Columbus as a pilot. . . . The man's name is given as Rice de Galuey. In St. Nicholas' Church there is shown a tomb, erected in 1660, which is said to be that of a direct descendent of this Rice."[28]

We could, of course, disregard this set of tales as simply another of the many post-1492 efforts to discover some kind of mysterious "pilot" who guided Colón to America. No such "pilot" appears in the lists of crewmen for the 1492 voyage or in the notations in Colón's diary, and there is no evidence for such a person.

The lists of crewmen, as reported by Colón six years after the voyage, include

> Pero Arraes, marinero (pay received by Vicente Yáñez)
> Juan Arraes, son of Pero Arraes (received by Vicinte Eañes)
> Juan Quintero, son of Argueta Arraes
> Juan Arias, portugués, son of Lope Arias, citizen of Tavira.

The hometowns or nationalities are usually given for the crewmen, and no one is listed as being from Galway or Ireland.

The idea that an Ires from Galway sailed with Colón in 1492 arose from a list published many years later of forty men who had died in the Indies and whose heirs were compensated by the Spanish crown in 1511. This list included both a "Guillermo de Ires: natural de Galney en Irlanda" and a "Tallorte de Lajes: ingles." Careful research has shown that *none* of these forty men, including Ires, sailed on the first voyage.[29]

In any case, the current tradition in Galway can perhaps be boiled down to a sad attempt to attract revenues to the St. Nicholas Church, an Anglican (Church of Ireland) institution since the Reformation in a Roman Catholic-dominated city. The church brochure states that "it costs

£100 per day to keep this church going. Your contribution will be greatly appreciated."

But before we write off the entire tradition, let us consider the possibility that it is based on a genuine albeit altered notion of an ancient contact between Galway and the land to the west. In other words, the Galwegians had a memory of the arrival of Americans, which led them to say after 1492: "Yes, we knew already of people to the west." From that tradition, the mystery pilot with Colón may have evolved.

Interestingly, there is possible genetic evidence that Native Americans reached Ireland and that their ancestry descends among the modern Irish. In Australia a "caucasian woman" and four of her relatives, "all of whom are of caucasian (Irish) stock," were tested in connection with a blood donation to the Red Cross. It seems that the Irish lady in question made a donation that was incompatible with other blood samples and it turned out that she had cells that were positive for the Diego gene (Di(a+)).[30]

The Diego gene is a characteristic of the blood found among some Native Americans, with its heaviest concentration in the Venezuela-Brazil-Andean region, but with a distribution around the entire Caribbean to North America and Puerto Rico as well. Thus it is a circum-Caribbean characteristic, not found among Inuit people in North America, nor among the overwhelming majority of Caucasians and Africans. On the other hand, some Asian groups tested show low percentages of the antigen, as do some eastern Europeans.

I would argue, then, that when the Diego antigen appears that it is a possible marker of Native American ancestry, since its clearly defined place of concentration is in the circum-Caribbean region. Unfortunately, although I have communicated with medical authorities in Australia I have been unable to find out from what part of Ireland the woman's family stemmed. Also since Native American sailors could have put in at Irish ports in the post-1500 years on occasion it is impossible to be certain when the Diego antigen reached Ireland, but it would seem much more likely that she was part-American rather than part-Asian.

It is intriguing to think that the Americans of 1477 and other people from America may have had a genetic impact upon the Irish. Such an idea, incidentally, does not surprise some modern Galwegians, some of whom have told me that the local people, and especially those of the Aran Islands, show some hint of Native American features. Equally intriguing is the fact that the seal and otter stories and beliefs of these coastal peoples remind one very much of Native American stories. Strikingly similar are Irish seal and sea-otter stories and Miluk (Oregon) stories of marriages of humans with sea-otters and swordfish, for example. Perhaps there are ancient American influences among the peoples of Ireland and Scotland, influences to join with the potato as key markers of Irish and British life.[31]

3.

Seagoing Americans: Navigation in the Caribbean and Vicinity

MARITIME NAVIGATION by First American peoples stands as a very neglected subject, especially since the topic extends to modern times, with Native People serving as sailors with the Portuguese, British, United States, and other navies and merchant marines. The subject is significant not only for the study of issues such as the diffusion of genetic characteristics but for establishing Native Americans as active participants in the process of travel and discovery and the resulting spread of cultural inventions to Europe, Africa, the Pacific, and Asia.

Much information has now been lost and must be reconstructed from the often fragmentary records left by early European observers or from archaeological and oral historical sources.

We must also bear in mind that the Spanish and Portuguese intrusions into the Americas after 1492 must have had a very chilling effect upon American navigation, even as the Portuguese thoroughly disrupted Indian, Malayo-Indonesian, and other shipping in the Indian Ocean and South China Sea region.[1] Native Americans were soon subject to seizure as slaves or forced laborers (*naborías*) almost everywhere from the Carolinas to South America, and after the English entered the field, along the New England to Nova Scotia coast as well. The Portuguese also kidnapped many persons from the Newfoundland-Labrador and Brazil regions. Thus, it probably became increasingly dangerous to go out to sea after the 1490s, and especially in parts of the greater Caribbean. The descriptions of Native shipping must reflect the need to be secretive and therefore many things are probably hidden from our present view.

Nonetheless, what we do know suggests that Native Americans of the Caribbean could have been justly referred to as "the polynesians of the Americas" and that shipping was also very important along the west coast of the continent, at least from Peru north to Mexico and in California and the Pacific Northwest. Thor Heyerdahl has stated that Native Americans had levels of navigational expertise and culture to match anything in the Old World. J. Eric S. Thompson, an expert on Maya peoples, has referred to the Putun (Chontal-Acalan Maya) both as "the Phoenicians of the New World" and as the "Argonauts of the Western Caribbean."[2] Their exploits in the period from circa 800 to the sixteenth century will be discussed below.

Let us first look at the testimony of the earliest European invaders. One of the items of evidence that motivated Colón to voyage to the west was, of course, his meeting Americans in Galway sometime around 1477. The evidence would seem to indicate that they had arrived in Ireland on two logs or two dugout boats, probably lashed together to make a more stable vessel for travel on the high seas. As we shall see, this is very much like a technique used by Lenápe (Delaware) people in sailing from New Jersey to Virginia.

During the 1480s, presumably, Colón also learned from a settler of the Azores that persons had seen "covered barks" that seemed to be built in such a way they "never could sink." Las Casas refers to these boats as "almadías o canoas con casa movediza," as dugouts or canoes with houses, vessels that could not sink, but that were blown about by the winds from island to island. Why wouldn't they sink? Most likely because they were double-hulled or outfitted with outriggers or other stabilizers. The fact that houses were built on them suggests that the sides were built up with planking.[3]

These boats may well have resembled a large trading vessel, probably of the Putun Maya, seized by Colón off of the Honduras coast at one of the Guanaxa Islands. This trading boat was apparently coming from a copper-rich region, or at least from an area close to such a region. Hernando Colón, a firsthand witness, tells us that "there arrived at that time a canoe as long as a galley and eight feet wide, made of a single tree trunk like the other Indian canoes; it was freighted with merchandise from the western regions around New Spain. Amidships it had a palm-leaf awning like that which the Venetian gondolas carry; this gave complete protection against the rain and waves. Under this awning were the children and women and all the baggage and merchandise. There were twenty-five paddlers aboard." The Spaniards quickly seized the freight boat while

Admiral Colón (Hernando's father) "gave thanks to God." Then, "he took aboard the costliest and handsomest things in that cargo: cotton mantles and sleeveless shirts embroidered and painted in different designs and colors; breechclouts of the same design and cloth as the shawls worn by the women in the canoe, being like the shawls worn by the Moorish women of Granada; long wooden swords with a groove on each side where edge should be, in which were fastened with cord and pitch, flint knives that cut like steel; hatchets resembling the stone hatchets used by the other Indians, but made of good copper; and hawk's bells of copper, and crucibles to melt it." The cargo boat was also outfitted with provisions, including "such roots and grains as the Indians of Española eat, also a wine made of maize that tasted like English beer. They had as well many of the almonds [Cacao beans] which the Indians of New Spain use as currency."[4] Colón's act of piracy revealed a Caribbean trading vessel of the kind that could easily have traveled to the southern United States or along the northern coast of South America. The palm-leaf matting used as an awning suggests also a knowledge of sailing, since such matting can easily catch the wind and be used as sails. Sails of woven matting were used along the Pacific coast and also by the Caribs of the Antilles.

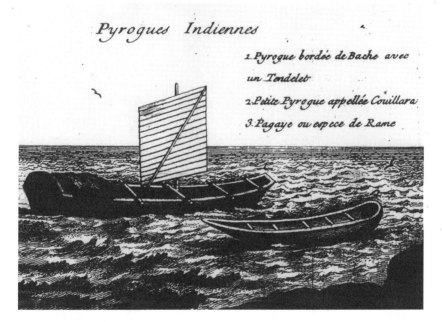

Small Carib canoes, one with a sail. From Pierre Barrere, *Nouvelle Relation de la France Equinoxiale*, 1743, 28.

On his third voyage, Colón also saw a very large boat, reminiscent of the ones that were seen in the Azores. He states: "Their canoes [in the Gulf of Pariá-Venezuela area] are very big and of better workmanship than those others, and lighter; and amidships in every one there is an apartment like a cabin, in which I saw that the principal men went with their women." It would seem likely that those large boats with covered areas and cabins were not simply dugouts but had been augmented by planking (to make a width of eight feet, for example).

The use of planking is known for larger Caribbean vessels, as we shall see. Nicolo Syllacio, a Sicilian philosophy instructor, had a friend on Colón's second voyage, Guillermo Coma, who supplied him with information on the Caribbean. He states that the larger Carib boats "are made of boards fastened together and are eighty feet long; they stand five palms above the water and the same number of palms in breadth. Instead of oars, they use broad paddles like bakers' peels, but somewhat shorter. In this manner they sail to the neighboring islands. . . . Sometimes they go

Americans of the Florida region transporting goods in a dugout without raised sides. "Historia der Innwohner Americae," in De Bry, *America 1590* (Munich: Verlag Konrad Kolbl, 1970), plate XXII.

greater distances, even as far as a thousand miles, in search of plunder."[5] Syllacio may not be a very reliable source, being one of the early perpetrators of the sensationalistic story of Carib cannibalism. Probably the boats he describes (at secondhand) were only partly built up with planks on a dugout base. Nonetheless, the impression of Carib navigational ability and boat size is probably accurate.

Now let us review Colón's impressions of Native American boats and navigation on his first voyage. In his letter to Santangel (February 15, 1493) Colón said that the Americans were

> of keen ingenuity and people who navigate all those seas, so that it is marvelous the good account they give of everything. . . . In all the islands they have many canoes resembling rowing *fustas* some smaller and some larger, and many are larger than a *fusta* of 18 oar-banks. They are not so wide because they are made of a single log, but a *fusta* could not keep up with them in rowing because they go faster than one can believe and in these they navigate [to] all those islands, which are innumerable, and carry their merchandise. One of these canoes I have seen with 70 and 80 men in it and each one with his oar.[6]

Some of Colón's comments in his 1492 diary are worth citing. On October 13 he noted that the Americans "came to the ship with *almadias* [dugouts] that are made from the trunk of one tree, like a long boat, and all of one piece, and worked [carved?] marvelously . . . and large enough so that in some of them 40 and 45 men came. And others smaller, down to some in which came a man alone. They row with a paddle like that of a baker and go marvelously. And if it capsizes on them they then throw themselves in the water and they right and empty it with gourd containers."[7]

On November 30 Colón reportedly saw "a handsome dugout or canoe 95 *palmos* in length, made of a single timber; and in it a hundred and fifty persons would fit and navigate." A short distance away they saw "an inlet in which he saw five very large dugouts, which the Indians call canoes, like very handsome *fustas,* fashioned in such a way that it was, he says, a pleasure to see them. . . . The canoes were under very thick trees."[8] Not only was Colón impressed with the size and beauty of the American boats but he also commented upon their seaworthiness. Near Haiti "he found in mid-channel a canoe with one Indian alone in it. The Admiral marveled at how he was able to stay afloat, the wind being great." Frequent reference was also made to the sighting of canoes with large numbers of persons on board. For example, on December 17 a canoe arrived at Haiti from Tortuga

Americans fishing from a smaller dugout boat. "Der Landschafft Virginia," in De Bry, *America 1590* (Munich: Verlag Konrad Kolbl, 1970), plate XII.

Island with some forty men on board. At Haiti also "many large canoes" were used to unload a Spanish vessel of "everything from the ship," thus indicating large capacities for carrying gear. In 1498 at Iere (Trinidad) Colón was met by a canoe with twenty-five young men, all armed with shields, bows, and arrows; but generally after the first voyage, references are no longer made so frequently due to fewer firsthand written sources, greater familiarity with native cultures, and an overwhelming preoccupation with slave-raiding and military conquest. Exceptions will be noted below.[9]

Colón also frequently referred to the great numbers of *canoas* that were seen. In the Trinidad-Gulf of Paría region he reports that "there came again an infinity of canoes loaded with people." On other occasions he referred to up to 120 boats in one place and to the "numberless canoes" of the Caribs.[10]

The Caribbean Natives also had boat sheds and ports from which to land and unload cargo, all of which indicates the high development of maritime activity. On November 27 Colón saw "a handsome dugout, or

American maritime warfare as imagined by a European artist. "Das Dritte Theil," in De Bry, *America 1590* (Munich: Verlag Konrad Kolbl, 1970), plate LIV.

canoe, made of one *madero* [log], as big as a *fusta* of 12 rowing benches, drawn up under a shelter or shed made of wood and covered with big palm leaves, so that neither sun nor water could damage it." It was in this vicinity that the Castillians also saw the boat of ninety-five *palmos* in length and, in a different place, five very large boats. "And going along a path that went out to them they came upon a very well arranged boat shed, covered in such a way that neither sun nor water could do harm to the canoes; and under it there was another canoe made of one timber like the others, like a *fusta* of 17 benches, and it was a pleasure to see the decorations that it had and its beauty."[11]

Thus, repeatedly, the Europeans were impressed with the size, beauty, decorations, seaworthiness, and mobility of the American craft. Of course, the greater number of boats were not seen by Colón, since he only succeeded in visiting parts of the Cuban and Haitian coasts and a few other islands. Many boats were probably out of sight (or kept out of sight) and thus we do not know from 1492 a lot of details about how people were seated, how cargo was stored, about the use of sails or masts, and so on.

Colón, while still in the Bahamas, learned about both Cuba and Bohío (Haiti) through "signs." "The Indians that he brought [from Guanahani] said that from the islands to Cuba was a journey of a day and a half in their *almadias,* which are little boats [*navetas*] of a log [*madero*] where no sail [*vela*] is carried. These are *Canoas.*" Some authors have taken this to indicate that Colón never saw any sails on any boats in the Caribbean, but it is quite certain that the above remark was made only after being in the Bahamas for ten days and *prior* to seeing any boats from Cuba or Haiti. Moreover, in those ten days messengers may well have warned the Americans to hide their boats and to stay away from the intruders, who, after all, had already kidnapped people. Finally, it is likely that the term *vela* would *not* be used for sails made of matting. Such is the case at Lake Titicaca even today.[12]

Interestingly, on the second voyage the Castillians found in a house on Guadalupe Island (Guadeloupe)

> un madero de navío, que llaman los marineros quodaste, á que todos se maravillaron, y no supieron imaginar cómo hobiese allí venido, sino que los vientos y los mares lo hociesen allí traído, o de las islas de Canaria ó de la Española, de la nao que allí perdió el Almirante el primer viaje.

While ransacking some empty Carib houses they found a timber that seemed to be a mast from a ship and they speculated that it might have been carried by wind or currents from Haiti, where Colón had lost a ship, or from the Canary Islands. Another explanation is, however, that the Caribs themselves had carried the mast to Guadeloupe or that they had made it and used it when needed for sailing.[13]

We do have some information on the kind of supplies carried in Caribbean watercraft. Some native fishermen were found to have nets, hooks, and calabashes (gourds) filled with drinking water. Another group of canoes had "bread and fish and water in clay jars and seeds of many kinds that make good spices." We have already noted the contents of the large freight canoe found in the Guanaxa Islands that had "all the products of that country," including "provisions" such as roots, grain, maize wine, and cacao beans. Mention has also been made of the gourds used to bail out any canoes that turned over. Thus, we can postulate that most American boats that might have been driven by storm into the Atlantic would have been equipped with a great many necessities for long-term survival, including water containers, food, and fishing gear. There is also much evidence that Americans were strong swimmers, being able to swim "a full half league from land," a mile and a half or more. Incidentally, bottle gourds (Lagenaria siceraria) have been found in Florida and Mexico, dated 7,300 and 7,000 years ago.[14]

The Colón sources also supply a great deal of information on the extent of geographical knowledge and travel experience possessed by Caribbean Americans. Perhaps the most intriguing is the fact that Colón on his first voyage learned from the natives of Haiti of the precise Caribbean islands that lay closest to Spain and the Canary Islands. In his letter to Santangel, written prior to his arrival in the Azores, Colón wrote that

> I have neither found monsters nor had report of any, except in an island [Caire or Dominica] which is the second at the entrance to the Indies, which is inhabited by a people who are regarded in all the islands as very ferocious and who eat human flesh; they have many canoes with which they range all the islands of India and pillage and take as much as they can. . . . There are those who have intercourse with the women of Matremomio [Matininó or Martinique], which is the first island met on the way from Spain to the Indies [partiendo despaña para las yndias], in which there is not one man.

Here Colón presents the myth of cannibals and of an "Amazon" island, but of greater interest is the question of how he knew that Martinique was the first and Dominica the second islands "met on the way from Spain to the Indies."

American vessels landing on an
island, with Europeans captured.
"Dritte Buch America, Das Dritte
Theil," in De Bry, *America 1590*
(Munich: Verlag Konrad Kolbl,
1970), plate XXII.

The answer is that he learned about these islands and their *exact* geographical locations from Americans on Haiti. In Colón's diary he refers
several times to the "island of Carib" and then "he has learned that . . .
on the island of Carib and in Matininó there was much copper . . . and
that from there [Carib] their island was visible and that he had decided
to go to it, since it is on the way, and to the island of Matininó which,
he says, was populated entirely by women without men, to see both and
to capture, he says, some of them." Then four youths came to his ship

"and they seemed to the Admiral to give such a good account of all those islands to the east, on the same route that the Admiral was to follow, that he decided to take them to Castile with him." When Colón lifted anchor to return to Castilla he said that he wanted to go "to the island of Carib" where the people "with their numberless canoes . . . travel through all those seas." But in leaving Haiti he sailed "east by north" and "east," then "northeast by east," indicating that his intention to reach Carib and Matininó referred to his intended return voyage.

It should be noted that Colón also states that he found a lot of seaweed in a bay of Bohío "of the kind they found in mid-sea when he came [on the out-bound voyage] because of which he believed that there were islands straight to the east of the place at which he began to find it, because he considers it certain that the weed originates in shallow water near land. And he says that if this is so, these Indies are very near the Canary Islands, and . . . less than 400 leagues distant."[15] The voyage from the Canary Islands to Dominica in 1493 is said to have been of 750 to 800 leagues in distance, thus indicating that Colón believed that some islands existed about mid-way or a little west of mid-way, perhaps southwest of the Azores.[16]

According to Andrés Bernaldez, Colón "from the signs which had been made to him by the people in the islands . . . discovered on his first voyage and which indicated the direction in which the Carib islands lay, he had steered his course toward them [on the second voyage], both because they were much nearer to Spain, and also because he thought that that route was the most direct way to Española. . . . And . . . this was as direct a way thither as if the path had been well known." He also noted that "these islands [Matininó, etc.] lay in the direction of Spain, though the admiral had failed to strike them on his first voyage, and he believed that there were islands forty or fifty leagues nearer Spain."[17] Thus it is clear that the islands of Carib and Matininó were not the same as these hypothetical "seaweed" islands (because the Carib islands were not so far from Haiti), which leads us to believe that when Colón refers to Matininó as being "at the entrance" to the Indies he is referring to a concept based wholly upon American information and upon some specific facts that they must have provided. What would these be? That Matininó and Caire were the farthest east of the Antilles? That they were the first islands to be reached if one utilized the Northern Equatorial Current coming from near the Canary Islands? That Americans had utilized the latter current and returned from the Canary Islands with its help? That Canary Islanders or other strangers had arrived via that current?

Matininó and Caire are *not* the farthest islands to the east (Barbados being much farther out and others of the Antilles being virtually as far east). Thus I believe that it was a knowledge of the currents and of their use by human beings that Colón learned about from his American informants. Moreover, I believe that Colón's decision to use a more northern route, via the Azores, on his return voyage in early 1493, was prompted by

Native American expertise, since by going east by north he was doubtless able to avoid combating the prevailing currents during the entire trip.

It must be stressed that on the return voyage of 1493 as well as on the westbound second voyage later in the year, Colón had the benefit of Native American expertise, since he had Americans on board who were doubtless becoming ever more skilled in the Castilian language. That some of the Americans were geographical experts also is shown by the fact that several whom Colón took to Europe drew maps there. For example, the King of Portugal, desirous of knowing all the details of Colón's voyage, obtained a bowl of beans and by signs ordered an American

> que con aquellas habas pintase o señalare aquellas tantas islas de la mar de su tierra quel Almirante decía haber descubierto; el indio, muy desen- vueltamente y presto, señaló esta isla Española y la isla de Cuba y las islas de los lucayos y otras cuya noticia tenía.

The king ordered one of Colón's captives to draw or mark the islands he knew, and quickly, very confidently, the American drew the islands of Haiti and Cuba and the Bahamas and others of which he knew.

Then the king, after a time, ordered a different American to draw the lands from which Colón had brought him.

> el indio, con diligencia y como quien en pronto lo tenía, figuró con las habas lo que el otro había figurado, y por ventura añidió muchas mas islas y tierras, dando como razón de todo en su lengua (puesto que nadie lo entendía) lo que había pintado y significado.[18]

The Native American with diligence and very readily marked with the beans that which the other had drawn but also added "many more islands and lands, giving a complete explanation in his own language." Thus we have evidence for the first geographical lessons about the Americas ever offered in Europe being offered not by Colón but by his very teachers, the indigenous experts. Clearly, Colón was accompanied by well-informed persons who were capable of guiding his travels. And, indeed, the 1493 voyage back to the Caribbean followed the precise route suggested by Native American informants.

After some twenty days of sailing from the Canary Islands, Colón's second fleet reached Dominica (Caire or Quariqui) in early November. Very shortly thereafter, he veered north to Maríagalante (Ayan) and then to Quaréquena or Kerkeria (Guadeloupe). Hernando Colón, writing more than thirty years later (and with his text surviving only in an Italian translation with many apparent mistakes), tells us that "an iron pan" was found this time, although he also states:

> I personally believe that some ignorant person found some shiny stone or flint that looked like iron; for up to now no one has found any articles of iron among them, nor did I ever hear the Admiral mention it. . . . Even if the pan was of iron, this was no great marvel; for the Indians of that island of Guadalupe being Caribs who went sailing and robbing as far as Española, they may have stolen that pan from the Spaniards or Indians on that island; or they may have taken it from the hull of the ship that the Admiral lost . . . or from the wreck of some ship carried by winds or currents from Europe.

Subsequently, when speaking of Colón's return voyage to Europe of 1496, when the fleet went south and east via Guadeloupe, Hernando tells us that the admiral's men looted Carib houses and found "iron which the Indians used to make little hatchets." This fascinating information is, of course, in direct contradiction to his assertion regarding the 1493 voyage's "iron pan" discovery. What are we to make of it? That he didn't re-read his own text? That he was careless in his use of sources for events in which he was not a participant-observer? That the Italian translator made a mistake?

We could argue that some Caribs had obtained iron in the Canary Islands or elsewhere that they had brought home to America. Of course, it is also possible that a wreck may have been the source, but a wreck would ordinarily have produced other articles of recognizable European or African origin. Finally, it is possible that the Caribs had helped the Haitian natives in their police action against the vicious Spaniards left behind in early 1493 at the colony of Navidad by the admiral. (These men had soon started to quarrel among themselves and had begun "taking as many women and as much gold" as they could, precipitating appropriate retaliation by the Americans. Each European had reportedly gathered some "four or five wives" apiece, thus doubtless contributing to the spread of venereal diseases on the island.)[19]

In any case, Colón appears to have become a rather improvident and careless admiral by his 1496 return voyage. Admiral Colón, instead of going north or northeasterly, sailed at first eastward against the prevailing winds and currents. "As the winds were easterly, his provisions running low, and his men tired and in bad humor, on April 6th he bore away south for the Caribbees, which he reached three days later. . . . Next day he set sail again . . . because the men complained that since they were searching for food, [they need not stay in port on Sunday]."

They then sailed to Guadeloupe, where some Caribs resisted their landing. The Spaniards then entered the Americans' houses "looting and destroying all they found." But also "being familiar with the Indian method of making bread, they took their cassava dough and made enough bread to satisfy their needs [for the return voyage]." Colón also captured a female leader (an "Amazon" *cacique*) whom he took back to Spain along with her daughter and thirty other Americans from Haiti.

Prior to reaching the coast of Iberia, the Spaniards on board became so hungry that they reportedly wanted to either eat the Americans with them or throw them overboard. This illustrates the improvidence of Colón in not taking on adequate supplies prior to leaving Haiti and instead depending upon obtaining them from Guadeloupe. Supposedly he had enough on board after stealing bread from the Caribs for twenty days, a length of time adequate perhaps for a rapid westbound voyage but not for an eastbound battle against the currents and winds. The voyage took almost fifty days (from April 20 to after June 8), thus illustrating the radical difference between sailing *with* the sea, as opposed to sailing *against* it.[20]

Hernando Colón tells us that "at that time men had not learned the trick of running far northward to catch the southwest winds."[21] In other words, they hadn't learned of the Gulf Stream and the favorable currents and winds north of the Bahamas. Perhaps, however, it was greed that took Colón southwards to the Antilles, since he continued to believe that more gold could be found to the south. Even more likely is Morison's suggestion that Colón's earlier plans to attack the Caribs in the Antilles included the "real object . . . to obtain Carib slaves for shipment to Spain" because no gold had been found on Cuba or Jamaica.

There can be absolutely no doubt that the Caribs of the Antilles were extremely well acquainted with the westward-moving currents and winds of their area, every island having an obvious lee side and their voyages to the Guianas and Borinquen (Puerto Rico) always having to contend with the former. But Hernando Colón's account of the 1496 eastward voyage suggests that his father still had not learned about winds and currents from the Americans, as I had argued earlier, or that his greed and desire to obtain slaves caused him to ignore the information.

One other significant item comes from Hernando Colón's account of the 1496 voyage which is that the Carib "women also seemed more intelligent than those of the other islands; for the others only measure time by the sun by day and by the moon at night, while these women kept count of time by the other stars, saying: When the Car rises, or such and such a star descends, then is the time to do so and so." This knowledge indicates an advanced stellar astronomy that would be very important in navigation. One caution must be made, and that is to ask who had the capability to understand the Carib women? Doubtless a Taino-Spanish interpreter was used, one who could converse with a bilingual (Taino-Carib or Island Arawak-Taino) woman, but all of this could be subject to misinterpretation. (On the other hand, and in contrast to the many stories about cannibalism, the Spaniards would have gained no propagandistic value from falsifying astronomical information in this way.)[22]

The voyages of Colón also provide us with a great deal of additional information on the extent of geographical knowledge possessed in the 1490s by Caribbean Americans. According to Bernaldez, the Caribbean people "had no diversity in language, and this may be the result of navigation, for they were masters of the sea, and it was because they had no means of navigation that in the Canaries they did not understand one another and each island had its own language."[23]

In the north, the Lucayo (or Yucayo) people of the Bahamas were knowledgeable about the North American mainland, Cuba, and Haiti. Colón wrote: "I will leave for another very large island . . . which they call Colba [Cuba]. In it they say there are many and very large ships and many traders [or sailors]. And from this island [I go to] another which they call Bohío, which also they say is very big. . . . But I have already decided to go to the mainland." The natives that Colón kidnapped said that Cuba was a journey of one day and a half by canoe. "They tell him by signs that there are ten big rivers; and that with their canoes they cannot circle it in 20 days. . . . And the Admiral understood that large ships from the Grand Khan came there and that from there to *tierra firme* was a journey of ten days."[24] This probably indicates that the Lucayo people were also familar with Yucatan or Mexico, since North America would have been less than ten days from Cuba and "large ships" would probably refer to Mesoamerican or South American freight boats.

Colón also learned (by signs) that people from the Northwest "used to come to fight them many times," presumably referring to people from the Florida area.[25] In this connection we can refer here to information found in Pedro Mártir de Angleria's *Decadas del Nuevo Mundo* after he had discussed the seizure of some forty thousand *indígenas* of both sexes carried off for slave labor in Cuba and Haití by the Spaniards to satisfy "their inexhaustible hunger for gold." The "Islas Yucayas" by the 1520s had become a "desert," but referring back to an earlier period he describes how three Yucayos attempted to escape on a raft from Haití but were apprehended two hundred miles to the north by a Spanish vessel returning from Chicora (South Carolina). Pedro Mártir goes on to relate that "so many *palomas* (pigeons) live in the branches [of the *jaruma* trees], that the inhabitants of the great island of Bimini and of the territory of Florida come there to hunt them and they return with their boats full of *pichones*." It is also told "that the Yucaya women are so beautiful that many inhabitants of the nearby lands, attracted by their beauty, abandon their own homes, in order to establish themselves, for love of them, in these places, as a new country. This is, they say, the reason that many of the Yucayas islands have customs which are more civilized like those farther away of Florida and Bimini, regions of older [*mayor*] culture."[26] López de Gomara, writing several decades later, repeats the story that "many men of the Mainland, such as from Florida, Chicora [South Carolina] and Yucatán, took themselves to live with [the beautiful Lucayo women]; and for that reason they had more public order among themselves than in other islands, and much diversity of languages." He also notes that "there are so many *palomas* and other birds, living in the trees, so that people come from the Continent and from Cuba and Haití to take them, and they return with the canoes full of them."[27] It seems likely that López and Mártir obtained their material from the same source. Nonetheless, it seems quite clear that the Lucayos had contact with the mainland of North America and that Americans would have crossed the Florida Channel frequently, thus being directly exposed to possible journeys (involuntary or otherwise) in the Gulf Stream.

Interestingly, the Yuchi Nation (now of Oklahoma) has a tradition of having, in part at least, originated on an island of the Bahamas (Lucayo). This could be related to the possibility that Lucayo people successfully fled to the coast of Chicora during the 1500–1520 period in order to escape Spanish slave raids. Evidence of this can be seen in the fact that the so-called Cusabo people of Chicora in the seventeenth century used the term "bou" for river, as in their name for the Savannah River, Westo-bou, river of the Westo. "Bo" is an Arawak word meaning river or water. The Yuchi lived for a time at Augusta, Georgia, not far from coastal Chicora, and could have absorbed Arawakan refugees from the Bahamas. Interestingly, some scholars have argued that baby hammocks used by the Yuchi may reflect a Caribbean influence.[28]

Colón's diary also reveals that the Cubans knew of Haití and that "behind" it lay "a landmass of exceedingly large size," which must have been North America. The Americans of Haití knew that "behind" Cuba to the south "there is another big island . . . called Yamaye [Jamaica]. The Admiral says he also learned that toward the east there was an island where there were women only [Matininó]. . . . And that the island of [Haití], or the other island of Yamaye, was near mainland, ten days' journey by canoes, which would be 60 or 70 leagues, and that the people there were clothed." Thus the Haitians knew of Cuba and Jamaica and a mainland beyond, doubtless Yucatan or Mexico, and also the Antilles as far as Matininó. The Italian, Cuneo, understood on the second voyage that "Lamahich" was five days from Cuba, with a difficult voyage going or returning, doubtless because of currents. This reference may well be a mixing up of Jamaica and Yucatan, due to the misinterpretation of signs. There is also strong indication that Cubans traveled to Florida and even established some settlements there.[29]

According to Colón's testimony, his belief in the existence of "a very great continent" to the south of the islands was due, in part, to the information about South America received from Native Americans of Guadeloupe, St. Croix, and Borinquen. Hernando, the son, tells us that Colón learned from women on Guadeloupe "that to the south were many islands, some of which were inhabited. This woman and the others called those islands Yaramaqui [Antigua], Cairoaco [Curaçao], Huino, Buriari [Bonaire?], Arubeira [Aruba] and Sixibey. The mainland, which they said was very large, both they and the people of Española [Haití] called Zuania [Guania or Guayana?]. They said that in former times canoes had come from that land to trade, bringing much gold. . . . From the same women they learned where the island of Española lay." Thus the people of the Antilles knew of the South American coast and islands from Guiana [Zuania] to Aruba and also knew of Haití to the north. The people of Haití are also said to have known of Guiana and the southern mainland.

There is no question that the Caribs, in particular, were in frequent contact with South America. On Guadeloupe the Spaniards found *guacamayos* (parrots) that "are only found on the mainland in the coast of Paria and beyond."[30] Evidence that the Caribs traveled great distances, 150 leagues or more, is frequently found. Supposedly much of this travel was for military purposes, but the subject is complex and the widespread trade in *guaní* or *guanin,* an alloy of copper, gold, and other metals, along with other commerce from the south, suggests that the "raiding Caribs" may be a European invention in order to produce an "enemy" population eligible for enslavement.[31]

Evidence of widespread travel is also provided in the diaries and letters by reference to exotic items or words. One example includes cow skulls that Colón saw in the Bahamas. These skulls can most likely be interpreted as buffalo skulls traded over vast distances from North America. A second example consists of the South American parrots already noted. Other examples include honeycombs found on Cuba that must have come from Yucatan, and feathers of the red spoonbill heron exported from Cuba to Mexico.[32]

Reference has already been made to Taino people from the Bahamas to Cuba and Jamaica being acquainted with Yucatan and other areas of the mainland: when Spaniards reached the area of Yucatan in 1517 and again in 1518 they found that the Maya people were already partially aware of what had transpired on the islands invaded earlier by the Europeans. The Maya at Cabo de Catoche in 1517 "made signs to us with the hands asking if we came from the direction of the sunrise, and saying 'Castilan,' 'Castilan' and we could not comprehend what they meant by Castilan." This is according to Bernal Díaz del Castillo, a very unreliable authority. Díaz also tells us that in 1518 the Spaniards met an American woman from Jamaica on the island of Cozumel. She told them "that two years earlier she had started from Jamaica with ten Indians in a large canoe intending to go and fish near some small islands, and that the currents had carried them over to this land where they had been driven ashore, and that her husband and all the Jamaica Indians had been killed and sacrificed." It seems more likely that the Jamaicans had fled from their home to avoid Spanish slave-raiders and that they did not want to fall under European control, thus her story. We must bear in mind that Díaz was writing some fifty years later, that Cubans taken to Yucatan by Juan de Grijalva in 1518 were uniformly treated well by the Maya (when sent to Maya villages unaccompanied by Spaniards), and that Oviedo, a secondhand source but one closer in time, mentions only that some of the Jamaicans had been killed and that the others had fled somewhere else.

In any case, it seems likely that Jamaicans had reached Yucatan and that the Maya knew of "Castilans" (Spaniards, Castilians) from them or other native people.[33] As we shall see, there is also archaeological evidence supporting ancient contacts between Mesoamerica and the Caribbean islands, although Caribbean cultures on balance are more closely connected with South America in trade, cultural relationships, and in myth. The *guanin* traded throughout the Caribbean seems likely to have been derived from the Cauca Valley of Colombia primarily, reaching the islands via the Paria region.[34] The antiquity of contacts will be discussed below.

As regards the construction of rafts by Caribbean Americans, Pedro Mártir tells us that a Lucayo man who was taken as a slave to Haiti attempted to escape in the following way. He had "exercised in his homeland the office of carpenter of buildings" using stone axes. On Haiti "he cut a beam of jaruma wood, hollowed out the middle (spine), placed in it grains of maize and gourds full to the brim with water, to be close at hand for the trip. He compressed together [lashed?] both faces of the trees, dropped the beam into the water, and embarked, admitting on board two relatives, a man and a woman, good swimmers, using oar power to try to reach their native homeplace."[35] The use of this raft-like boat is of great significance, since it indicates a tradition that could have easily supported the lashing together of two boats for greater stability in stormy seas. Perhaps the craft seen by Colón at Galway in 1477 was based upon some such adaptation.

We have already discussed early descriptions of Taino boats, but with one or two exceptions we have not yet referred to the character of boats built by the Antillean Caribs or by the coastal peoples of northern South America and the Guianas. Sven Loven, a Swedish scholar, argues that the Caribs had craft superior to those of the Tainos, but I cannot find any factual basis for such an argument, since the Spaniards failed to fully describe either the Tainos' or the Caribs' boats.[36]

The evidence tends to support a continuity of navigational ability all around the inner Caribbean, in the islands, and along the Guiana coast. Jeronimo Benzoni, in the early 1500s, joined a Spanish expedition to capture slaves along the coast of Venezuela that utilized "very large piraguas, boats employed by the natives, which could hold up to fifty persons." In 1596 the Englishman Doctor Layfield described the people of Dominica:

> wee were met with many Canoes . . . the cause of their comming was to exchange their Tabacco, Pinos, Plantins, Potatoes, and Pepper. . . . Their canoes are of one Tree commonly in breadth, but containing one man, yet in some are seene two yonkers sit shoulder to shoulder. They are of divers length: some for three or foure men that sit in reasonable distance, and in some of them eight or nine persons a rowe. . . . they speake some Spanish

words: they have Wickers platted something like a broad shield to defend the raine, they that want these, use a very broad leafe to that purpose, they provide shelter against the raine.[37]

Thus Layfield saw no really large boats but did notice that the Caribs had wicker-work (which could perhaps be used as mat sails) and plantains.

In 1604 Captain Charles Leigh voyaged along the Guiana coast as far as the Amazon estuary. To the north, on the River Wiapogo, "plantons" were obtained from the Americans (along with honey). Subsequently, the English learned of Caribs arriving "in eight warlike Canowes," one of which was subsequently abandoned. Leigh notes that "their Canowes . . . are able to carry twentie men and victuals for ten dayes."[38]

Two years later Henry Challons reached Santa Lucia and Dominica on a voyage to Virginia that miscarried. At Santa Lucia they "saw certaine of the Savages there about fortie or fiftie, came unto us at our Ship in one of their Canoas, bringing unto us Tobacco, Potatos, Plantins, and Cassavi Bread."[39] They then proceeded to Dominica, where they met a Spanish priest in an incident that will be discussed below, as it involves the question of the use of sails.

Large boats were also made along the Orinoco River. Antonio Vázquez de Espinosa, in the period between 1612 and the 1620s, described boat-making among the Tibitibes people: "They are so patient and ingenious that from a tree which they call *vice,* and from another called *vagasa,* which are of monstrous height and thickness, they manufacture with a scrap of iron which they whet and sharpen like an adz, a boat or dugout which will hold from 400 to 600 jugs of wine and 60 persons with all that is necessary for their food and maintenance."[40]

Fernandez de Oviedo, writing a century earlier, tells us that the Americans of the Cartagena region were able to utilize huge trees "in making canoas, which are boats in which they navigate, so large, that in some go one hundred, and one hundred and thirty men, and they are of a single piece of one tree. And some are wide enough so that a barrel or cask can be held and people can still pass on each side. And some are as wide as ten or twelve palms [spans]."

William H. Sears notes that historical sources seen by him document canoes in the sixty- to eighty-foot range for both the Antilles and northern South America. He goes on to assert that "physical laws" make a "comparatively narrow dugout a very easily propelled form. Paddles could easily move such hulls, without strain, to speeds in excess of six knots. Twenty-four hours at such speeds covers a lot of water."[41]

As regards the Caribs of the islands, some of our best descriptions come from a work credited to Charles de Rochefort (sometimes known as Cesar de Rochefort), from the middle of the seventeenth century. The author (perhaps one "Father Raymond" Breton) states that the Caribs of Dominica took great pain in the making of their "*piragas*" or vessels "wherein they go to sea. . . . These vessels are made of one great Tree, which they make hollow, smooth, and polish with an unimaginable dexterity: The greater sort of *Piragas* are many times rais'd higher all about, especially towards the poop, with some planks. . . . These Shallops are so large as many times to carry fifty men with all their Arms." Before acquiring metal tools "they were obliged, as the Virginians, and some other Savages were, to set fire at the foot of the Trees . . . and so they undermined the Tree by little and little." Among the officers of the Caribs was a "Captain of a *Piraga* . . . and these are named *Tiouboutouli Canaoa*." Also "amongst those who have every one the commande of a Vessel in particular, they have also an Admiral or General at Sea, who commands the whole fleet: Him they call *Nhalenè*." On war expeditions, next to the "care they take about their Arms, they also provide themselves sufficiently with belly timber, and take along with them in their little vessels good quantities of *cassava*, boiled Fish, Fruits, and particularly *Bananas*, which keep a long time, and the meal of *Maniac*." They also, along with Native Brazilians, "take along with them to the Wars a certain number of Women, to dress their meat, and look to the *piragas* when they are got ashore." Their custom

> is to go from Island to Island to refresh themselves, and to that end they have Gardens even in those which are desert, and not inhabited. They also touch at the Islands of their own Nation, to joyn their Forces. . . . Their ancient and irreconcilable Enemies are the *Arouacas* . . . [*Alouagues*], who live in that part of . . . America which is known [as]. . . . Guyana or Guayana. . . . The cause of this immortal enmity between our Insulary *Caribbians* and those people hath been already hinted in the Chapter of Origin of the *Caribbians*, to wit, that those *Arouagues* have cruelly persecuted the Caribbians of the Continent, their Neighbours, the Relations of our Islanders . . . and that they have continually warr'd against them to exterminate them, or at least, to drive them out of their habitations.

The Caribs of the islands were not themselves directly attacked by the Arawaks. Island Caribs came from as far away as Santa-Cruce (St. Croix), a distance of three hundred leagues, to attack the Arawaks of Guyana. Rochefort also notes that the Caribs, in defending themselves from

Spanish slave-raids, were often able to capture Spanish ships, which they looted and then burned. "True it is, they pardoned the *Negro-slaves* they met with, and having brought them ashore put them to work in their Habitations; thence came the *Negroes* which they have at present in St. Vincents and some other Islands [perhaps ancestors of the later Garifuna of Belize after intermarrying with Indigenous Americans]."[42] One can see that the Island Caribs were certainly very capable at sea, with enough experience to allow them to survive voyages across the Atlantic if necessity required.

Some scholars, notably Marshall B. McKusick, have doubted whether the Carib *piraguas* (pirogues) were actually built up with plank sides prior to European contact. Jean Du Tertre (1667) described planks being added as follows:

> Without using nails they lash and fit these planks upon the pirogue with cordage made of *mahot* fiber. They next caulk the joints with oakum made from the beaten bark of *mahot*. Over this caulking they bind small sticks with *mahot* cordage. . . . This is indeed very watertight, but it does not last long and must be done over and over again . . . . These pirogues are usually 40 feet long and 7 to 8 feet wide. . . . The pirogues sometimes carry 50 people and all their luggage, and run by sails or paddles. . . . They sometimes go 200 to 300 leagues in fairly bad weather.

It seems quite likely that this use of planks to enlarge the boats was pre-European, since, as noted earlier, Nicolo Syllacia (from Guillermo Coma) mentioned such a feature in the 1490s, and since the method of attaching the planks seems non-European.

Antonio Vázquez de Espinosa saw tremendous use of dugout boats by Americans in the Caribbean-Venezuelan region between 1612 and 1620, a use apparently little changed by European intrusion because the region around the Windward Islands, Trinidad, and the Orinoco mouths was still basically in American hands. Dugouts were used on all of the rivers for inland travel but also for extensive voyaging at sea. "The navigation and route of the natives of the island of Trinidad . . . pass through the Dragon's Mouths, which lie 7 leagues from the island of Trinidad; they are exceedingly dangerous at all times because of the strong currents and riffles." In spite of the dangerous waters, the Americans navigated as far as Margarita Island, off of Venezuela, as well as southward.

The Caribs of the Grenada area, called "Camajuyas," along with other Windward Islanders, went "with their dugout navies on robbing expeditions along the whole coast of the Spanish Main, the island of Trinidad and Margarita and others." The Camajuyas had captured a Portuguese slave ship and had colonized five hundred Africans from the ship on a small island ("Potopoturo").

According to Vásquez de Espinosa, a naval war between Araucas of Trinidad, with 60 dugouts, and the Garina Caribs of the Orinoco, with 120 dugouts, was fought in 1596 on one of the channels of the great river. Thus it is clear that American navigation in the southwest part of the Caribbean persisted well after European intrusion.[43]

The Warao people, ancient inhabitants of parts of the Orinoco delta region of Venezuela and Guyana, are well known as a notable seagoing and canoe-using people. Johannes Wilbert, who has worked extensively with the Warao, states that "besides easily accommodating one hundred people, the Warao boats can take three cannons, as they did in the seventeenth and eighteenth centuries." It is believed that the Warao were pioneers in the earliest settlement of the Antilles and Florida (Timucua being a related language) since the "place names throughout the Caribbean . . . are definitely Warao. They can be interpreted without stretching the language in any way."

Haburi, the ancient culture-hero of the Warao, invented canoes prior to people existing on the earth. Canoe-making is considered "divine-service," accompanied by chants and poetry. A canoe-maker must go through spiritual preparation and receives great recognition for successful voyages. The Warao as early as 1595 were trading with Trinidad for tobacco but their "seafaring goes back to prehistoric times." The voyage from the Orinoco to Trinidad is difficult, but the Warao also recalled when the shallow depression between the two areas was not filled with water, thousands of years ago.

Warao canoes often have planks to heighten the sides, lashed together to the gunwale with vines. The hull is also widened by means of fire, hot water, and cross poles. They also use "sails of leaf-stalk matting or triangular ones of cloth" in the Upper Delta. The mast for the sail "rests in a step mounted on the bottom of the boat." It is also supported by two "mast partners." The Warao's large canoes are categorized by Wilbert as "seagoing vessels" with a paddle mounted at the stern, lashed to the gunwale as a rudder. We can assume, I believe, that other Caribbean-area American groups had canoe-using customs and procedures similar to the Warao.[44]

Turning to the region of Central America and the Maya, we find that later sources confirm what Colón had found: that the Americans were builders of large boats and were active maritime merchants. When Spanish corsairs began to touch upon the Yucatan coast between 1517 and 1519 the crewmen noted the extensive Maya use of boats. One writer saw "about one hundred boats" in one location. Another author notes that "more than 100 canoes or boats" with about three thousand people came towards them (or about thirty persons per boat). The same writer also specifically refers to a Maya boat with thirty men on board. Navigation across the rough waters of the strait between Cozumel Island and Yucatan was also described as a frequent occurrence by Spanish writers of the period.[45]

López de Gomara, writing at secondhand, describes Maya boats in connection with the invasion armada of Hernán Cortés (1519). He states that during a period of furious wind a canoe was seen crossing from Yucatan to Acuzamil (Cozumel) a *la vela*. This is extremely significant because it shows that Mayas were capable of navigating in bad weather and also with a sail.[46]

The use of sails by the Maya is apparently confirmed by Bernal Díaz del Castillo, although he writes fifty years after the events and had read López de Gomara prior to writing. Díaz notes that in 1517 he saw "ten very large canoes, which are called piraguas, full of Indians native to that population, and they came by oar and sail. These canoes are made like troughs, and are large and of thick logs and carefully dug out until hollow; and all are of one log, and there are many of them which can hold forty Indians." The next day a dozen large canoes were seen, with Indian oarsmen. Díaz also noted that with their boats the Americans navigated by oars from "coast to coast."[47]

A letter written within a few months after the invasion of Cortés into Mexico states: "The next day at noon, a canoe with sail was seen coming in the direction of the island [Cozumel]."[48] Aside from the use of sails, there is also evidence that the Maya and Aztecs used planks to raise the height of their boats and that there may have also been the use of "a boat of two canoes tied together." Such a craft was seen at the lagoon of Bacalar in 1641. Wharves seem to have also been constructed by the Mexicans on Lake Texcoco and are known archaeologically for the Maya in Quintana Roo and Belize. Some two thousand years ago the people living on Chetumal Bay in Belize were trading great distances. They expanded their seafaring culture as time went on, developing a dock for their boats.

By the end of the eighth century, a series of "strategic coastal strong-holds was established by canoe seafaring peoples. These people were called the Itzá by archaeologists. . . . Eventually, these merchant warriors founded a permanent port facility, on an island off the northern coast . . . [Cozumel] where they could command a rich trade." A small island was transformed "into a simple round and massive platform with masonry docking along its entire periphery for the large dugout canoes used by these peoples."

Evidence of pre-Columbian navigational activities is also derived from a study of pictures of boats, many with raised ends, found in various codices, murals, and sculptured walls of the Mexico-Yucatan region.[49] A great deal is known about the incredible maritime trade maintained along the Mexican-Central American coast by American navigators. This regular sea trade is especially well documented between Tabasco, around Yucatan, and on to Honduras, with additional trade in gold and other products extending from Nicaragua and Panama to Veracruz.[50]

The coastal area of Tabasco, with its numerous bays and navigable rivers and channels (like the mouths of the Orinoco and other great rivers) is a perfect place for the evolution of maritime skills. It is also a region, with adjoining southern Veracruz, where a significant number of language groups came together and sometimes overlapped, including Nahuatl (Nahuat), Maya, and Mixe-Zoque. While Tabasco came to be an area of Putun Maya dominance, several Nahuat-speaking towns were located in the midst of the Maya, and one prominent trading center, Xicalango, was especially connected to the "Mexican" (Nahuan) people. Evidence indicates that the Triple Alliance of the Valley of Mexico (the so-called Aztec Empire) and its predecessors maintained a trading connection with Xicalango, although there is contradictory evidence as to whether they controlled it. In any case, the Putun Maya came under considerable "Mexican" and "Mixteca-Puebla" cultural influences, which they helped to spread by sea southward as far as Honduras.

The Putun appear to have expanded along the coast at least by the 800s CE, soon establishing a major mercantile center at Cozumel, an island along the east coast of Yucatan. They also expanded their commercial dominance to the Chetumal region, along the Belize coast, and down to Nito and Naco in the Guatemala-Honduras region. Putun merchants were permanently stationed in these areas. Jeremy A. Sabloff tells us that "they were expert sailors and canoers." Their language became a "lingua franca" of trade from Veracruz to Honduras. They were "waterborne traders *par excellence* and helped institute econopolitical trends which came to characterize the Post-Classic Period."[51]

Arthur G. Miller adds that "it is known that there was extensive trade via seagoing vessels from the east coast of the Yucatan Peninsula along the Caribbean coast as far as Nicaragua and Panama," this in addition to the vessels plying from Tabasco to the east coast of Yucatan. Added to this was the evolution of Cozumel and later Tulum as holy shrines of the female spirit-power Ix Chel, associated with the moon, childbirth, procreation, weaving, and medicine. Miller suggests that the east coast of Yucatan "became a kind of mecca for the Maya and possibly for many people from the rest of Mesoamerica. Pre-Columbian pilgrims came to this area [Tulum-Tancah] to be renewed, reborn." An "international" culture with "Mixteca-Puebla" influences developed as a result, one that was flourishing when cut down by Spanish imperialism in the sixteenth century. The people who built Tulum up after 1440, presumably Putun Maya, "controlled the sea."[52]

Earlier, in the 900s, the Putun had either conquered or helped to conquer the inland city of Chichen Itzá (918). Subsequently, around 987 they facilitated the movement of Toltecs from the inland Tula north of present-day Mexico City. The Toltecs, led by the banished Quetzalcoatl-Kukulcan, traveled to the Gulf Coast and then reached Chichen Itzá—apparently with the help of the Putun Maya fleets and marine facilities. The Putun and their allies continued to be powerful maritime factors until at least 1536, when they sent an expedition of fifty war canoes from Chetumal to aid Ulua, Honduras, against the Spaniards. Later, disease and warfare "almost eliminated the Indians of coastal Honduras," with the surviving Maya probably being absorbed by Jicaque survivors. Inland, in Tabasco and Chiapas, however, the canoe-using Acalan-Putun were able to remain independent until 1695 in part of their former territory.[53]

The significance of Putun Maya and related maritime activity can hardly be overrated. Hernan Cortés, speaking of interviews with men of Xicalango and Tabasco, noted that some of them had been to most of the towns along the coast and could describe them as far as the residence of Pedrarias Dávila (Panama). We also know that their influence reached up the Veracruz coast and into the interior as far as Tula, Hidalgo. We can suggest that they were also in contact with the Caribbean islands, from evidence cited earlier and from archaeological and ethnological evidence to be discussed below.[54]

In the future, perhaps, other scholars will be able to enlighten us with detailed studies of Americans as pilgrims to sacred sites as well as of regular routes of maritime trade.

Mesoamerican navigational skills also extended southward along the Pacific Coast into Cuscatlán (El Salvador) and Nicaragua. In 1586 Fray Alonso Ponce made a trip across the Gulf of Fonseca, ferried by American seamen. The boats "which went on that journey are not very long, but wide, for in the hollow part by the floor they are a *vara* and a half wide, and as much high, and they gradually get narrower until the sides are only a little more than two palms apart at the top." The boats are made from very thick trees.

> Those canoes navigate well, and they make them in that form in order that they will better withstand the large waves and heavy seas ordinary in that region. Ordinarily, they propel them with paddles although sometimes they heist sails of cotton cloth or straw mats [petates]. . . . In each canoe . . . there were eight oarsmen, and for each friar there was a little awning, four palms wide, made of little mats with rods forming an arch from one edge of the canoe to the other . . . between the awnings were the oarsmen.

This use of sails seems to be aboriginal, since as J. Eric Thompson has pointed out, "it is . . . well known that sails were used on the west coast of South America."[55] Clinton R. Edwards and other writers have also documented the use of balsa craft and other vessels with sails on the Pacific Coast of South America and Mesoamerica. Benzoni noted the common use of sails in the early 1500s.[56]

In summary, we can be reasonably confident that the Americans of Mesoamerica were acquainted with the use of wind power for navigation, as well as with the specific use of both cotton and matting sails. This is strongly reinforced by Fernandez de Oviedo's assertion that the Americans of Cartagena navigated their canoes "con dos velas, que son la maestra y el trinquete; las cuales velas ellos hacen de muy buen algodón." That is, they used two sails in their boats, a mainsail and a foresail, both made of very good cotton.[57] Fernandez de Oviedo was in the region very soon after the initial Spanish attempts at invasion and thus his observation should be accurate (especially since he was inclined to give his fellow Europeans credit for any positive influences upon the Americans).

Now let us return to the Antilles. Georg Friederici favored the idea that the Caribs' use of sails was of pre-European contact in origin. In part this was because of a study of the Island Carib language that revealed twenty-six words relating to sails. McKusick, on the other hand, rejected the idea, basing his argument on a single piece of evidence. He states: "it can be clearly demonstrated that the Island Carib adopted sails from Europeans." He then quotes from the account of Henry Challons's voyage in 1606 to Virginia, as written by the pilot John Stoneman some time afterwards. Stoneman, it should be stressed, was unable to speak Spanish. In any event, he states that at the island of Dominica they saw a white flag approaching that proved to be a Spanish friar in a canoe with some Caribs. The friar "cried aloud in the Latine tongue" asking them to rescue him from his American companions and stating that he had been a prisoner for sixteen months, two other Franciscans having been killed. "We demanded of him then, how he got so much favour to preserve his life. . . . He answered, because he did shew the Savages how to fit them Sayles for their Cannoas, which greatly pleased the Savages as appeared, for we saw them to use sayles in their canoas, which hath not been seene before." The sails were allegedly made from linen cloth recovered from three Spanish vessels that had shipwrecked on the island of Guadeloupe. He also informed them of gold or copper he had discovered in a stream on Dominica, as well as sugarcane plants growing there.

The English sent the Caribs away "much discontented" and carried "Friar Blaseus" off towards Puerto Rico, where all were captured by the Spaniards and taken to Spain. Nothing more is said of the Franciscan, nor did he help the English prisoners in Sevilla, where he was from and where they were held captive for a time.

McKusick accepts the above account as proving not only that the Caribs of Dominica acquired a knowledge of sailing from a Franciscan friar from Sevilla, but that the Caribs of Martinique, Guadeloupe, and every other island did so as well! I won't attempt to analyze the entire story, but suffice to say that the Caribs had perfectly fine cotton cloth and matting of their own manufacture and did not need castaway linen; that the good friar is unlikely to have known any better than any other non-sailor how to make sails, erect and attach masts in a dugout canoe, adjust a canoe for the effect of the use of sails, and all of the other intricacies of navigation by sailing; that Stoneman, not knowing any Spanish (or probably much Latin) could not be expected to have understood everything he had heard; and, finally, that Friar Blaseus's two fellow Franciscans could have easily been enlisted by him in his alleged sail-making and lived, if the story were true.

In brief, one little secondhand story of doubtful accuracy does not a navigational complex make! Friar Blaseus's story would have us also believing that gold or copper and sugarcane were present on Dominica in 1606, information to be questioned at the very least. As for Stoneman's not having seen canoes with sails before, it would appear that his previous sailing experience was in North American waters rather than in the Caribbean.

Supplementing Stoneman is the report of John Nicholl, an Englishman who had reached the Carib region around 1605, a year before. Nicholl states: "before our arrival, three Spanish ships were cast away, and much of the goodes these Indians had saved with their Boats, and hid it in the Woods, they had so much Roan cloth, that all their Periagoes had sayles thereof." To give a single Franciscan the credit for such a wide use of sails would seem very unlikely indeed.[58]

Certainly, later French visitors to the Antilles found the Caribs very adept at the use of sails. Rochefort notes that "the sails of the Caribbians are made of cotton, or a kind of Mat of Palm-leaves. They have an excellent faculty of rowing with certain little Oars, which they move very fast. They take along with them also some *Canows,* which are their least kind of Vessels, to attend their *Piragas.*" When on journeys

> Their Arms and Provisions are well fastened to the *Piragas,* so that if the Vessel comes to overturn, which happens often, they set it right again without losing any thing of what was in it: And upon those occasions, being so good Swimmers as we have reported them, they are not troubled for their own persons, so far that they have sometimes laugh'd at the Christians, who, being neer them upon these occasions, endeavor'd to relieve them. Thus the Tapinambous [Tupinambas of Brazil] laugh'd at some Frenchmen upon the like accident, as De Lery relates.[59]

It seems clear, then, that the Caribs (and other Americans) were ideally prepared for stormy seas, being able to swim great distances and having their supplies protected from the vessel's overturning.

It would also seem highly likely that the Caribs, like the natives of the Canary Islands, knew how to use sails of palm-matting prior to European contact.[60] Only such a tradition could have allowed for the transition to cotton or other cloth sails, since one must first know how to fasten the sails to the boat. It does little good to have a cloth sail if the technology of erecting and securing masts and harnessing wind power is lacking. But especially compelling is the evidence already cited for Cartagena and Yucatan, coupled with reports relating to the use of sails in the Orinoco and Amazon basins.

The use of sails (cotton or matting) by Americans is well documented for the Pacific coast of South America and Central America. It would be incredible if such use did not also occur on the Caribbean side of the Isthmus of Panamá. Giroalmo de Benzoni depicts a sail on an American raft around 1550, while a description of the huge freight raft captured by Spaniards in 1527 off of Peru includes reference to "masts and yards of very fine wood, and cotton sails in the same shape and manner as on our own ships." A sail has been recovered, along with toy rafts, from aboriginal graves in northern Chile.

Pierre Barrere includes in his *Nouvelle Relation de la France Equinoxiale* (published in 1743) a drawing of Carib pirogues from French Guiana, one of which has a sail made of palm matting. It is flat, supported by a wooden pole as a mast. He also refers to pirogues of thirty to forty feet length and describes the use of planks.[61]

Evidence relating to the knowledge of sailing principles and to the general navigational capabilities of the Caribbean natives is provided by the case in 1516 when seventy or eighty Spaniards in a caravel and a *bergantín* (brig) sailed from Santiago de Cuba to the Guanaxa Islands off of Honduras (now Roatan). There they enslaved many peaceful Guanaxa people and carried them in the caravel to Havana, Cuba. The Americans were subsequently able to overcome a few Spanish guards, seize the sailing ship "y haciéndose a la vela, cual si fueran expertos navegantes, volvieron a su patria que distaba más de doscientas lenguas."[62] In short, the Americans were such "expert navigators" that they were able to sail from Havana to Honduras, a distance of more than two hundred leagues, in a European vessel with no assistance from any non-Americans; and this after having been kept below decks during their journey to Havana. Clearly, they knew something about sails. It seems very likely that they also had prior experience navigating between Cuba and the Gulf of Honduras.

Many other examples of long voyages undertaken by Americans under adverse circumstances can also be cited. In 1738 or 1739 some Native Peruvians managed to escape from servitude in the Juan Fernandez Islands in a "simple canoe" without provisions and supplies. They successfully made their way eastward to Valparaiso, some 360 miles over open ocean, in spite of difficult winds and currents.[63]

Turning to the Atlantic coast of North America we find that Americans also went out to sea. On the South Carolina coast, for example, the Sewee outfitted boats with sails and on one occasion a group of them reportedly decided to visit England. They outfitted a canoe with sails and went out into the Atlantic but were picked up by a British vessel and sold as slaves. This apparently was prior to European colonization.[64]

In 1524 Verrazano saw dugout boats, perhaps near Chesapeake Bay, that were twenty feet long and four feet broad, while canoes were seen at or near Narraganset Bay, going out to sea with fourteen or fifteen men in them. He also saw how dugouts, large enough to hold ten or twelve persons, were made. One report from a later date states that Americans navigated between New Jersey, New York, and the Chesapeake Bay, using canoes especially outfitted with sails and decks. "But when they want [to go] a distance over the sea, as for instance to Virginia or New Holland, then they fasten two punts [canoes, dugouts] together broadwise with timbers over them, right strongly put together, the deck made completely tight and side board of planks; sails of rugs and frese [cloth] joined together; ropes and tackle made of bast and slender spruce roots; [and they] also mason for themselves a little fireplace on deck."[65]

In 1643 Roger Williams published his *Key Into the Language of America* in which he included many words relating to *Kitthan,* the sea. An Indian boat or canoe made of pine, oak, or chestnut was called *Mishoon.* Of greater interest is the word *Sepakehig* for "a sayle" and *Sepakehommaûta* for "Let us sayle" and *Wunnâgehan* for "We have a faire wind." Williams notes: "their owne reason hath taught them to pull of[f] a Coat or two and set it up on a small pole, with which they will saile before a wind ten, or twenty mile." He then goes on to add additional sailing expressions. "It is wonderful to see how they will venture in those Canoes, and how (being oft overset I have my selfe been with them) they will swim a mile, yea two or more safe to land: I having been necessitated to passe waters diverse times with them, it hath pleased God to make them many times the instruments of my preservation." Their word for anchor is *Kunnósnep,* thus showing that the Narragansetts of Rhode Island were well equipped for sea navigation and for survival at sea.[66]

Indeed, an Englishman writing twenty years earlier noted that the Massachusetts Americans were "very adventurous in their Boates," although reportedly not going all the way to Virginia. Horace P. Beck, in his study of Native Americans as sea-fighters after European contact, provides numerous examples of superb seamanship in the northeastern region, including the capture of European longboats and vessels equipped with sails. Beck cites sources that assert that Americans were operating a "Biscay shallop" with sails, oars, and eight crewmen along the Maine coast in 1602 and that seven years later "the countrypeople" possessed two French shallops somewhere near Penobscot Bay. Beck then goes on to give many examples of Native seamanship in New England during the seventeenth and eighteenth centuries. He also cites evidence that Americans were harpooning whales in New England waters as early as 1605 and that they may have taught the later white settlers how to take whales at sea.[67]

There is also some evidence for the use of sails in the St. Lawrence River in pre-Columbian times and one archaeologist thought that he found evidence for the use of sails in a pre-European contact site in the southeastern United States.[68]

To the south, along the Brazilian coast, the Portuguese and other Europeans also witnessed American navigation at sea. An Italian traveling with Magellan in 1519 noted that the Brazilians' boats were made from the trunk of a tree: "son tan grandes estos árboles, que en una sola canoa caben trienta y aún cuarenta hombres, que bogan con remos parecidos a las palas de nuestros panaderos." Thus the boats held thirty to forty men, according to Pigafetta. In the 1550s Hans Staden noted that the dugout boats of the Santos-Rio de Janeiro area could hold up to thirty men, were four feet in width, with some being larger and some smaller. "In these they move rapidly with oars, navigating with them as far as they wish. When the sea is rough they take the canoes ashore until good weather comes again. They do not go more than two leagues straight out to sea but along the coast they navigate far."[69] In 1565 the Jesuit Jose de Anchieta stated that the Americans of the same region had dozens or more *canoas*

> que hazen de una corteza sola de un árbol cada una, poniéndoles otros pedaços de la misma corteza por bordos muy bien atados con vimbres, y son tan grandes que lleva cada una dellas viente y 25 y más personas con sus armas y victualles, y algunas más de 30, y passan ollas y mares tan bravas que es cosa espantosa y que no se pode creer ni imaginar sino el que lo ve, y mucho mejor de quien no las passa; y si se las anega, échanse todos el agua y sácanla fuera a la playa, o en la misma mar la esgotan y se tornan a meter en ella y van su caminho; y acaesce muchas vezes que con la grande furia de la tempestad se las haze pedaços, y ellos nihilo-minus vanse a tierra.

Thus the Brazilian boats were also very well made, were very fast and maneuverable, and could be righted at sea if necessary. They were used to carry thirty or more persons and supplies considerable distances along the coast, as, for example, from Santos (Sao Vicente) to Rio de Janeiro.[70]

It is also interesting that evidence exists for the large-scale migration of South Americans by canoe, such as the movements of the Tupí from the south coast of Brazil up to the Bahia area and then up the Amazon a great distance. Similarly, evidence exists for Carib movements by water to new homelands.[71]

In general, it would appear that the Americans of the Caribbean and adjacent coasts built the biggest boats and were more accustomed to going far out to sea, while the Atlantic coastal groups (south of the Guianas and north of the Bahamas) were more oriented to staying within a certain distance of land (six miles or so). On the other hand, all were capable of being carried out to sea by strong winds and currents and yet surviving rough water, especially since most were used to being overturned and had learned how to anticipate that danger.

The indigenous people of Terra Nova or Newfoundland also were accustomed to venturing out to sea, but in a totally different kind of watercraft. In 1613, for example, some Englishmen met two "canoas" holding eight men or women "for commonly in every Canoa there is one woman." Further,

> Their Canoa, are about twenty foote long, and foure foote and a halfe broad in the middle aloft, and for their Keele and timbers, they have thin light pieces of dry Firre, rended as it were lathes: and instead of Boordes, they use the outer Burch barke, which is thin, and hath many folds, sewed together with a thred made of a small root quartered. They will carry four persons well, and weigh not one hundred weight: they are made in forme of a new Moone, stem and stern alike, and equally distant from the greatest breadth: from the stem and sterne here riseth a yard high a light thin staffe whipped about with small roots, which they take hold of to bring the Canoa ashore . . . and will never put to See but in a calme, or very faire weather: in the middle of the Canoa is higher a great deale then in the Bowe and quarter, they be all bearing from the Keele to the portlesse not with any circular line but with a right line.

The Newfoundlanders had acquired sails from the Europeans but were using them as coverings it would seem, although, one report has them using sails at sea by 1769.[72]

In 1618 another visitor wrote of the Newfoundland boats as follows: "The Natives . . . have great store of red Oaker, which they use to colour their Bodies, Bowes and Arrowes, and Cannowes withall, which Cannowes are built in shape, like the Wherries on the River of Thames; but that they are much longer, made with the rinds of Birch trees, which they sew very artificially and close together, and overlay every seame with Turpentine."[73]

Much earlier, in 1508 or 1509, seven Americans were picked up at sea by a French vessel and taken to Rouen in France. The description of the American boat indicates that it was either manned by Newfoundlanders or by Micmacs from the Cape Breton region. Two original accounts exist describing this event, the first of which is added as an appendix by either Joannes Multivallis or Herricum Stephanun (Henri Estienne) to the *Chronicon* of Eusebius for the year of 1509. The account states, in abbreviated late Latin:

> Septe hoies sylvestres ex ea insula (quae terra nova dicit) Rothomagu adducti sut com cymba vestimetis & armis eoru. Fuliginei sut coloris, grossis labris, stigmata in facie gerentes ab aure ad mediu mentu, instar lividae venule per maxillas deductre. Crime negro & grosso ut equa iuba. Barba p tota vita nulla . . .

Translated, the above means that seven "sylvan" or "rustic" men were brought from an island called terra nova to Rouen, with their boat, clothing, and weapons. They were of a darkish complexion, with thick lips, with marks on their faces extending along the jaws from the ears to the chin like livid veins. Their hair was black and thick like a horse's mane: "cymba eoru corticea qua homo una manu evehat in humeros." Their boat was of bark and a man may raise it aloft to his shoulders, with one hand.

The above account, published in 1512, has been alleged to refer to a voyage undertaken by Thomas Aubert of Dieppe in 1508. The latter is given credit for bringing the men to Rouen in the following year by several later sources, including an anonymous letter of 1539 written by a Frenchman of Dieppe and published by Giovanni Ramusio (in Italian) a few years later. Pierre Biard, writing in the early 1600s, also refers to Aubert's bringing the Americans to Europe, but it is likely that he was copying Ramusio, since he states that he read about the event.[74]

It should be noted that the 1539 letter only states that Aubert "was the first who brought hither [to France] people of the said country" from Newfoundland or Cape Breton. Likewise, Biard does not mention any number but only "some of the Natives." The reason this could be important is that Cardinal Pietro Bembo in his chronological history of Venice refers to the same or a similar incident for the earlier year of 1508. He states: "Navis Gallica dum in oceano inter non longe a Britannia faceret, naviculum ex mediis abscissis viminibus arborum que libro solido contectis edificatam cepit: in qua homines erant septem mediocri statura, colore sub-obscuro, lato & patente vultu." Translated, the above states that a French ship in the midst of the ocean not far from Britain found a small boat made from halved, cut-off wicker-work from trees (bark) that was made solid and fastened together, in which there were seven persons of medium stature, of a somewhat darkish color, with broad and open countenances.

The Italian version of Bembo is very similar in stating a French ship sailing in the ocean not far from England found a little boat of wicker-work in which were seven men "e d'una cicatrice di violato segnata." That is, the men had scars or marks of violet color. They were also taken to Rouen.[75]

It seems quite likely that the seven men of 1508 and the seven men of 1509 were one and the same, but it does make a difference whether or not they were discovered by Aubert near Newfoundland-Cape Breton or by some other French vessel near Britain. I am inclined to believe that the former is the case; however, other writers have interpreted Bembo's evidence to support the idea of Americans being able to drift to Europe. It may well be that the Parisian source should be regarded as the more accurate but that the Americans were picked up somewhere between Newfoundland and Britain.[76]

A North American archaeologist, E. F. Greenman, has argued that people utilizing bark craft of the kind described above for the Newfoundlanders, or using skin-covered Inuit-type kayaks, could have traveled across the North Atlantic during the Pleistocene period (forty thousand to ten thousand years ago) when an archipelago of ice sheets and icebergs might have existed from France and Britain to Newfoundland and New England. Some of the issues involved have been discussed earlier, but the concept will be discussed further in the next chapter; here it is sufficient to note that Greenman places great emphasis upon Newfoundland-type bark boats and Inuit skin-covered boats as vessels available for traveling across the North Atlantic, taking advantage of ice islands as places for drying out the boats en route. These ice islands presumably existed prior to ten thousand years ago and also, on occasion, in more modern times as when large numbers of polar bears were brought to Iceland on floating ice sheets, presumably from the coast of Greenland, after the Norse occupation of Iceland. Inuit navigation will be discussed in chapter 6, focusing upon the arrival of kayaks in Europe.[77]

How far back in time did American navigational abilities extend? This is a question very difficult to answer, because materials made of wood, bark, and skin do not usually survive well archaeologically. Nonetheless, we will deal with this question below and in chapter 4, showing evidence that Americans were utilizing boats several thousand years ago. Moreover, I believe that an argument can be made to support the notion that American shipbuilding and navigation may have been more advanced in ancient than in modern times. The pattern of cultural influences that existed along the Pacific coast from Bolivia (Tiahuanaco), Peru, and Ecuador north to western Mexico suggests regular intercommunication by sea at a very early date, probably back to five thousand years ago. Similar cultural connections probably existed between Louisiana, Mexico, and Peru from 5000 BP (before the present).

Similarly, the intensive and extensive influence of Mesoamerica in the southeastern United States and the Ohio Valley suggests regular maritime contact that probably diminished after about 1450 CE. It should be noted, however, that when the English invaded Virginia in 1607 they learned of rumors to the effect that several Powhatan leaders were of Mesoamerican origin (Wahunsonakak and Opechkankano); that is, they had come from "New Spain." On the whole, however, it seems likely that Mesoamerican contact must have been greater in the pre-1450 period than later. For example, the art work found on shells at the Spiro Mound, Oklahoma (1000–1500 CE), seems to this writer to be part of the Mesoamerican culture area, and the shells used were from either Vera Cruz or Florida. At Cahokia, Illinois, a marker resembling the Maya time symbol has been found from the same general period.[78]

Archaeologists and other scholars are developing a better understanding of the antiquity of navigation and maritime trade in the Caribbean region. William H. Sears tells us that "Starting thousands of years before the birth of Christ, one trait or cluster after the other points to contacts and origins across the Caribbean and the Gulf of Mexico. . . . To me, the accumulated evidence strongly suggests movement up through the Antilles and/or across the Gulf of Mexico by many groups of people over several millennia." Such groups brought to North America (especially Florida) the Timucua language, shell tools, maize horticulture especially adapted for Florida's topography, methods of preserving maize, fiber-tempered pottery, and certain forms of decoration. Important also was the spread of *nicotiana rustica* and the tobacco complex from South America, an event that would appear to extend back to very ancient times.

There are numerous South American influences in the Caribbean but there are also important Mexican-Yucatecan influences, such as the ritual ballgame complexes of Puerto Rico and the Dominican Republic, featuring the use of Mesoamerican-style yokes or collars.

The Timucua language of Florida connects with Warao of the Orinoco in about 75 percent of its basic structures and processes. Both languages also have a "proto-Arawak" stratum. A split of about 2000–3000 BCE is suggested. Sears argues that about three thousand to five thousand years ago movements by sea occurred between South America to Florida, with influences continuing.

Donald W. Lathrap commented in 1977 that the entire Caribbean area was "a wide-open avenue" as early as 3000 BCE, with the Taino perhaps dominating early trade with Mesoamerica. Honduran obsidian has been found underwater in Jamaica, illustrating one possible item of trade. There is also some indication of seaborne raiding of the Yucatan coast by "Caribbean peoples."[79] In addition, there is evidence of the linguistic influence of Arawak and Carib languages upon Maya and other Mesoamerican tongues, suggesting periods of intensive contact by sea.[80]

In the next chapter we shall see that maritime activity in North America extends back to at least eight thousand years ago. Along the Pacific Coast of America, trading between the Americans of the Santa Elena Peninsula, Ecuador, and the west coast of Mexico goes back to 1500 BCE. The South Americans were also trading with Costa Rica between 100 BCE and 600 CE. "Between about 1500 and 1100 BC, the Machalilla [of Ecuador] . . . were in contact with the northern Andean highlands, with the west coast of Mexico, and possibly with Soconusco [Chiapas]." Allison C. Paulsen also sees a possible relationship between the Chavín de Huantar culture of Peru and the Olmecs of Veracruz, Mexico. Paulsen argues for "a long-term, long-range network of maritime trade along the Pacific coast between southwest Ecuador and western Mesoamerica."[81]

The widespread use of rafts by American peoples should also be discussed. Antonio Vázquez de Espinosa, writing of the years 1612 to 1620, when he traveled in Central and South America, makes frequent reference to various types of rafts used on rivers and lakes, as well as upon the ocean. Some were built upon bamboo floats while some (off of Peru) were erected upon seal-skin floats. At Siete Corrientes, on the Río del Paraguay where it emptied into the Río de la Plata, he noted that "one goes on board rafts built of dugouts" perhaps similar to the one used by the Americans who reached Galway in the 1470s. Rafts were most common on the Pacific side of America, but the Chocó used "dugouts or rafts" in the Panama region.

Typically, longer rafts usually had a compartment built up on top of them. On the Río Cauca, Colombia, "they build large rafts on it, of 40 or 50 bamboos, which they call guáduas. They fasten these together and build a compartment on them, which they call a barbacoa [barbecue, or cooking place?]; here they stow their stuff or merchandise, so that it will stay dry."[82]

Great freight rafts were used along the Pacific coast of South America and north to Central America and Mexico (as noted). These rafts, resembling Thor Heyerdahl's "Kon Tiki" but sometimes larger, were incredibly seaworthy and quite capable of traveling over vast distances, but they were less commonly used in the Caribbean and Atlantic apparently (although in general concept they do resemble the compartments built upon a framework of dugouts).[83] Nonetheless, they were used by the Cuna and also in Brazilian waters, especially in the mouth of the Amazon and around Bahia, Ceará, and Pernambuco. In 1940 the latter type of raft, called a *jangada,* was being used to reach fishing grounds "as much as one hundred miles offshore" and was staying out to sea for three days. In 1922 one crew sailed atop a *jangada* from Recife to Río de Janeiro and back, a 2,144–mile journey. The *jangada* is attributed to the Tupi people, but we cannot be sure how far back in time such use extended.[84]

A scholar in Massachusetts, Fox Tree, has reproduced a painting from "a ceramic ware" in a "private collection" that is "dated from 500 bce to the early Medieval period," which arguably could depict a three-sailed ship or boat. Unfortunately, "naviforms" (drawings that resemble boats) aren't always accepted by all scholars as depictions of boats, especially when no humans are shown sitting in them or standing with oars in hand.[85]

In conclusion, we can establish that Americans were often very capable navigators and sailors at the time of the European invasion, with the circum-Caribbean region being a major area of marine activity, but with other seagoing activities extending along both the North American and South American Atlantic seaboards. In addition, we can argue that this ability in maritime affairs extended back in time, at least predating the settlement of the various islands of the Caribbean and of the Cape Breton-Newfoundland region and probably extending well back into very ancient times.

This marine activity should establish the distinct likelihood that Americans took advantage of the prevailing winds and currents to visit Europe, or were storm-blown involuntarily to Europe, on various occasions before 1492.

4.
Ancient Travelers and Migrations

MOST PEOPLE have probably never heard of the idea that ancient Americans might have traveled to other parts of the globe, so strong is the fixation with the "newness" of America. "Mainstream" archaeology in the twentieth century exhibited hostility toward any ideas that suggest a remote antiquity for humans in the Americas, or to the idea that Americans might have "spilled over" into Siberia and other parts of Eurasia.[1]

During the nineteenth century, scholars were open to the possibility that humans might have appeared on earth in extremely ancient times and that they could, therefore, have established homes in most parts of the globe, perhaps a million or more years ago. The twentieth century, however, witnessed a tendency to restrict the age of modern Homo sapiens and immediate predecessors to a very brief time span (one hundred thousand to two hundred thousand years) and to restrict the history of Native Americans to from five thousand to thirty thousand or forty thousand years (with a majority of conservative archaeologists favoring an "arrival" date of some ten thousand to fifteen thousand years ago).

The result of the newer theoretical orthodoxy has caused a great deal of earlier evidence to be ignored. The recent use of genetics to unravel human history has not changed the orthodoxy, for on the contrary, existing theories of the antiquity of humanoids have served to determine the accepted speed of mutations (changes), which in turn determines the dating of changes in DNA and mtDNA. Thus, genetic evidence is not always able to serve as an independent source of chronology, but instead is partially predetermined by standardized geological and hominid dating.

It is not my task here to become embroiled in the controversies surrounding the age of humans, nor to endorse any specific theories of American origins. Instead I hope to present some of the existing theories relating to American movements and to discuss some general issues relating to human migrations.

A few years ago, when I was examining early census records for Nebraska, I was somewhat surprised to note that very few Missourians were arriving (in the 1850s and 1860s) and even fewer southerners. Instead, people were coming into Nebraska from Canada and from the tier of states adjacent to Canada. I soon realized that there was a very good reason for this: that farmers from southern, warmer climates lacked the cultural skills to cope with the Nebraska climate and probably also lacked the psychological preparation for long, cold winters.

I then began to think about the large, warm barns to be seen in Germany and Switzerland, with animals and humans often living in the same structure, the animals either on the ground floor or at one end of the solid structure. I thought also of the planning needed to store hay and other food for cows, horses, pigs, and so on, to live off of during long, snowy winters and contrasted that with the often "open" conditions for animals found in more southern climes, not to mention "open" houses for humans.

My conclusion was that while humans can migrate from a colder to a warmer region, they cannot ordinarily migrate from a warm area to a cold one (except under modern urban-industrial conditions, or when coerced, as with enslavement or a desperate need for work, as with farm laborers).

I believe that conditions in the northern hemispheres of the earth for many thousands of years have created a very strong likelihood that migrations will ordinarily occur from north to south except where climatic influences (such as the Gulfstream and North Atlantic current) create uniform conditions in a south-to-north region; or they will occur in an east-west one or west-to-east direction, when climate remains much the same.

I would argue, then, that a people adapted to the Arctic and especially to its maritime zones, will migrate into similar areas but may find it difficult to push south into the harsher interior. On the other hand, their ability to move south (especially along maritime areas) will be much superior to that of warm-climate interior groups moving north (unless perhaps under extreme pressure).[2]

If we examine known migration patterns, we can document the movements of such groups as the Celts from north-central "Germany" to Asia Minor, Gaul, and Spain; the Goten (Goths) from southern Sweden to east-central Europe and then on to Italy and Spain; the Vandals southward from the near-Baltic as far as Spain and North Africa; several Germanic tribes from the Baltic southwards into Switzerland with incursions into France, Britain, and Italy; Teutonic movements to Britain; the Norse invasions of Scotland, Ireland, France, and Italy; the Danish invasions of Ireland and England; the migrations of the Turks, Tartars, and Mongols southward and southwestward as far as China, India, and Asia Minor; the movements of the Persians and related groups south to Iran; the migrations of Aryan tribes into India from central Asia; the southward push of the Chinese and the similar migrations of the Thai and Vietnamese peoples; the movements of Swedish (Ros) "Vikings" into Russia and on to Constantinople, and on and on.

Migrations to the north from warm or temperate regions are far fewer and are usually of a special character. The Romans, for example, did push northward but they did so in a relatively mild climatic zone as far as England and a somewhat less mild zone in the Balkans. In any case, the Romans utilized native troops whenever possible, including large numbers of Germanic tribesmen and Thracians. They also never seriously penetrated the colder areas of interior central Europe, that is, beyond the Rhine. The Greeks and the Carthaginians, the Macedonians of Alexander, and most of the old empires never conquered northern regions.

Of course, there are exceptions. One finds, for example, the Norse moving up the coast of Samiland to North Cape, but only in a warming period and within the influence of the warm waters of the Gulfstream-North Atlantic current. Movements can also be east to west and west to east if they follow along a similar climatic zone, as in the German push east into Prussia and the European migrations across North America.

It seems to me that this overwhelming pattern of cold to warm, north to south, or same climate movements in recorded human history must be given great weight when we turn to think about ancient human movements. In fact, one can argue that the tool-kits (material and psychosocial) carried by our ancient ancestors would be even more crucial in early times because they would tend to be more climate-specific than in later evolutionary times, and the ancients would probably tend to lack subcultural variations and diverse environmentally significant specializations within specific communities.

In North America we can document the recorded movements of many nations since European contact. For example, the Blackfeet Confederacy, the Assiniboine, Lakota, Cheyenne, Arapaho, Sutaio, Crow, Shoshone, Comanche, Kiowa, Ojibwe, and Cree all have moved from east to west. In the vicinity of the Black Hills or the Rockies, all of the nations that push that far tend to turn southerly. None turn northerly, with the exception of some Cree groups west of Hudson Bay in pursuit of fur-bearing mammals. The Pikuni swing south into Montana; the Kiowa and Comanche push south into Oklahoma and Texas; the Cheyenne, Arapaho, and Sutaio follow the former; and the Plains Apaches are either pushed ahead of all of these or join the Kiowa.

On the east coast we find the Yuchi, Shawnee, and probably Catawbas and Saponis pushing southward (although some Shawnees return northward to Maryland and Pennsylvania after wars in South Carolina). The Tuscarora and some other remnant groups also move north to join the Six Nations, but they do so gradually and under severe white pressure.[3]

In the Plains area we find an exception in that it is arguable that Plains Apaches, after acquiring horses, might have pushed northwards to the Black Hills only to begin retreating southwards (as noted above) after their neighbors also acquired horses and the Apache were placed under pressure from the east as well. This northward movement occurred, however, within the High Buffalo Plains zone, similar in many respects from West Texas north to southern South Dakota.[4]

Many tribes who were driven from the eastern woodlands made notable transitions to new ways of life, abandoning permanent villages, pottery, and agriculture in favor of tipis, leather containers, and major dependence upon buffalo hunting. This transition was, however, greatly facilitated by the acquisition of horses and by the fact that much of their new "plains" culture was amplified from elements already present in their woodlands life. Moreover, as noted, they did not swing north into colder, forested climatic zones, but tended southward/southwestward.

When we move back in time we must, of course, deal with climatic conditions that are quite different from recent centuries. Nonetheless, we must, it seems assume that human movements in remote antiquity would follow similar rules. For example, movements would follow the

Arctic shore or the Imakpik (Bering) shore, circling the upper rim of the globe where feasible, or movements might follow the tundra belt and the edge of glaciers, or migrations might stay within forested zones of a similar climatic character, and so on.[5]

Of course, groups could arguably be forced into new and hostile environments by such phenomena as advancing glaciers or hostile neighbors; however, it is also possible that many such groups were not able to survive. Extinction due to starvation and dietary inadequacy are very real possibilities, as can be seen in many Inuit stories of starvation and in the example of the Norse Greenlanders, who were allegedly unable to adapt to a colder environment (caused by climatic changes that were favorable to the maritime-hunting Inuit people but perhaps fatal for the Norse).

Some scholars have imagined that humans from southern climes have managed to migrate into northern Siberia and from thence into North America, as with early theories of proto-Australoids and south Asians migrating from southeastern Asia and eventually leaving descendants in Baja California or South America, and so forth. It seems much more likely that if Asians did cross into North America via Imakpik, they did so after having lived for extremely long periods of time along the Siberian Arctic shore, in the cold interior of the northeast, or along the shores of Kamchatka and eastern Imakpik. Likewise, when Americans crossed over into Asia (as seems likely around 10,000 BP and later) we can be confident that they tended to move within the same climatic bioregions, as they had originated, at least for very, very long periods.[6]

During periods in which the northern hemisphere was heavily glaciated much of Alaska and Imakpikia (the Imakpik sea bed exposed by a lowered sea-level) would have virtually constituted a separate "continent," probably cut off from the balance of America by a solid zone of glaciation from the Pacific Coast of Canada to the Atlantic (some have argued for a so-called ice-free corridor to the east of the Rocky Mountains for a certain period of time towards the close of the last glacial period; however, this is simply a wishful-thinking type of theory at this stage of knowledge).[7]

In any event, all migration theories must grapple with the difficulty of people moving into more frigid climatic zones or into other demanding bioregions. They must also deal with the fact that population pressures such as are found in the period of written evidence would most likely be lacking and, therefore, the motivation for moving from favorable (or familiar) environments to life-threatening ones would be largely absent. Movement, then, would be extremely slow and probably not unidirectional. We cannot accept any idea of trailblazing groups being pushed ahead all the way from Imakpikia to Patagonia in a few generations. Instead, we can expect great confusion and unevenness in the process due to the ability of small groups to constantly filter past one another in a sparsely populated environment. Nor can we imagine our American ancestors to have been explorer-adventurers with modern desires to discover new lands for the sake of their riches or merely to satisfy curiosity. If they were anything like our recent indigenous ancestors, they would have become firmly attached to sacred homelands, mountains, and ceremonial sites that they would be extremely loath to abandon.

The theory has been sometimes put forth that ancient humans (or some of them) were avid big game hunters and that they followed migrating herds of animals in an endless trek across vast regions (as in crossing Imakpikia). This is, of course, unlikely for two reasons: first, because herd animals tend to migrate within a fixed area, thus allowing hunters to also remain within that area; and second, because without very effective spear points or projectiles and cutting tools people are not likely to be hunters of large game! Thus the people who crossed Imakpikia were not following herds of animals, judging from the absence of suitable projectile points in pre–13,000 BP times, if we accept the conservative archaeologist's rejection of the Lewisville (Texas) sites 37,000–33,000 BP date for a Clovis-type point. Even if the latter is accepted, it still leaves the northeast Sibera-Imakpikia region bereft of early points.[8]

It is worth mentioning here that long before modern sapiens appeared east of the Sinai, other types of humans such as "European Man" (Homo Neandertal) had long been living in cold climates in Europe while various types of Homo erectus were distributed over southern parts of Eurasia and well up into China. Presumably these physically "robust" types had long adjusted to frigid climates and doubtless paved the way for entry into the farther north as glaciers retreated in the several inter-glacial periods. But their relationship to the origins of Americans or most Asians is totally unclear. Did modern sapiens evolve from them outside of Africa? Did they intermix with modern humans? Did they teach sapiens to cope with specialized environments not found in Africa or western Asia? Interestingly, a recent find in the Republic of Georgia places perhaps three types of humans in the same site, apparently living in the same area.

Did "European Man" (Neandertal) or Homo erectus ever reach America? For whatever it is worth, a number of American nations do have traditions of being preceded by, or of fighting with, "giants" or more robust people. The bones of "giants" were allegedly found on occasion, but no scientific investigations seem to have verified such.[9]

In any case, I want to now briefly review some of the ideas about the antiquity of humans in Abya Yala (one native name for America). This is a very controversial subject and we can begin by stating categorically that no one knows the answer. Early sites have been systematically rejected by conservative archaeologists following the lead of the notorious Ales Hrdlicka, a Czech physical anthropologist who came to dominate Euro-American studies of American antiquity early in the twentieth century. Nonetheless, we must keep an open mind, since many of the ancient sites were sometimes found under conditions similar to famous sites in Eurasia that are fully accepted by the majority of scholars (such as the finds that gave us Java Man, Peking Man, Heidelberg Man, and so on).

Older archaeological evidence, based on geological dating, could place Homo sapiens in the Americas as early as one to three million years ago.[10] More recent evidence, such as that of Hueyotlaco, Mexico, could take modern humans back to 250,000 years ago.[11] Unfortunately, however, such early dates conflict sharply with the opinions of contemporary bio-historians who believe that modern humans first appeared in Africa about 200,000 BP and did not begin to migrate out until about 100,000 BP, appearing first principally in North Africa and Western Asia. According to this notion it took about one hundred thousand years for modern sapiens to reach the near area of Western Asia, but then only fifty to eighty thousand years to migrate all the way to America, adapting to arid environments; cold but temperate mountain environments; cold, treeless steppes of Central Asia; even colder mountains of Mongolia or forests of Siberia; frigid treeless zones of northern Siberia, and mountainous, partially glaciated regions of northeast Siberia or Arctic coastal environments. Alternatively, humans might have crossed through warm and tropical South Asia and southeast Asia, entering China, and then gradually migrating northwards into ever more frigid and/or arid environments until reaching eastern Siberia. Needless to state, the number of radical adjustments would be extremely great, especially with the route via India, Burma, and China.[12]

Aside from the problem of having "southerners" migrate *against* the weather, to colder climates, many of the theories of ancient migration assume a certain plasticity of culture, namely, that desert nomads could become mountain-dwellers, then learn tropical forest culture, go on to the colder and drier climates farther north, or become coastal maritime people, and so on. But we need to have better evidence about how inland hunters become fisher-folk, or how fisher-folk make the change to hunting, or how people adjust to a steppe environment after being in forests, or vice versa. How many bio-historians and archaeologists have studied in detail such transitions? Do we have examples of coastal maritime people shifting to inland ways of life, or of inland people mastering a marine technology (without borrowing a tool-kit from already existing sea-folk?).

The question of why Homo sapiens sapiens would leave temperate climates to move into frigid Siberia has never been answered. The old-fashioned theory was that small groups of hunters followed herd animals, generation after generation, finally crossing Imakpikia (the Imakpik or Bering Sea) when it was open tundra. But does this view make any sense, when one looks at northeastern Siberia and notices all of the transverse mountain ranges that, coupled with the harsh environment, would not have made for ideal range for herd animals?

Werner Müller has argued that Siberia (from the Urals to the Kolyma River) is actually culturally unrelated to America and that it constitutes a barrier, with cultures expanding northerly along south-to-north rivers, but not east to west. He also, following others, sees the Chukchi and other northeastern Siberian peoples as being essentially "Americanoid" and perhaps the result of migration ("backflow") from America.[13]

In any event, it would seem much more likely that human beings would have followed the coast, being adapted to a semi-maritime way of life, whether along the north coast of Siberia or the coast of Kamchatka and the north Pacific. The edge of the landbridge (if it existed) would not have been particularly attractive to maritime cultures, I would think, since sea-life is perhaps most abundant along rocky shores rather than along alluvial fans and mud flats. Nonetheless, bird life and such would perhaps have made up for the lack of seaweed and other foods found along rocky shores.

White scholars seem to be uniformly convinced of the existence of the Imakpikia landbridge during the late Pleistocene.[14] I am not so sure of its existence or width for a variety of reasons, which I will only cite briefly: (1) What happened to the currents that flow through the Imakpik from the Arctic Ocean to the north Pacific? Would that current have been so weak that it could not maintain a channel to the Pacific, cutting through the silt continuously? And what did the whales do who normally migrate against that cold current to the Arctic? (2) Has anyone calculated the annual silt deposited by the Yukon and other rivers and subtracted the silt that has been deposited for ten thousand years now from the depth of the Imakpik? (3) Has anyone calculated the effect of North America moving west over the Pacific Plate on the increased elevation of the Imakpik region since 10,000 BP? (4) Why did a number of animals not cross the bridge, such as the Siberian horse, the northeast Asian tiger, the American bison, the American wolf, and a number of other species? Surely, if humans could reach Imakpik the tough Siberian ponies could have crossed as well, one would think.

In any case, migrants to and from America did not require a landbridge if they were maritime-oriented and were capable of using rafts, dugouts, or other floating devices. I believe that the latter was the case, for two reasons: first, the evidence from Australia that humans were able to cross from island to island, reaching Australia by 60,000–40,000 BP;[15] second, that Americans were apparently able to reach Iceland by about 9000 BP (to be discussed later).

Most Native Americans in North America believe that they were created in America. But there are also traditions suggesting migrations across the Pacific (the Hopi and some South Americans), while some Guaraní-speakers are recorded as looking to the east, to Africa perhaps, as a place of origin. It is interesting that trans-Pacific origins would point toward very, very early navigational skills and would certainly suggest coastal migrations upon arrival in America. Some scholars are suggesting that the most ancient American skeletons (which are very few) resemble south Asians rather than later northeast Asians.

Such terms as "south Asian" are, of course, very general and one has to ask, Does this term refer to the very rare Asian skeletons in southern Asia of 50,000–10,000 BP (let us say) or to the modern peoples of Vietnam, Laos, Kampuchea, Malaysia, and so on, among whom there are great physical variations from "Negrito" (Black African) to mixed features, including African elements and various Asian elements related to East Asia as well as to the Indian subcontinent; along with immigrants from south China?

In any event, a trans-Pacific route would seem to be ruled out by the late dates for settlement in Polynesia. If various kinds of "Asians" reached America by maritime means, they must have utilized the Japan Current and not any trans-Pacific routes. In that case, it would probably be incorrect to term them "south Asians."[16]

Physical variations among Ancient Americans should not surprise us at all. The current interest in the subject may spring from a conscious or subconscious desire to make the claim that "other peoples" were the "true First Americans" and that "Indians" were later arrivals. This effort to discredit "Indians" surged with the controversy over "Kennewick Man," an individual portrayed initially as a "white man" or "European" and later as perhaps some type of Asian, in spite of Kennewick's obvious resemblance to later Native American individuals of a "longheaded" variety, including (as I pointed out) a Nez Perce leader from the same region.

In the early 1960s I wrote:

> It should be borne in mind that the Native Americans were themselves the result of ancient inter-ethnic relations, and that they were not a uniform group when the Europeans arrived. These groups also had distinctive physical characteristics. There was, for example, very little similarity between a heavily-bearded, round-faced central California native and a lightly bearded, sharp-featured plains dweller. Variations in color, facial type, beardedness, height, body build, and other features were very pronounced, especially in certain regions; and changes could be observed within short distances.
>
> Thus the Native Americans themselves may represent a process of amalgamation of diverse stocks which was not yet complete at the time of European contact. On the other hand, they may originally have been a relatively uniform people who formed separate groups through the process of isolation, genetic drift, and differential re-amalgamation.

I have been teaching for over forty years:

> The physical characteristics of Native American peoples were at one time thought to link them with the so-called Mongoloid peoples of Asia, but the problem is now generally seen to be much more complex than was formerly supposed. For one thing, the American Indian peoples did not comprise a physically uniform population. Although the variations in physical type found in the Americas are not as great as those found in Eurasia or Africa, they nonetheless are great enough to suggest that perhaps several different ancestral groups mixed either before or after migration to this hemisphere.
>
> In any event, it would be a mistake to think of Native Americans as part of a "Mongoloid" racial family since several of the more important characteristics of the so-called classic Mongoloid type are virtually absent among American Indians (such as B and AB blood types and the epicanthic eye-fold). This writer would suggest that Native Americans, by and large,

comprise a population standing somewhat between the extreme Caucasoid and Mongoloid types and may represent either the end-product of the mixture of several Mongoloid and Caucasoid type groups or the survival of the type from which Mongoloid and Caucasoid are both derived. The reader should, however, be aware that such terms as Caucasoid, Mongoloid, Negroid, et cetera, are almost completely discredited as referring to "races" (groups of people who are genetically distinct). (See Jack D. Forbes, *Afro-Americans in the Far West,* 1967, for a discussion of the concept of race.)

Nonetheless, we find that some archaeologists continue to use such antiquated terminology, apparently being unfamiliar with modern genetics and with the variations found both in Eurasia and America.

One becomes a bit irritated when one finds, for example, one writer attempting to contrast "paleoindians" with the supposed non-Indians ("first Americans") who allegedly preceded them. The modern Native Americans or American Indians (whatever term we use) are certainly descended from *all* of the groups who entered America and *all of these ancestors are "Indians" if any of them are "Indians."* (But, of course, "Indian" belongs to India and any true "paleoindians" would be living in or near India, not America.)[17]

The truth is that all "races" are essentially geographical groupings. Thus when we speak of an "American race" we are simply referring to all persons who have intermixed in America from the beginning of human settlement for the next fifteen to fifty thousand or more years, until 1492. The "American race" is not a genetically separate population from other geographical populations such as Asians, Pacific Islanders, or perhaps even Europeans. But it is a "race" (race means a branch, not a separate, distinct group) that has obviously absorbed or evolved many variations in appearance as well as ways of life. These variations are such that anyone familiar with living Native American peoples has to be a lot more careful about saying that a given skull (without hair and flesh) does not look "Indian" or does not look like a "Nevada Indian" or does not look like a "Pacific Northwest Indian," and so on. The reconstructed heads that I have seen look like people I have known! And we must remember that diet and weight will change the way a person looks (just look at a modern, tall Japanese-American man walking next to his short, delicate mother or grandmother).

Certain Euro-American scholars have advanced the idea that similarities seen by some in North American cultures as compared with European cultures, especially in stonepoint technology, suggest a migration route from Europe to North America in Pleistocene times. This theory is based primarily upon the supposed similarity between the Solutrean points of Spain and southern France (dated 24,000–16,000 BP) and the Clovis points of North America (dated usually at 11,200–10,800 BP, if the early 37,000–33,000 BP date at the Lewisville site is ignored). The idea, advanced by E. F. Greenman in 1963, and repeated more recently by others, is that Europeans traveled by raft or boat from western Europe to North America along the edge of glaciated and frozen ice in the North Atlantic.[18]

Such a theory goes against all knowledge of currents and winds in the Atlantic (as already discussed) and actually defies common sense as well. Why would big-game hunting people (using Solutrean points) decide to become maritime folk, setting out in unknown seas, against winds and currents, with a totally foreign ice-edge environment to confront? It would make more sense to have Iberians drift southerly to the Canary Islands and Morocco than cross (after centuries perhaps) to Trinidad and the Caribbean. But then we would find the Solutrean in the African islands and Morocco, and it would show up in the Caribbean earlier than in mainland North America.

It would also make much more sense to see the occasional similarities between America and Europe as being due to shared cultural needs or common psychic evolution, or to Americans actually carrying innovations to Europe. As noted earlier, it is incredibly easier for Americans to reach Europe, while it is virtually impossible for Europeans to reach America (except from off of north Africa) before the advent of sails and techniques of tacking against the wind.

As noted earlier, the North Atlantic was probably very dangerous in Pleistocene glaciation periods, with strong westerly winds and currents clashing directly with sea ice and permanent ice. A great deal of turbulence could be expected, where westerly driven waves crashed against ice cliffs or huge bergs. The experience of Inuits along the east shore of Greenland illustrates that sea ice does not always calm wind-driven seas. For east-to-west travel the situation would be nearly impossible because the occasional easterly winds found at high latitudes would be blowing over frozen ice, not over open sea, in all likelihood.

Still further, the route from Iberia north to France and Britain would have been extremely difficult because of prevailing northerly summer winds that make the job of reaching northern destinations quite difficult. Moreover, the crossing of the Bay of Biscay could be extremely dangerous, as noted earlier.

More recently, some proponents of the Solutrean theory have considered a southern route from off of southern Spain or north Africa, but again, why not find the Solutrean in Africa, Madeira, the Canaries, or the Azores, in that case? And a landfall in America would still be in the Bahamas or the Caribbean, not on the east coast of North America. Certainly no early European big-game hunters would end up on the Powhatan (James) River in Virginia. If they did make a landfall in the Bahamas or Caribbean, by the time they or their descendants would have migrated to Virginia their tool-kit would have certainly changed greatly in a small-tool, maritime direction.[19]

In any event, in our discussion of American visits to Europe we shall be considering all Americans of pre-1492 as being equally Americans; whether long-headed or broad-headed, robust or delicate, tall or short, with high cheek-bones or not, with all of the same diverse variety we witness among unmixed Native Americans of modern times.

In the nineteenth century and earlier there was a ready reception for the idea that pre–Columbian Americans had become travelers to distant continents. Some even supposed that human beings of the modern variety had originated in America, while others argued that Americans had helped to civilize the Egyptians, Indians, Japanese, and others by spreading the learning of the Mayas and other American nations. The Argentine scholar Florentino Ameghino proposed that South America was the origin place of modern humans after finding Homo sapiens skulls in geological formations reputed to be more than one million years old.[20]

Other early scholars repeated the stories about Atlantis, derived from Plato and Theopompus (Theopompe), and later writings by Poseidonios, to the effect that people from the west had invaded and conquered either parts of the Mediterranean or the Celtic regions of Europe farther north. These accounts were then linked up with the supposed origin of the Iberian peoples in the west, so that the Iberians were seen as descendants of the Atlanteans (or Americans). Proof was then found in the language and character of the Basques, as the last speakers of an Iberian tongue, whose resemblance to Americans was strongly believed. Basque was, in fact, stated to be an American language.[21]

Is it possible that these traditions reflect the actual arrival of Americans in Europe? Do they perhaps reflect ancient Iberic traditions later acquired by the Greeks or by the Egyptians? In any case, theories of Eskimo (Inuit) migrations to Europe also developed, based in part upon skull shapes but also on the resemblances seen between European Mesolithic cultures and those of Arctic peoples.[22] In more recent times such theories have been revived by scholars including Werner Müller and Jeffrey Goodman. The latter takes much the same data used by E. F. Greenman and others (who argue for a Solutrean movement from Spain to America) to argue that radiocarbon dates favor the exact opposite, that the movement was from America to Europe via Siberia. Goodman suggests that there were probably "several migrations from North America to Europe and back again." He cites the strong evidence of a North American "backflow" into Siberia about 10,000 BP to help build his case. He cites Gordon Willey to the effect that "American-invented blade and point forms diffused . . . from North America to Asia in the early post-Pleistocene." Points of American type also appear near Lake Baikal at 8000 BP.[23]

But Goodman also argues that Americans crossed over to Asia at much earlier times, sending Homo sapiens into Asia and Europe. He states, "I believe that Paleo-Indians from the New World, the first fully modern men anywhere in the world, traveled to the Old World and woke it from its sound evolutionary sleep . . . the path of migration was from North America to Siberia, Asia, and then Europe." This movement occurred perhaps in a warm interglacial "about 170,000 to 70,000 BP" or in another "relatively warm" time about 35,000–27,000 BP.[24]

In 1989 Werner Müller published a book devoted entirely to a similar thesis, except that he regards central Siberia from the Urals to the Kolyma River as a "gap" or "barrier" separating similar American and European ancient cultures of the Paleolithic and Mesolithic. Thus Müller favors the movement of Homo sapiens (of American origin) from North America directly to Europe via the Greenland-Iceland-Spitzbergen zone. Like Goodman, he sees proto-Europeans living in the American Arctic but he identifies them with the Tunit (Tornit), a people supposedly preceding the Thule Inuit across northern and eastern Canada.[25] Müller is able to compile an impressive amount of evidence to argue for an American derivation for post–40,000 BP Europeans, evidence centered around the Siberian "gap" (already mentioned), a number of cultural resemblances, and, most especially, an Arctic origin for the first post–Neandertal European cultures. Müller argues that Americans could have followed the same route to Europe as did the Pleistocene *Rangifer arcticus* reindeer, a species found in North America and then again anciently in northwest

Europe (the two areas being separated from each other over most of Eurasia by *Rangifer tarandus,* a different variety). A land connection in the early Quaternary in the most northerly regions is cited, as well as vague references to later possibilities.

Müller states that "The American continent was not the recipient but the initiator . . . as things now stand, the American continent passed on its development to Asia in the west as well . . . [the Calaveras skull is cited]. Only a reexamination of the discoveries from the last century could definitely establish the presence of man in the New World during the early Quaternary. Then it will become apparent that America is the only typically sapiens continent."[26]

Of course, the theories of Müller, Goodman, and earlier advocates of an American origin for modern humans fall completely outside of the conceptual framework of most contemporary North American archaeologists or European/North American paleontologists. They are, in short, not even considered. For my part, I believe that we must keep an open mind on all of these questions, since the accepted theories of today may well be the repudiated theories of tomorrow. For example, the predominant idea of today that modern sapiens came out of Africa about 100,000 BP is contradicted by Chinese findings of sapiens' remains allegedly dated at 300,000–400,000 BP, as well as by theories that modern humans evolved from Homo erectus-like ancestors all over the globe.[27]

I believe that Goodman's theory of American migrations to Europe via Siberia faces tremendous physical obstacles in terms of Siberian realities, while Müller's idea of a North Atlantic route must await evidence relating to ancient navigation. One certainly cannot visualize any crossing of the North Atlantic by "dog-sled" even if one could show that sleds and dogs were available. However, as I hope to show, there is a great deal of evidence to show that Americans did reach Iceland and Europe at later dates (after 10,000 BP) by means of watercraft. But that date is too late, of course, to explain European cultural and physical evolution after 40,000 BP. Nonetheless, any significant genetic interchanges between America and Europe, or America and Asia, or America and Polynesia, after 10,000 BP will still be of great importance.

In this connection, studies of mtDNA, the genetic material passed from mother to distant descendants only in the female line, have located a rare type, called "haplogroup X," which is found (apparently) only among a small percentage of Native Americans in both North and South America. The significant thing about "X" is that it appeared before European exploration and is also found (rarely) in Europe and Asia. "The source area for the X lineage is not clear," but already its existence is being taken to support theories of ancient European visits to America. On the other hand, I would argue that it could better support theories of ancient American visits to Europe and the Mediterranean.[28]

Today, of course, the use of genetic data to shed light upon historical problems has become widespread. The data available to "bio-historians," as I call them, have changed radically in the last fifty or so years, with many new and complex tools of analysis now available. Unfortunately, most geneticists and bio-historians are usually poorly trained in ethnohistorical methodology and know very little about the documented movements and mixtures of human beings during recorded history.

Many thousands, if not millions, of Americans were enslaved after 1492 and their bondage often included being shipped to Africa, the Canary Islands, Portugal, Spain, and elsewhere. One would expect, therefore, to find a certain number of persons living today in the Mediterranean, Iberian Peninsula, and African coastal regions who could well possess American mtDNA or American "Y" chromosome characteristics, as well as blood types and other markers. Confusion could be added by the fact that many of the Americans were derived from areas in Brazil and the Caribbean where few (if any) unmixed Native Americans now live. Thus they could pass on to Europeans genetic markers that would not be known to geneticists studying contemporary Indigenous Americans.

Huge numbers of Taino/Arawaks, Caribs, and other peoples from many regions, especially along the east coasts of America from Newfoundland and then from Massachusetts/New Hampshire over to Argentina, have disappeared in the sense of unmixed populations. Survivors may have African and European ancestry and probably have been partially or largely ignored by genetic researchers. But until the genetic characteristics of all of these "missing" Americans are reconstructed, we cannot be sure about the kind of biological heritage possessed in 1492 by America's nations. Thus, current generalizations often seem extremely premature (and this includes ones from the study of American teeth, skulls, and languages as well, since in all cases many examples have disappeared).

The impact of diseases introduced by Europeans from 900 CE onward, and especially after 1492, also needs to be considered. Such diseases as smallpox, malaria, bubonic plague, syphilis, and so on, may have had the effect of eliminating certain populations or selecting for certain genetic characteristics. This might especially be the case where large populations have disappeared (as in the Dorset area of eastern Canada about 1000 CE) or in malarial zones of tropical America.[29]

The subject of Native American migrations to, or contacts with, Europe ultimately depends upon when Americans acquired the navigational skills necessary to cross the Atlantic, either totally by sea or partially on land (Greenland, Iceland) and ice islands. The fact that persons seem to have reached Australia by 50–60,000 BP or that Homo erectus might have crossed stretches of water even earlier do not necessarily establish that Americans possessed such skills in Pleistocene times (before 11,000 BP).

An early site on Santa Rosa Island, California, dated at around 35,000 BP could indicate early navigation on the west coast, and certainly artifacts on nearby San Miguel Island, dated at 13,000 BP, would seem to prove the same. Farther north, boats seem definitely to have been used for the early settlement of Unmak Island in the Aleutians (dated 8400 BP), unreachable by land. Actually, initial settlement could have been even earlier, since the shoreline for earlier millennia was under water after 8000 BP and thus sites older than that are simply not available for examination.[30]

On the east coast of North America, a site at Miami indicates that Americans were eating reef fish caught from "seaworthy vessels" by 9000 BP. At about the same time, Americans were possibly reaching Iceland, according to Kevin Smith, an archaeologist and Chief Curator at the Haffenreffer Museum of Anthropology, Brown University. He has reported on the discovery of a microblade core, similar to ones manufactured in the region from northwestern Canada to the Imakpik region between circa 10,700 and 8000 BP. But this core was found in Iceland at a tenth-century Norse site "in good stratigraphic order, suggesting that the core was found or disturbed during the 10th century and carried to the site." The site was "in proximity to the ca. 9000 BP coastline in western Iceland."

Significantly, the microblade was manufactured from jasper, which "only matches well, geochemically, with western Icelandic jasper." Smith states: "I'm left with the unavoidable conclusions that (1) the core was made in Iceland by someone who knew how to make and use this typically Arctic technology, (2) there is no evidence anywhere that 10th century Norse knew or used this technology, and (3) that there is yet no evidence for additional related material at the site."

Another possibility, although remote, is that some Greenlanders of the pre-Dorset "Independence I" culture or of the Dorset culture managed to reach Iceland and were imitating microblade technology of a much earlier period. Smith notes that the pre-Dorsets and Dorsets lived in eastern Greenland: "an area from which intentional or unintentional travel/drift to Iceland would have been relatively easy, given the short distances involved and the presence of the East Greenland Current, which runs from the NE coast of Greenland and then splits around Iceland, regularly depositing icebergs, driftwood, and the occasional polar bear on Iceland."

In any case, it seems clear that some Americans reached Iceland, perhaps as early as 9000 BP, but possibly a few thousand years later. It is interesting that far to the west high ocean levels continued in the Aleutian Island region from about 8000 to 3000 BP, and if this is also true for the North Atlantic, then the shoreline could be of varying age. Nonetheless, one would seem to have evidence for navigation by the 10,000–9000 BP period.[31]

Hundreds of dugout canoes have been found at the bottoms of lakebeds in Florida. The oldest seems to be six thousand years old, while others have been found that are between three and five thousand years old. The canoes are up to twenty-two feet long, and many have rounded sterns and bows.[32] On the northeast coast of America, one finds coastal cultures, with maritime adaptation, advancing northward after 9000 BP and reaching northern Labrador by 4500 BP or earlier. Newfoundland was settled by 5000 BP (4900–3600), while the important L'Anse Amour Mound site in Labrador yielded a child's burial with charcoal dated at 7530 BP. This latter site has a very strong marine adaptation, with "a probable antler pestle for applying or grinding the paint and a quantity of red ochre" found under the body. A walrus tusk "suggests sea mammal hunting" and a "true toggling harpoon and a crescentic hand-held toggle leave no doubt that sea mammal hunting techniques were very sophisticated . . . by 7,500 years ago. The toggling harpoon . . . just might be the oldest such weapon found anywhere in the world."

This "Red Paint" maritime tradition of coastal Labrador seems to have been a continuous one from about 9000 to 3000 BP, with gradual stylistic changes.[33] It is suspected of being ancestral to Algonkian-speaking nations of more recent times, and more southern locations. It will be reviewed again in more detail below.

Across the North Atlantic, types of boats seem to have appeared by about 9000 BP (when they were needed probably to take the first settlers to Ireland) and early specimens are dated at 9500 BP (Star Carr in

Britain, a paddle) and 8000 BP (Holland, a dugout boat). Britain was still connected directly to the continent until 8000 BP but Ireland apparently was separated from Britain by a channel and then by the Irish Sea (during the last glaciation and afterwards).[34]

During the height of the last glaciation (up to 13,000 BP) it is suspected that the Gulf Stream shifted southwards from the Cape Hatteras "gate" off North America to head "straight across toward Spain" instead of heading toward Britain. The Stream "ran from 2 to 4 degrees centigrade cooler than at present, but . . . its system carried tropical species farther east than it does today."[35] Nonetheless, it would appear that southern Ireland (below the Shannon and Leinster), and coastal Glamorgan in Wales, the Severn estuary, and southern England were all ice-free, thus indicating that the Stream approached the southern coasts of Ireland and Britain, making perhaps a sharp curve between Brittany and England before heading south (since the English Channel did not then exist, as noted).[36]

I would suppose that during interglacial periods the Gulf Stream and North Atlantic Drift resumed their movement in a northeasterly direction, passing the west coasts of Ireland and Scotland, passing Iceland and the Faeroes, and along the west coast of Norway, towards Murmansk. I would have thought that the warmer water helped to slow down the freezing of the North Atlantic and perhaps even led to partial open water even at the height of the glaciation periods. But in any case, it would appear that no people were living in Ireland, Iceland, or the Faeroes before 13,000 BP to welcome visitors. Britain did, however, have small populations during the warm periods, but, more than likely, any Americans reaching Europe during interglacial or glacial times would have arrived in France or Iberia or perhaps farther south, in the Canary Islands. If any did reach Britain during interglacial periods, their numbers would have simply blended in with the British inhabitants and all would have retreated to southern England and Wales during the last glacial advance.

Interestingly, the Romans found a somewhat darker-skinned, dark-haired people, the Silurians, living in that section of Wales that was probably non-glaciated between 18,000 and 13,000 BP, but, of course, they could have arrived much later and been related to similar peoples found in the Mediterranean region.

As regards Native Americans reaching Iberia before recorded history, it is interesting to note that two probable Amazonian (Brazilian) ground-stone hand-axes have been found in Galicia. One was found on the beach of Lapamán (San Martiño de Bueu, Pontevedra), at the edge of the sand.

The other was located at Hío in a nearby area (Cangas) at Pontevedra, also near the Atlantic coast. After careful examination, Ramón Fabregas Valcarce is of the opinion that they are definitely not Iberian, and not "Oriental," and that they very closely resemble examples of Brazilian hand-axes found along the length of the Amazon. How they reached Pontevedra is not known. It is possible that a modern collector brought them to Spain, but then why would they show up along the coast, one of them broken apparently because of long exposure to the elements?[37]

As we shall see, this section of Galicia or nearby Portugal was visited by an American navigator during the Middle Ages of Europe. In any case, one would expect to find scattered American-made objects in many places in coastal or island Europe, out of archaeological context. Most would probably never be recognized as being American, except by knowledgeable archaeologists familiar with American artifacts. Reported Inuit harpoon heads, found in Scotland and Ireland and dating apparently from pre-1492 times, provide other examples of American objects found along cobble beaches or other coastal sites.

As noted in chapter 2, the Gulf Stream has left great evidence of its action in terms of carrying logs, flotsam, seeds, and other debris from the Caribbean and North American waters to the coasts of Ireland, Wales, Scotland (the Hebrides especially), Iceland, Norway, and the Faeroes. Presumably during the last glaciation this flotsam was carried in greater quantity to France, Iberia, and, as later, to the Azores and Canary Islands. In chapter 2 I cited a great deal of evidence relating to the frequent arrival of this material in Europe, with evidence from charcoal dated about 2000 BP to show the continuity of this "American export."[38]

In all likelihood, we can reasonably suppose that (conservatively) at least once every century a major storm carried Americans out into the Atlantic from, say, 9000 BP onward. That would equate to ninety involuntary voyages before 100 BP. At one voyage per each half-century, we would be looking at 180 such trips. After about 50 BCE we can definitely document a few of the voyages, which we shall do in the next chapter, but there is no reason to suppose that the voyages began simply because literate Europeans were available to record them.

As mentioned earlier, it is interesting that the blood types of Native Americans (O with some A) resemble extreme western Europeans. The Irish have "large and moderately long heads and, particularly in the west and north, a relatively high proportion of blood group O, a feature which is characteristic also of Scotland, Iceland, the Basque country and the western Mediterranean region, that is, its distribution is markedly peripheral in Europe, which generally has a relatively high A frequency." The Aran Islanders, near Galway, who frequently gather drift from America, "have relatively high frequencies of blood group A," thanks perhaps to the stationing of English troops there several centuries ago.

Also interesting are what some persons refer to as the "peculiar features" of Irish Gaelic that are said to have analogies in non–Indo-European languages such as Basque, North African, Berber, and other languages. The majority of Irish ancestry is undoubtedly pre-Celtic or at least pre-Gaelic, being derived from the Firbolgs (Bag-Men) and other ancient peoples. Did Native Americans contribute at all to the ancient settlement of Ireland and Scotland?[39]

During the post-glacial era (after 13,000 BP), some scholars believe that Americans from South America and perhaps Mesoamerica moved north, occupying formerly tundra and taiga regions as they became more temperate. These Americans would doubtless have been able to penetrate much of North America long before the populations of the Imakpik region could have headed south and, indeed, if proto-Eskimos/Aleut people were the primary Imakpik population (perhaps including Chukchee and other future Siberians) their cultural adjustment to cold regions might well have precluded much of a southern movement. Indeed, the linguist Johanna Nichols believes that all American languages except Eskimo-Aleut evolved south of the ice during the period 40,000–13,000 BP.[40]

There is interesting genetic evidence to support the migration from South America, namely the disbursal of the Diego antigen (discussed briefly earlier), a marker concentrated in Colombia, Venezuela, and Brazil among some Caribbean, Carib, Arawak, and other indigenous language groups. There the percentage of Native Americans in South America possessing the antigen is often 20 to 30 percent or higher. Significantly, both the Carib and Arawak families are suspected of having originated farther south, perhaps in Amazonia. We can, therefore, postulate a northward migration of the marker, among several language groups, eventually crossing the Caribbean and the Isthmus of Panamá to Mexico and the southeastern United States, and then to Canadian border regions.[41]

What is especially interesting about the Diego antigen is not merely that it probably traces South American ancestry in North America, but that it has also spread beyond America. For example, as noted earlier, persons of Irish, Polish, Japanese, and other ancestries have shown up with the Diego antigen. An Irish woman with the marker was living in

Brisbane, Australia but, unfortunately, we cannot trace her ancestry to a specific place in Ireland.[42]

Some scholars have attempted to see in the Diego antigen a marker developed in Asia or Siberia that was carried into America. But this is obviously a difficult thesis, given the circum–Caribbean-Amazonian-Andean character of the antigen and the documented movements of Americans across the Atlantic and Pacific oceans.[43]

It is certainly possible to suggest that maritime navigation skills could have emerged or advanced during the period before 13,000 BP, since the waters along the Caribbean coasts, with several islands visible from shore or nearby (such as Tobago, Aruba, Curaçao, and others), would have encouraged water travel. Trinidad became separated from the mainland as ocean levels increased. My own belief is that ocean navigation is encouraged by the presence of offshore islands and, conversely, that it is unlikely to develop early where islands do not exist.

Contact between North and Meso and South America during the period of 5000 BP on also needs to be cited as evidence of maritime activity of a more than casual kind. As an example, the construction of monumental structures of a mound or pyramid type commenced almost simultaneously in Louisiana, Mexico, Guatemala, and the coastal regions of Ecuador and Peru, between 5000 and 3000 BP. The architectural accomplishments argue for a high degree of social development and, at the same time, a ready (and steady) means of communication. It is certainly reasonable to assume that the large boats seen by Columbus in the 1490s were already in use in the Caribbean by 5000 BP and that boats or sailing rafts of the kind later used along the Pacific Coast between Mexico and the Andean Coast were also in use. The migration of the Tarascan (Purepecha) people, apparently from the Andean region to western Mexico, seems to have been the end-result of a long period of communication. Dillehay tells us that "South American civilizations were far older and more sophisticated than we once imagined. . . . New excavations in Peru and Ecuador have turned up large pyramids and other monuments dating back nearly 5,500 years, to about the time when the Great Pyramids were being constructed in Egypt."[44] Americans of that period were not only in communication over a vast area, largely by sea, but they apparently possessed the social systems capable of sustained trade and exploration.

In 1987 Bullfrog Films released *The Mystery of the Lost Red Paint People*, directed by T. W. Timreck (with W. N. Goetzmann), a survey of the Red Paint (Red Ochre) people of the region from Maine to Labrador, otherwise known as the Maritime Archaic culture. This remarkable American tradition lasted from about 8000 BP to some 3500 BP, as noted earlier. Some believe that it was the "most advanced Native American culture ever to have inhabited the Northwest Atlantic zone." The Red Paint people developed "one of the world's great maritime adapted cultures," featuring elaborate artistic items and a deep-sea fishing and hunting orientation.

The Red Paint people utilized both barbed and toggling harpoons, including one of the latter dated at 7500 BP, as well as killer whale effigies, water bird drawings, a Great Auk beak (suggesting that they may have followed the auk's migrations), well-organized communities, stone pinnacles placed along the coast, and numerous stemmed points, plummets, and engraved pendants. Locations selected were often near the sea, at very dramatic and prominent locations, as in Labrador at Ballybrack.

Timreck and Goetzmann present evidence suggesting that the Red Paint people contacted Europe, leaving influences in places such as Brittany, Denmark, Norway, and elsewhere. The use of red ochre in graves is cited as an example, along with tools of slate, spiritual beliefs, art forms, and designs. They cite the work of Gutorm Gjessing, who saw evidence of an ancient circumpolar culture linking America and Europe and east Siberia (but not central Russia).[45]

Gjessing has commented that

> with great certainty we can construct a continuous culture belt in the Arctic and sub-Arctic regions. . . . For the present this cultural connection can be established most securely in the sub-Arctic and boreal frost regions; but important cultural manifestations such as the use of slate, the skin boat, and the Eskimo harpoon suggest that the connection in the Arctic sea-hunting cultures is also very old. Strangely enough it looks as if the British Isles had also been touched by this circumpolar Stone-Age culture.

He goes on to say that "on the whole there would seem to be so many Arctic elements in early British culture that it is very desirable that the problem should be taken up for investigation."[46] Like Werner Müller, Gjessing wanted to explore whether there is a connection "between the West European Paleolithic culture and the Eskimo cultures." He notes that J. Pokorny has argued on philological evidence that "the Arctic harpoon with line and bladder was present in Ireland in pre-Celtic times." The "Eskimo harpoon" with "an open socket" had spread to the Kola Peninsula of Scandinavia in the Bronze Age, according to Gjessing, and by 1335 CE the Basques were using a harpoon with a line and float instead of a bladder.[47]

Whether the harpoon of that type was an Inuit invention or whether it is older in "Red Paint" cultures of northeastern America remains to be seen. As noted, a "true toggling harpoon" was found in Labrador dated at 7500 BP and the possibility exists that it "just might be the oldest such weapon found anywhere in the world." In any event, it would appear that the harpoon used for Arctic-style hunting is an American invention that spread to Asia and Europe, clearly by human contact.[48]

Stuart Piggott tells us that in the Orkney Islands north of Scotland, as at Skara Brae, there are sites reflecting circumpolar culture of the kind still surviving among Eskimos and allied peoples, dated late in the third millennium BCE (4500–4000 BP).[49]

The use of red ochre in burial mounds and burials seems to extend south to Virginia (about 11,000 BP or earlier) but is especially characteristic farther north. In southern Labrador "Red Paint" burial mounds are dated to 7500 BP and 6900 BP, associated with maritime-oriented cultures. Farther south it extended back to 8000 BP, or earlier, and persisted in some areas to 3500–3000 BP, when climatic change (a cooling trend) seems to have led to a decline in open-water hunting and the harpooning of swordfish, especially in the Gulf of Maine area. The burial mound culture of 7500 BP represents an advanced development. Older sites may have been destroyed by rising sea-levels after 8500 BP.[50]

That the "Red Paint People" were excellent sailors is illustrated by their pursuit of the very large and difficult swordfish as prey. Not only were swordfish caught off of Maine, after 5100 BP, but swords were made from them. Heavy woodworking tools in graves, for boat-making, and related items "all argue for the conclusion that relatively large dugout canoes were being used for fishing, marine hunting, and transportation."[51] Effigies of whales in Massachusetts and of seals and porpoises in Maine also illustrate the maritime orientation.[52]

During the "Red Paint" era, there is some evidence that the Gulf Stream may have gone further north along the northeast coast of America before turning eastward toward Ireland and Britain. If this is true, then voyagers from northeast America might well have been brought more directly to northern Scotland, Orkney, Shetland, and Iceland during the period before about 3500 BP. This would help to explain the alleged Red Paint influence in Britain and the microblade found in Iceland. After 3500 BP a cooling trend seems to have begun in the North Atlantic, with a shift away from marine hunting in the Gulf of Maine. Farther north, the Dorset culture replaced the Archaic Maritime (Red Paint) tradition during the 2000s BCE, perhaps an example of the Dorset adaptation to colder, ice-hunting conditions.[53]

Although there is a shift to the use of birch bark canoes (for river and lake use), dugout boats continue to be made in New England into the seventeenth century of our own era.[54]

The arrival of Americans in European waters might be expected to lead to a series of tales and legends about islands of mystery beyond the western horizon. Indeed, we know that such is the case, not only in the writings of ancient Hellenes, but in the belief in "sea paradises" located to the west of Ireland. Beliefs in an "Elysium" in the western ocean could in fact be based upon vague traditions about strangers arriving from the west. It may be that the reputed voyage of St. Brendan from Ireland in the fifth century CE (written about in the ninth century) was inspired by an American visit, or the tradition of one. Such an inspiration might be needed to cause a navigator to sail out of sight of land, against the winds and currents. Thus in all of the tales of mysterious islands to the west, common to several parts of Europe, may we not see a pale reflection of American voyages and, perhaps, of the stories told by Americans upon discovering Europe?[55]

5.

From Iberia to the Baltic: Americans in Roman and Pre-Modern Europe

MANY AMERICAN NATIONS have traditions pointing towards animals as teachers of human beings; and it is certain that the Ancient Americans learned much from carefully and consistently observing the lessons offered by the natural world and its living children. Indigenous Americans often seem to have made it a major part of their lives to watch the animals, birds, and other living things in order to learn their secrets, in order to understand the patterns of their behavior.[1]

I believe that we can be absolutely sure that Americans of old, putting out in boats into the waters of the Caribbean, off the mouth of the Amazon, in the Florida Straits, or in the Gulf Stream farther north, would have studied the moving rivers with infinite care, would have, in fact, mapped out the precise movements of the currents and winds with extreme exactitude, and certainly would have observed the onward traveling of huge numbers of logs, branches, debris, and, what is more important still, the behavior of animals in the streams.

The logs and the animals, such as the marine turtles of America, were clearly going somewhere, but where? And for the people in the Amazon-Caribbean region, it was obvious that floating things were also arriving from the east. Certainly there were rivers in the oceans that formed great circles of going and returning.

But the turtles of American waters are especially important, particularly the great Leathery Turtle. One was washed ashore at Harlech, North Wales, in 1988, weighing 2,106 pounds and measuring about ten feet in length and nine feet across the span of its front flippers.[2]

In point of fact, it is very rewarding to look at the behavior of American marine turtles because their movements, going back millions of years, provide a ready guide for watchful human hunters and sailors. There is absolutely no doubt that American turtles followed the Gulf Stream to Ireland, Wales, Scotland, Cornwall, the Isles of Scilly, and Devonshire's coast, as well as on occasion to Iceland, Norway, and, in one case at least, to Murmansk. They may have even returned to the American tropics, as will be discussed below.

The earliest European drawing of an American turtle is from the 1100s CE. E. Charles Nelson, who has written about drift seeds, notes that a churchyard slate of the twelfth century in Cornwall (Tintagel Island) has "a vivid thumbnail sketch of a Common Loggerhead turtle. These animals, natives of the American coast, are frequently stranded on Cornish shores."[3] Five species of turtles have been reported from British waters in modern (post-1700) times. They are the Leathery, the Common Loggerhead, Kemp's Ridley, Green, and Hawksbill (rare). The first three are the most common. The Leathery nests primarily in Guiana, South America, but also along east Florida. Leatherys are seen often off northeast America (Connecticut to Newfoundland) "where they feed on jelly-fish in waters up to 15° C colder than those in which they nest in Florida. The turtle's temperature may be as much as 18° C warmer than the surrounding water." In 1958 a Leathery was seen off Norway at 69°18 N and another off of northern Iceland in 1963. A Common Loggerhead was caught in a fishing line off Murmansk in 1964. The "powerful Leathery Turtle may well have the stamina to return south."

R. D. Penhallwick tells us that "the circulation of the oceans makes it unlikely that turtles of any species from the Mediterranean or West Africa would reach British shores, as this would entail swimming for hundreds of miles against the prevailing currents." He goes on to inform us that "evidence from other organisms, some the food of Leathery Turtles, as from inanimate objects, all point to the West Indies and the northern shore of South America as the origin of turtles stranded on British and Irish shores . . . as recently as December 1986, a speed-boat turned up at St. Ives, in all probability from the southern United States." Penhallwick also reviews the evidence supplied by Charles Nelson and others relative to the drift seeds and other American items that turn up on the coasts of Cornwall, western Ireland, and Scotland. "Indeed, the earliest European reference to them comes from Cornwall where they were collected by Dame Catherine Killigrew before 1570[,]" who said that the "faith of the

Cornish folks" was that they drifted from the "New World" because of the winds. Most of the seeds turn up on the north coast of Cornwall and in the Isles of Scilly, as many as twenty-four species being represented.

The huge Leathery Turtles, incidentally, often could be seen traveling or floating on the surface of the water, as were three seen together on two occasions off of the southwest coast of Cornwall in 1967 by a British trawler's crew. They are accompanied, apparently, by Pilot Fish (*Naucrates ductor*), which have been seen with them off of both Cornwall and Norway.[4]

Loggerhead Turtles also reach European Atlantic waters, after nesting along the Georgia and Florida coasts, in the Dry Tortugas, and along the Mexican coast. Loggerheads reach 300 pounds or more, but those reaching Britain are usually juveniles or sub-adults (who, reportedly, when just hatched, make rapidly for the warm Gulf Stream waters). "The specimens reaching European Atlantic shores are probably of American origin. Indeed, some have been washed ashore, as in Cornwall in 1938, in company with Kemp's Ridley which cannot have come from anywhere else." Hawksbill turtles, from Guyana, Guiana, and the Caribbean region, are rarer in British waters but in 1867 one was recovered in the English Channel and in 1983, a 280–pound one was netted off of Cork, Ireland.[5]

The "discovery" of Europe by American marine turtles is, I believe, of great significance, especially as we look to the meeting of "Classical America" with "Classical Mediterranean/Roman Europe," the topic of this chapter. It seems beyond doubt that American seafarers, especially from turtle-watching regions, would have noted the traveling patterns of the turtles, especially since they surface frequently and are of huge enough size to be followed day after day. Turtle-following, as well as other maritime activities, undoubtedly took many mariners far, far out to sea, but I would suggest that there would often be the curious few who would pursue the turtle's watery path all the way to Europe, and then perhaps to return along the same path to America once again, following its southern, southwestern, and western arcs.

A study has shown that Florida-born Loggerhead Turtles can navigate across the Atlantic and return to American waters using "subtle signals of Earth's magnetic field." The signals help baby loggerheads to stay within the circular ocean current of warm water moving clockwise from America to Europe and then back again via the coasts of Spain and northwest Africa, then turning west to complete the circle. This turtle migration path is some 8,000 miles in length. Is it not possible that Americans were able to learn of this phenomenon and how to use it to their advantage, navigationally?[6]

Passing from turtle travel to human movement, it has been suggested that clay figurines and other arts of Mexico contain images suggestive of European, Semitic, African, and (perhaps) Asiatic features. If so, then we might be looking at very concrete evidence that Americans not only visited Europe and Africa, but brought back mental images that they were able to share with their countrywomen/men. This possibility is strengthened by an alleged Roman-like head found in a Matlatzinca (Calixtlahuaca) pyramid and by an alleged Hebrew (or other Semitic) inscription found in a Cherokee-area cave, under burials, and dated in the second century CE also.[7]

The alleged Roman-type terracotta head has recently been dated by a thermoluminescent age test with a date of 215 CE (±400 years). This is rather interesting because it makes the terracotta roughly the same age as a bronze head of an American (?) now housed in the Louvre in Paris. In any case, the head seems to have been found in either Mound 5 or Mound 6 at Calixtlahuaca in the 1930s. It was found with pottery of the 1476–1510 period and above a twelfth century level, as part of a burial offering.

Scholars involved in the latest analysis of the "cabecita de barro" suggest that the Matlatzincas, as allies of the Aztecs, participated in two war expeditions between 1440 and 1469, one to the coastal area of the Huastecas from which they "returned with a rich booty." Thus they might have acquired the head from the Huastecas, who presumably might have held it for a millennium or more.

Of course, a number of "ifs" remain in this story, but nonetheless it does suggest an American (Huasteca?) voyage to the European area (Gaul, Iberia?) and a return voyage to the Gulf of Mexico. The authors of the latest report (Romeo Hristov and Santiago Genoves) express the normal Eurocentric idea of a Mediterranean vessel being "swept away from the Canary Islands, Madeira or Cape Verde to the American coasts." On the other hand, let us emphasize that while we have quite a number of references to Americans reaching Europe, to be discussed, we have absolutely no references to Europeans reaching America by any route prior to Norse navigation. Given the extent of Roman, Greek, Carthaginian, and other historical sources, and given the existence of numerous geographies written by people such as Pliny, Strabo, and Pomponius Mela, I think that we can say that the ball is in America's court and not in Europe's. (I am, of course, not arguing against the theoretical possibility of a Roman drift voyage, but I am saying that when we find terracottas, coins, or other relics of supposed European origin in America, we must give primacy to American agency, not European).

European or Euro-American writers almost always see such items as evidence of European (or Semitic) voyages to America, but given what we now know about American seafaring and cultural sophistication, it is much more likely that they are things seen by American travelers, images brought home after voyages, and shared by means of art. But, of course, not everyone will agree on their authenticity, in any case, given the long-term interest of some religious sects and nationalities in "proving" the truth of their own particular ideology. The "salting" (intentional contamination) of archaeological sites always remains a possibility, along with the misinterpretation of such items as clay heads with beards or other specific features.

Nonetheless, I will argue that we must accept the probability of American agency, and that the art pieces must be viewed as a kind of "photographic" record of indigenous travels. In Perú a woven cotton textile of alleged pre-Columbian origin depicts persons riding on horseback, something clearly to be seen in Europe or Asia, but not in pre-1492 America. Since one cannot imagine a European or Asian producing Andean cloth, one must assume that an American made the textile with its illustrations, thus indicating a visit to Europe, Africa, or Asia and a return to Perú, provided, of course, that the *tejido* has been properly dated. Indeed, the section of the cloth depicting horses is rather non-Andean in appearance and suggests a post-Spanish conquest date.

As regards the clay heads in Mexico that are alleged to depict Africans, Europeans, and Asiatics, Donald Cordry, an authority on Mexican masks, has stated: "any attempt to date a mask . . . becomes an extremely questionable estimate . . . the inability to date Mexican masks stems from a temporal ambiguity in Mexican culture, an ambiguity that is one of its essential characteristics and charms. It is not uncommon to find pre-Conquest ideas and beliefs existing side by side with modern ones." He further notes that "one of the more common methods of dating artwork is to use stylistic trends as criteria. However, . . . the cultural diversity and complexity of Mexico . . . precludes the identification of traditional styles in any but the most general terms, far too vague to base any estimate of a mask's age upon." The popularity of "negrito" (African) masks in post–Conquest Mexico, along with the common production of masks with European features, raises many questions about the dating of alleged "pre-Columbian" figurines. Perhaps only a chemical analysis can actually date such materials.[8]

The use of art to support pre-Columbian contacts can also be extended to American arrivals in Europe and the Mediterranean. For example, I possess a photograph of the figure of an Egyptian man of "tête salt" from the "14e siècle avant J.C." (fourteenth century before CE), which decidedly resembles an American. The carved or ceramic figure has high cheekbones, large almond eyes, and a prominent nose. Such a figure could be completely ignored, I suppose, except that John T. C. Heaviside argued many years ago (1868) that Americans had influenced ancient Egypt and, more recently, Stephen C. Jett has written about evidence of nicotine (tobacco) leaves being found in the cadavers of ancient Egyptian mummies (such as that of Ramses II, second millennium BC). Samples of mummies at the Munich Egyptian Museum, of ages from 1070 BC to CE 395, were found to contain both nicotine and cocaine. Jett also presents data suggesting that cocaine and nicotine have been found in mummies from parts of Europe and Nubia, as well as Egypt, all dating to ancient times. Since both nicotine and coca (cocaine) appear to be of American origin, their appearance in Egyptian mummies suggests early trading expeditions to the region from America.[9]

Early contacts between America and Italy are also suggested by wall paintings uncovered in the Roman port city of Pompeii, a municipality covered over in an eruption of Mount Vesuvio on August 24, 79. The paintings include a portrait of a husband and wife. The man is very "Mexican" looking with brownish skin, high cheekbones, large semi-Asiatic eyes, and dark hair. He also has a very scanty moustache and very sparse beard (perhaps added later by a graffiti artist). He is definitely not "Mediterranean" in appearance, although his wife appears Italian. He also does not remind one of a North African or Middle Easterner, in general.

Another mosaic from the Vesuvius area, around Pompeii, appears to feature representations in color of a pineapple, and red chili pepper (both American fruits), along with several lemons (?) and a rooster or large hen. The anana or pineapple would have been from South America, while the peppers could have been from the Caribbean as well. Thus, again, we are justified in suggesting ancient American contact. The relationship of such possible journeys to the spread of syphilis will be discussed below.[10]

In the context of art, it is interesting that by the nineteenth century, scholars noticed that a Roman bronze housed in the Louvre of Paris very

much resembled an Indigenous American. In connection with my research, I located the bronze and photographed it because it does, indeed,
resemble a native of the Americas. It so happens that this bronze may well
reflect an actual visit by "Indians" to northern Italy, and in all probability,
to Rome. In this case, the bronze probably does not represent a Roman
visit to America, first, because of the navigational difficulties presented,
and second, because we have a specific record of "Indians" reaching Europe in the same period that the bronze was produced.

At the current time the bronze in question is labeled "Vase en forme
de tête, IIème-IIIème s. après J.C. L'aspect physique du personnage est
particulièrement marque." It is from the "Collection Dinand, 1825. Br
2947." Nearby is a "Vase à parfume: buste de Noir, IIème s. après J.C.,"
also from Dinand 1825, Br 2946. Thus a bust of an African woman (rather
small) is located next to a vase or container in the form of a head, second
to third century CE, with "the physical aspect of the personage being
particularly marked."[11]

In 1859 Professor Emile Egger argued that the "Indians" who had
reached the Roman world in the 60s BCE (to be discussed below) were
Caribs from America "or other individuals of American race." He also
voiced the opinion that the ancient bronze head found in the galleries
of the Louvre represented one of those Indians and that it was a "repro-
duction of a type of the American race." In 1868 the existence of the
bronze was publicized in a catalog of ancient bronzes belonging to the
Louvre.[12]

Another French authority also felt that the bronze resembled an American of the type portrayed by the art of George Catlin. Paul Gaffarel concludes: "At the very first look, everything in this bronze makes us think
of the red race of the new world. The skull is dolichocephalous, receding
forhead, long and low ears, strongly arched brows, aquiline nose, big lips,
round lower maxilla. The total impression is striking. . . . Very well, this
is the type of an American, and of an American of the United States."[13]

Not everyone has agreed that the bronze represents an American of
60 BCE. Gaffarel (1892) said that it was "a hazardous conjecture" to assume that the bronze was of one of the Indians arriving in the 60s BCE,
even though he believed that it portrayed an American. Geoffrey Ashe
also doubted the connection, believing that the bronze appeared "more
Roman than Red Indian." He described the object as "a bucket (*situla*) in
the form of a human head. The projection on top is the handle, and the

Bronze head of a man with an American physical type, in the Louvre, Paris, France. Photographed by Jack D. Forbes, 1994.

Another view of the bronze head of an American (?), in the Louvre, Paris, France. Photographed by Jack D. Forbes, 1994.

cranium is hinged to open like a lid. It might possibly be a divining urn." William H. Tillinghast (1889) was aware of the bronze but regarded its identification with an American as "purely arbitrary."[14]

The association of the idea of a "divining urn" with a possible American head is intriguing, since it could indicate that as early as two thousand years ago the Romans began to associate mystical or spiritual matters with a Native American. Could it be that an American spiritual person reached Europe and became a practitioner there? Such a theory may seem far-fetched, but the dissemination of ideas, folktales, and other cultural traits often depends upon just such strange arrivals in the various ages of world history.

My own judgment is that if one covers over the ears on the bronze, which are perhaps excessively large in order to provide balance to the work of art, one sees an Indigenous American face, one with a combination of features found in many parts of North, Central, and South America.

Now let us proceed to examine the documentary evidence relating to American visits to Europe in the Roman and Teutonic periods. The initial source is a description of the world written by Pomponius Mela during the reign of Emperor Claudius (41–94 CE, probably written ca. 44 CE). Mela, in the process of discussing a then-current theory (attributed to Homer) that the Indian Ocean possessed a direct connection with the North and Baltic seas, introduced relevant information as follows:

> Cornelius Nepos, ut recentior, ita auctoritate certior; testem autem rei Quintum Metellum Celerem adjicit eumque ita retulisse commemorat: cum Galliae pro consule praesset, Indos quosdam a rege Boiorum dono sibi datos; unde in eas terras devenissent, requirendo cognovisse, vi tempestatum ex Indicis aequoribus abreptos, emensisque quae intererant, tandem in Germaniae litora exiisse.

> [Cornelius Nepos, a more recent and therefore more authoritative author, adds the testimony of Quintus Metellus Celer on this point and says that he gave the following account. When he was Governor of Gaul, some Indians were given to him by the king of the Boii. On asking where they had come from to these lands (their present whereabouts), he learned that they had been driven from the Indian seas by violent storms . . . and finally come ashore in Germany.]

Thus an author of greater authority, Cornelius Nepos, asserted that Quintus Metellus Celer (when Proconsul of Gaul) told him that he received some Indians (*Indos*) from the King of the Boi (a Celtic people located in present-day France and also farther east, perhaps to Bohemia), who asserted that they were driven by a storm to the coast of Germany (which then could reach to the Rhine area of the Netherlands) from the seas of India.

Other versions of Mela's text state that the Indians were delivered to Celer by the King of the Suevi, a "wandering" Germanic-speaking people located in the region of the Netherlands, north Germany, and/or northern France and Belgium, and closely associated with the Sequani, a Celtic-speaking group.[15]

Unfortunately, the geographical work of Cornelius Nepos is lost, but he seems to have obtained his information on the Indians from Celer directly. The event apparently occurred in the period around 62 BCE.

A later Roman writer who died in 79 CE, Claudius Plinii (Pliny) also had access to Nepos's writings, telling us:

> Idem Nepos de septentrionali circuitu tradit Quinto Metello Celeri, Afranii in consulatu collegae sed tum Galliae proconsuli Indos a rege Suevorum

[Sueborum] dono datos, qui ex India commerci causa navigantes tempestatibus essent in Germaniam abrepti.

[The same Nepos relates the following with regard to the northern passage: Indians were given as a gift to Quintus Metellus Celer (who was col-
league of Afranius in the consulship but at this time governor of Gaul) by
the king of the Suevi. The Indians had been sailing from India on a trading
mission but had been carried off to Germany by storms.]

This information was provided by Pliny in connection with his discussion of the supposed marine connection between India and the north
of Europe.[16]

To understand the circumstances under which Mela and Pliny wrote,
one must realize that everything to the east beyond India and the island
of Ceylon was only vaguely known to Romans and that it is likely that
any people thought to have been derived from Asia east from the Indus
valley to China and Japan would have been regarded as "Indians." In later
centuries, as we shall see, all parts of Asia east of the Ganges River were
called *India extra Gangem,* India beyond the Ganges, and all persons found
in southeast Asia, the Pacific, China, and Japan were regarded as being
"Indians" (as were the Americans from 1492).

What the Roman geographers did not realize was that the oceanic
connection between the Indian Ocean and northern Europe did not exist
except by way of the north Pacific and the Arctic Sea. Thus the "Indians"
of circa 62 BCE could not have come from the east as they imagined.
Instead, they came from the India of Columbus, which was, of course,
America.

Mela's (ca. 44 CE) map of the world shows Germania extending from
the Rhine River eastward. It also has India as a very large area at the
southeast corner of a Eurasian continent. The Ganges River and Seres
(China) face an ocean where the Pacific exists, but the latter connects
directly northerly with a Scythian Ocean that in turn reaches to the Hyperboreans, Caspian Sea, and to the Britannicus Oceanus. Scandinavia
is completely distorted in shape. Mela's map resembles that of Strabo (9
BCE–21 CE), adding some detail in the Baltic but also adding many fabulous
groups (such as "Amazons" near the Caspian, people with the hooves of
horses, and so forth). Strabo, incidentally, argued that the Atlantic was
navigable and that one could sail west from Spain to India, as taught by

his predecessor Eratosthenes. Mela doesn't seem to have considered that possibility.[17]

European geographers later come to realize that "India" (America and the Pacific–East Asia–East Indian region) could be reached directly by sailing westward from Europe, but apparently both Mela and Pliny were not conversant with ideas of voyages to and from the West (as was the case earlier, with Strabo, and in the days of the Atlantis story).

The clerical historian, Francisco López de Gómara, writing in the 1550s, was skeptical of the notion, which still persisted in his day (and in spite of the maps of Claudius Ptolemy), that one could sail from Scandinavia to east Asia through cold, freezing waters (as López put it) by way of the north of that peninsula. He noted that there were no memories among the ancients of anyone traveling by such a route with the one exception of the Nepos-Celer account. López concludes his remarks by saying of the latter's "Indians": "si ya no fuesen de Tierra del Labrador y los tuviesen por indianos, engañados en el color." Thus he seems to favor the ideas that the visitors were Americans from Labrador, taken for "Indianos" (the new Spanish name for Asian Indians) because of their color. Immediately thereafter López discusses the arrival of other Indians at Lubeck in the twelfth century.[18] His exact language is "If on that occasion they would not be from Labrador and they would hold them to be 'Indians,' deceived by the color; not a bit of it; besides, they say that in the days of the Emperor Frederico Barbarossa certain 'indios' made port at Lubec in a canoe." Thus López expresses his doubt that the Indians came around via Scandinavia, in spite of the promotion of such a route by his contemporary "Olao Godoz" (Olaus Magnus, a clerical refugee from the Swedish reformation, who died in 1558).

I will suggest that the "Indians" must have been from America, since the arrival of Sami (Lapps), Finns, Russians, or other northern Europeans is unlikely to have excited any special notice. Mela, for example, knew of the Hyperboreans, by which name he referred to such people as the Sami, Finns, Karelians, and north Baltic peoples. The Romans had already visited the Cimbri (now Denmark) and had entered the Baltic. The Teutonic nations of that region were trading and skirmishing with Rome, and Roman coins have been found in Denmark from the first century CE. Thus it would seem virtually certain that the term "Indians" was used for a totally strange people, probably with long dark hair and very brown skins.[19]

What is absolutely certain is that European geographers of the fifteenth century, when reading of Nepos's Indians, assumed that these Indians had crossed the Atlantic from the west. Such was the opinion of Pope Pius II, when, as Aeneas Sylvius Piccolomini, he wrote his *Historia rerum* (with "De Asia") in circa 1461. Christopher Columbus was directly inspired by the belief that Indians had sailed easterly to Europe and, indeed, wrote in the margins (as noted previously) of Sylvius's history that he had seen two such persons in Galway, Ireland, coming from the west.[20]

Aeneas Sylvius wrote: "Plinius nepotis testimonio utitur: qui Metello Celeri: Gallia proconsuli donatos a rege Sueuorum indos astruit: qui ex India commertii causa navigantes: tempestatibus esset in Germaniam arrepti [abrepti]." Thus he quotes Pliny about the Indians being tempest-blown to the coast of Germany on a trading mission. He then goes on to add the information about Indians reaching Germany in the twelfth century (which will be discussed below). Together these instances lead him to say: "in some manner, the greater part of the northern ocean is congealed [frozen] and not navigable; [but] away from the Columns of Hercules [Straits of Gibraltar] Mauritania, Hispania [Iberia], and Gaul form a circuit and nearly all west is navigable. The East is unknown to us."[21] Thus Sylvius was aware that the Atlantic Ocean was navigable. He was also aware that the distance to the east coast of Asia where "Indians" lived was an immense one going easterly (due probably to the travels of Europeans to China and greater knowledge of "India beyond the Ganges"). Since the Earth was seen as a globe by such thinkers, some contemporaries began to realize that the quickest route from Europe to India was directly west; that is, the Far East and the Far West were one and the same (since America was unknown as a large continent but was merely known, if at all, as islands).

The work of Sylvius influenced the geographer Paolo Toscanelli and Columbus, and part of that influence consisted in the references to Indians being blown by storm to the European coast. Sylvius, after citing Pliny, goes on to inform us that one Otto (probably Otto of Freising) indicated that during the reign of one of the German emperors, a "boat and Indian traders were caught on the German coast, to which place, from unwelcome contrary wind from the east blowing constantly, they arrived accidentally."[22]

This event seemingly occurred in the 1160s or thereabouts and perhaps was localized in the west Baltic or in the Frisland region between

Denmark and the Netherlands. But we are also informed by the Spanish writer López de Gómara, as noted, that

> también dicen cómo en tiempo del emperador Federico Barbaroja aportaron a Lubec ciertos indios en una canoa. El papa Eneas Silvio dice que tan cierto hay mar sarmático y scítico, como germánico y índico. Ahora hay mucha noticia y experiencia cómo se navega de Norwega hasta pasar por debajo del mismo norte ye continuar la costa hacia el sur, la vuelta de la China. Olao Godo me contaba muchas cosas de aquella tierra y navegación.

Thus López reports, from his sources, that in the time of Emperor Frederick I Barbarossa [1155–1190] a canoe-load of Indians reached Lubeck, (a Wendic-Slavic port of East Holstein which had been conquered and refounded by Saxons and Frisian merchants in 1138–43). He went on to tell the reader about Aeneas Silvius's continuing belief in an ocean connection from Scandinavia to India and then to relate the belief of Olaus Magnus about the possibility, noted above, of sailing to China from northern Norway.[23]

Were these the same Indians as reported by Otto of Freising, or were they a second group perhaps following up on trade opportunities? Since Lubeck was already a major trading center, it is possible that they were encouraged to go there after initially landing somewhere else.

In any case, Paul Gaffarel interprets López de Gómara as saying that the Indians of Celer and Lubeck could be from America. "Who knows if the Indians of Metellus Celer were not Americans from Labrador?" translates Gaffarel (but note my own earlier translation of López, which is somewhat different). Another early writer, Cornille Wytfliet, stated that "the Indians could not come from the fartherest Orient or Occident, but that they were from Labrador, from Estotiland, or other neighboring country; and one who knows about differences in climate would concur with me."[24]

Wytfleit also wrote, in his *Histoire Universelle des Indes* (ca. 1597): "Et si ne doute pointe, que les Indois qui fureint iadis poussez par la tempeste aux rivages de Sueviens, & d'Allemaigne, les quels le Roy Suevien donna à Quintus Metellus . . . estoyent de ces terres d'Estotilande [Newfoundland, Labrador], ou de quelques outres circovoysines . . ." In short, he believes that the Indians of Celer and Lubeck were from the Labrador-Newfoundland region, and he adds that Paolo Giovio, an Italian historian and cleric, was of the same opinion, but in addition, he is said to have offered the notion that Americans were coming to England and France to capture people for human sacrifice![25]

A more accurate source would seem to be that of Antonio Galvano who wrote in circa 1555:

> In the yeare 1153, in the time of Fredericke Barbarossa it is written that there came to Lubec . . . one Canoa with certaine Indians, like unto a long barge: which seemed to have come from the coast of Baccalaos [New- foundland region]. . . . The Germans greatly wondered to see such a barge and such people, not knowing from wence they came, nor understand- ing their speech, especially because there was then no knowledge of that countrey, as now there is: it may be credible that though the boate was small in respect of those huge seas, yet the winds and water might bring them thither.[26]

Those who have suggested that the "Indians" of Celer and Lubeck might have been Sami, Finns, or other northern European people have failed, I think, to understand the extent of trade and commerce that must have already existed throughout the Baltic and the multilingual capacities that would have resulted. British scholars have, for example, demonstrated that over a period of several thousand years, during the life of the Stonehenge sacred circle, that part of Britain as well as Ireland and Brittany and even more remote regions were in regular contact. During the century prior to our own era, Romans were in contact with large areas of the southern Baltic rim, as noted earlier, as well as specifically with the Cimbri Peninsula (Denmark and Holstein). It seems logical to assume that the existence of Sami, Finns, Slavic groups, and other Baltic peoples would be known and that one could find individuals in Gaul or the Rhine region who could translate from the many Celtic, Germanic, Slavic, and Finno-Ugric languages of the region, as well as even pre–Indo-European tongues still spoken in Roman times.

Tacitus (90s CE) and Procopius (530–50s CE) both were aware of the Fenni or Lapps. Tacitus described the Fenni as being hunters with skins for clothing. Procopius was aware of many Sami (Lapp) customs. It would seem likely that the Sami of that period were basically similar in physical type to other northern Europeans, except for stature, and that they would hardly be mistaken for Indians. Slavic peoples, Latvians, Lithuanians, and Finnish-Karelians were doubtless also part of the Baltic trading world, and this would be especially true by the 1100s CE. Lubeck at that time was in a state of transition from Wendic (Slavic) ascendancy to Germanic dominance and the trading center must have been very multilingual.[27]

Paul Gaffarel, a careful student of these matters, summed up the situation of both the Roman and Teutonic contacts by stating: "Therefore, it seems that the Greeks and Romans never went to America. On the contrary, there are Americans who, during the first century before the Christian era, might have come to Europe. Of course we are talking about the unintended trips of some Americans brought by storms onto the European shore. These trips are very much disputed. However, if they are not proved, they are at least very likely." After discussing other examples of Americans reaching European waters, Gaffarel goes on to say: "Therefore, it is quite possible that the winds brought some Americans to the European coast; for the distance in between is not so important that it cannot be traversed in a short time." In this connection, he cites the story of the Marquis de la Roche, who, in a small boat, was driven by a storm from Sable Island, Canada, to France in a very short time.[28] He also cites other examples of native travel that we will discuss below.

But perhaps the most important evidence is found in the opinions of Christopher Columbus as he wrote in the margins of Pierre D'Ailly's *Ymago Mundi* (written ca. 1420, published ca. 1480–83), Pliny's *Natural History,* and especially Aeneas Sylvius's *Historia* (1477 edition). Most of Columbus's marginal notes in those works were written in the 1481–90 period and they reveal the importance of the American visits to Europe.

Columbus was frequently impressed by evidence presented in both d'Ailly and Sylvius that India and Iberia ("Hispaniam") were not very distant, sailing westward from the latter. For example, Columbus wrote marginally in *Ymago Mundi:* "Quod inter hisppaniam et indiam est paruum mare": the sea that separates Spain [Iberia] and India is small. D'Ailly went on to say, "ad ultimu[m] habitabile ulterioris hyspanie pro occide[n]te & adultimu[m] idie ulterioris pro oriente." As Columbus interpreted: "India is at the extremity of the East and the end of the west is properly the extremity of Spain."[29]

D'Ailly also wrote that "India is immensely large," and has 118 peoples. Columbus's marginal note reiterates that "It is the third part of the habitable world" and "India gentes 118," or India has 118 nations.[30] D'Ailly continues that "from the extremity of Spain and the beginning of India is an area that is not great." Columbus writes marginally: "India est prope Hispania [*sic*]," India is near Spain.[31] Columbus also wrote 24 marginal notes in Pliny's *Natural History,* but 861 notes were placed in his copy of Sylvius's *Historia.* For example, Columbus writes: "Auctor docet quod totum oceanum septentrionaliem sit navigatum. . . . Auctor docet prout in Germaniam fuit inventum naves indorum cum homines et merces." That is, the author states that all of the northern sea is navigable, and, the author states that boats coming from the Indias that contained humans and merchandise reached Germany.

Columbus then goes on to write: "si esset maximam distanciam non potuissent venire cum fortunam sed aprobat esse prope." That is, "if the distance was extremely great [between Germany and India] the boats could not make the journey without mishap. Moreover it proves the two countries are close."[32] It is at this point that Colón goes on to describe his directly witnessing the arrival of two Americans in Galway, Ireland, in circa 1477, as discussed in chapter 1: "[Homi]nes de catayo versus oriens venierunt. Nos vidimimus multa notabilia et specialiter in galuei ibernie virum et [ux]orem in duabus lignis areptis ex mirabili [pers]ona." [People from Catayo towards the east they came. We saw many notable things and especially in Galway, Ireland, of a man and wife of marvelous form, with two dugout logs in their possession.]

After this most important statement, Columbus goes on to add: "Auctor oceanum septentrionalem non est concretum neque innavigable orientem nobis incognitum veteres tamen navigatum produnt." That is, "the author [Sylvius] says that the northern ocean is not congealed, nor innavigable. The East for us is unknown. However, the ancients claim that someone has navigated there" [from a French translation]. "Even if ancients went forth navigating" [from Latin].[33]

In short, not only did Columbus personally witness the arrival of Americans in Ireland, but he clearly interpreted the information from Pliny and Sylvius as referring to people crossing the Atlantic. Of course, there are other reasons for Colón's opinion, such as the references to boats reaching the Azores from the west, as discussed below, along with carved wood objects, and deceased humans of a non-European and non-African type.

There is also additional evidence of which Columbus's sources were unaware. A very prominent writer of books about maritime life, Jean Merrien, has provided us with two references to the arrival of an American on the west coast of Spain or neighboring Portugal. Merrien states in *Lonely Voyagers:* "In the Middle Ages there arrived one day on the coast of Spain a man 'red [rouge] and strange' in a craft described as a hollowed tree. From the recorded description, which specifically says that he was not a Negro, he might well have been a Native of America in a piragua—a dugout boat." Unfortunately, the man died before he learned to speak the local language. "He had been put in the care of a religious fraternity who . . . carried him off to their bishop so that he might be instructed and baptized. The journey was too much for him."[34]

Shortly thereafter Merrien wrote a book on Christopher Columbus in which he states: "according to the chronicle, a man had been found alive on the coast of Portugal, and had died without having been able to make himself understood, though he was taken to the Bishop."[35] Unfortunately, Merrien does not tell us which "chronicle" he used, and my efforts to trace his sources have been fruitless. However, it would seem that the "Red Man" arrived either in Galicia or the Oporto region, where the border of Spain and Portugal was obscure due to the fact that Spain did not then exist as a state and Portugal only emerged gradually between 997 and 1143. I would think that Merrien is referring to this general period, because after the 1150s the distinction between Portugal and Galicia (Leon and Castille) would be clearer.

Occasionally artifacts have turned up in Europe that suggest visits by Americans. These include harpoon heads of possibly Inuit origin found in Ireland and Scotland from much the same period just discussed, as well as numerous kayaks of a somewhat later date. These will be considered in the next chapter in connection with the northern or Inuit route from America to Europe. But here it is necessary to examine four baked clay "masks" now housed in the Pitt Rivers Museum of Oxford University.

The ceramic heads in question are called masks because of their lacking a back, being only rather thick representations of the front of a face. They lack eye slits, however, and therefore were perhaps never intended to be worn by humans, as in a dance or ceremony. They may have been funerary masks, used in some American cultures to cover the head of the deceased or otherwise to represent the deceased. They were perhaps originally painted but most of the paint has disappeared except for traces. The masks are described by English observers as "grotesque" and seem unlikely to have been the kind of objects that would be brought to England by a collector or by a dealer in antiquities. Now let us review their provenance and history, so far as I have been able to discover.

In 1884 Julian Pitt Rivers acquired two ceramic items as part of his original collection of artifacts. They were described as "Grotesque death's head face in coarse pottery," classified as "Figures Religion." At a much later date (1984), they were labeled as "Aztec" and said to be from "Mexico" by

The Pitt Rivers "Mexican" heads, from right to left: 1884.67.83 (painted); 1884.67.84; 1977.15.2 (probably from the Bull Inn site); 1977.15.1 (some paint, probably College Court site). Photographed by Jack D. and Carolyn L. Forbes; thanks to the assistance of Linda Mowat, of the Pitt Rivers Museum, Oxford.

Elizabeth Baquedano of the Institute of Archaeology, London University. They were catalogued as 1884.67.83 and 1884.67.84.

It is not known from whom Pitt Rivers acquired the two heads; however, I will suggest that they came from Gloucester City and specifically from an excavation in College Street of that city. In May 1883 the *Gloucester Journal* reported that College Street was to be widened. "It is proposed to take down the houses on the eastern side of the street, and re-erect a row of more imposing-looking buildings." At the same time the street was to be widened, but a "picturesque ancient gateway" on the west side would not be changed. The widening would provide a carriage route to the cathedral. As it was, the street "is a miserable lane, so narrow that there is barely room for one vehicle to pass along it at a time."[36]

All of this might mean very little except that a very similar (perhaps identical) head turned up as a result of an excavation in College Court, an alley very close to College Street, and also leading to the cathedral area. John Rhodes, then director of the Gloucester City Museum, informed me that the College Court head was probably found prior to 1930 and could even go back to the 1860s, when the museum was opened. The museum had held the object for years but there was no accession date or any other records of acquisition. The city also had no record of any excavations in College Court.

Mr. Rhodes earlier had written to me that the College Court head and one found at Bull Lane (to be discussed) "occurred in the city center which has been occupied more or less continuously from Roman times to the present day, and in any open ground (such as, in this case, the Bull Inn garden) was used for burying rubbish from medieval times up to the mid-nineteenth century."[37]

On December 5, 1967, Mr. Rhodes had sent to the Pitt Rivers Museum the head found in College Court, referred to as a "grotesque mask." He said that it is one of two found in building sites in Gloucester; hitherto "we have regarded them as possibly medieval local products, but yesterday a visitor told me that he had seen a similar object in your galleries labeled as a Mexican death-mask. If the enclosed really is of foreign origin, please do not trouble to return it." A reply was made on December 18 in which Mr. Rhodes was informed by Beatrice Blackwood that "the mask certainly bears a close resemblance to a specimen described in our catalogue as 'death's head, Mexico.' It is one of the original Pitt Rivers specimens and has no further documentation . . . and the resemblance even extends to the traces of white paint . . . it therefore seems likely that your mask does indeed come from Mexico; objects as exotic have been found on British sites, though how they got there remains a mystery." On June 6, 1968, Mr. Rhodes sent the other Gloucester head to the Pitt Rivers, this one being the one found in excavations of 1951 at the site of the Bull Inn, as mentioned above.

A few days later Ms. Blackwood responded that she had taken the first mask "to the Ashmolean Museum to show it to the medieval specialist. The latter stated that they do not know of anything remotely like them from medieval England. The resemblances between both of your specimens and the two Mexican 'death's head' masks we have are so detailed and striking that I have no doubt . . . that they are in fact Mexican . . . we shall be pleased to give them a home among our Mexican antiquities."[38] Unfortunately, the two new masks were mixed up so that it became impossible by the 1990s to tell which one was from College Court and which from Bull Inn. However, we do have a clue in that the Court head was mentioned as still having traces of white paint. The number 1977.15.1 has been assigned to the one with "much paint." Number 1977.15.2 is described as "very worn, cracked and mended." No. 1977.15.1 is virtually identical to 1884–6783, also with paint.

Perhaps now the reader will understand why I feel that the original Pitt Rivers heads stem from Gloucester also, from the College Street location that is very close to College Court and also to the Bull Inn location.

Now as to the Bull Inn find. The 1951 report of the Gloucester City Museum states that "a careful watch was kept for any possible traces of Roman buildings when the foundations for the extension of the telephone exchange were dug in the area between Bull Lane and Berkeley Street. A quantity of medieval and some Roman pottery was collected from this site." Any traces of Roman buildings must have been destroyed by the medieval pits that had been dug right down into the natural sand. Ms. D. M. Rennie, an archaeologist, had joined the staff in June 1951.[39]

A report on "Mediaeval Pottery from Bull Lane, Gloucester" was prepared by someone at the museum. It states that when the foundations for the Telephone Exchange building were dug (after the removal of the old inn): "a square of about 20 feet was completely excavated by hand to a depth of 10 feet and further excavation by hand took place in part of the area. . . . Pits several feet deep, which contained pottery of Mediaeval [written in] dates as well as Roman pottery ranging from 2nd to 4th century, were seen to have been cut into it." The "Mediaeval pits" had "evidently been cut through Roman levels." It adds that "as much pottery as could be rescued without delaying the men working . . . was collected and has been placed in the Gloucester City Museum."[40] The Mexican ceramic head was found as a part of this collection of medieval and Roman materials.

In a letter, D. M. Rennie states that the area dug up was not really done "by hand" but by "pick and shovel" instead of a "mechanical excavator." She kept watch "in case any remains of Roman buildings should be discovered, in which case we should have tried to make records, or, if the site seemed of sufficient importance, to carry out some archaeological investigation."[41]

I interviewed Ms. Rennie on May 6, 1994, in Oxford. She stated that she was primarily a Roman specialist and was principally looking for Roman ruins below ground level. As I recorded in my notes from the interview: "Workers worked by hand. Found rubbish pits—Roman layers of pottery and medieval layers. The medieval material was stored in Museum basement, including the mask. She didn't pay any attention to that material."[42] John Rhodes, who came to the museum in 1962, stated that a box of "delftware, slipware of the 17th and 18th centuries," was also found at the Bull Inn site, but he was not present at the excavation. In any case, it would seem that the mask was associated with a medieval rubbish pit, according to the person who was present (Ms. Rennie). Still further, Rhodes himself believed that the mask was of local medieval origin; as stated in his letter to the Pitt Rivers of December 5, 1967.[43]

The Bull Inn was a famous Gloucester inn built at an unknown date but "probably . . . before 1600" according to T. G. Hassall of the Royal Commission on the Historical Monuments of England. The site was previously occupied by a "College of Priests" or "priest's tenements" during the time of Henry III, up to and beyond 1455. The college was suppressed by Edward VI (1537–53), after Henry VIII's order of 1536. Rubbish was buried in back gardens throughout the Gloucester city center, such as behind the college and the later Bull Inn.

Bull Lane, on which the inn was located, was called Gor Lane in the Middle Ages. In 1455 the lane included several tenements of abbots and priors and then "the Chaplain and Proctors of the service of the Blessed Mary in the Church of the Holy Trinity hold diverse tenements, wherein divers priests dwell as in a college, held of the Abbot of Saint Peter of Gloucester; which in this time of King Henry III [1207–72] were called 'the land of Thomas Campeis,' and also afterwards." At about that time (1450) "New Inn" was constructed not far away to house pilgrims who came to visit the shrine of Edward II in Gloucester Cathedral (then the Abbey Church of St. Peter). New Inn still survives, at least in part.[44]

The priests' college was suppressed soon after 1536–37 and the Bull Inn was doubtless built on the site soon after. One can argue that the medieval rubbish pits were probably filled up during the period of the college occupancy, since material from the Bull Inn period would hardly be considered "medieval," I would think.

In any case, we have two presumed Mexican masks stemming from locations in medieval contexts, with the likelihood of four such masks buried in adjacent but diverse parts of the city center. How did they get to Gloucester and at what date? Why were they buried in different locations?

At my request, the Oxford University Research Laboratory for Archaeology and the History of Art carried out tests on the two Gloucester Museum masks for the Pitt Rivers Museum. The results indicated that 1977.15.1 is between 550 and 900 years from last firing (1093–1443 CE) and that 1977.15.2 is between 300 and 500 years from last firing (1493–1677 CE).

This would seem to indicate that the four masks in question (since one of 1884 is identical with 1977.15.1) perhaps were created in the 1400–1500 period or quite possibly prior to the Spanish conquest of Tenochtitlan.[45]

It would appear that the mask from College Court (perhaps 15.1) is very similar to 1884–6783 and that both were made by the same maker or from the same mold. Thus it is unfortunate that we do not know how deep in the ground the mask was found, or even in what context. Nonetheless, general conditions would indicate that the masks arrived in Britain *before* 1550–1600 (when Bull Inn was built), although a later date cannot absolutely be ruled out.

Gloucester, a very ancient city, is located on the Severn River and has long been an important port. In 1877, 549 foreign ships and 3,762 British ships entered the port. Thus it is a site that might have been reached by persons derived from a drifting American boat from Mexico or Meso-america, a boat that had perhaps entered the Irish Sea or Severn estuary. But, of course, a British or other ship might have brought the masks, but, in either case, when and why?

If we were to argue that the masks were brought from Mexico by a British subject, we face the difficulty of explaining why four somewhat rough and unspectacular ceramic objects would have been important enough to be smuggled past Spanish officials or stolen from a Spanish vessel (and why would they have been on a vessel in the first place?). In the early and later 1500s, English ships were entering the Caribbean and, more rarely, going to Mexico. For example, in 1555 an English ship went to Haiti and Mexico, where they found Thomas Blakes, a Scotsman, "who had dwelt there twentie yeares." The master and others were imprisoned and sent to Spain, but other voyages reached Mexico in 1564 and 1568. Most of these visits were hostile ones, especially during the Elizabethan period.[46]

One can imagine that a few spectacular or impressive Mexican objects might have reached Britain as a result of such activities, but I would argue that objects of purely ethnographic interest would not have been of enough value to steal or carry, at least until after Mexican independence (1821) and the rise of nineteenth-century antiquarianism.

Before concluding, let us return to the question of the meaning and function of Mexican masks. According to Donald Cordry, an authority on Mexican folk culture, Mexican masks traditionally constitute a "face" or "soul": "Mexican Indian groups . . . directly relate the face to the soul . . . covering the face with a mask is the equivalent of temporarily removing the identity and soul (alma) of the mask wearer from the everyday world

. . . masks substitute a 'new' face (i.e., new ego, persona, and soul)." Cordry is speaking especially of masks used in dances and ceremonies, but the "soul" concept also applies to death masks: "the surviving clay and stone masks are commonly classified as mortuary masks, as they were usually discovered in tombs . . . some of these masks have no eyeholes and were probably specifically made for the dead . . . all of this splendid work may have been done so that the wearer could wake up comfortably after death in another world." Masks were often used for protection against evil, against illness, and in funeral rites. Cordry notes that "when mortuary bundles were the custom, a mask of stone, wood, or possibly copper was tied to the top of the bundle." The early Spanish observer Gerónimo de Mendieta noted: "of the ceremonies with which they buried the lords, and those who were not . . . all assembled together, they put the dead body in order, wrapping him up in fifteen or twenty exquisite capes woven with a design[,] and when he was shrouded and his face covered, they placed a painted mask on top."[47]

It would seem that the Gloucester masks were either taken from the excavation of Mexican burials or were brought by Mexicans to Britain. Again, the excavation process was probably not initiated until after 1821 (although perhaps tomb robbing or looting might have been common in the early years of the conquest, but gold and other precious objects would have been sought). It is also possible that the Roman Catholic priests began to suppress the use of burials with "soul masks" soon after the Spanish conquest.

But if the masks arrived in Gloucester in late medieval or pre-1519 times, in the hands of American visitors, why would they have been carried across the Atlantic? I can only suggest two possibilities: (1) that the masks had religious significance, as described; and (2) that the Mesoamericans expected that they might perish on their long voyage and wished to have death masks along with them for that event. Finally, of course, there is also the possibility that English vessels kidnapped or otherwise added Mexicans to their crews while in American waters and that some of the latter somehow came to Gloucester with death masks in the sixteenth century. In any event, the finding of such objects raises important issues that must be dealt with, even if, at this stage, a certain explanation is not available.[48]

Americans continued to cross the Atlantic in the fifteenth and early sixteenth centuries. Bartolome de Las Casas, using Colón's notes and diaries, found that the latter had learned from Portuguese sources "que en la isla de las Flores, que es una de las Azores, había echado la mar dos cuerpos de hombres muertos, que parecía tener las caras muy anchas y de otro gesto que tienen los cristianos." Thus Columbus was told that two bodies had been washed ashore in the Azores of persons with very broad faces and features unlike those of Europeans. Moreover, "otra vez, diz que en el Cabo de la Verga . . . y por aquella comarca, se vieron almadías o canoas con casa movediza, las cuales por ventura, pasando de una isla a otra o de un lugar a otro, la fuerza de los vientos y mar las echó donde, no pudiendo tornar los que traían, perecieron, y ellas, como nunca jamás se hunden, vinieron a parar por tiempo a los Azores." Thus canoes or almadías (dugout-like boats) with removable houses had by chance been blown by the winds to the Azores while their original occupants had perished. The canoas were still afloat as they drifted from island to island.[49]

We do not know, of course, whether these Americans were on their way across the Atlantic in an eastward direction or, perhaps, more likely, had already been to European waters and were returning southwesterly, having become separated from the fastest-moving section of the ocean stream. In any case, their adventures can perhaps be best understood by mentioning here the fate of the seven Americans who, in 1508 or 1509, were picked up by a French ship as they traveled in the north Atlantic somewhere between Newfoundland and Britain, as discussed in chapter 3. These North Americans ended up in Rouen, France, at least for a time, but did they remain there or did some return to their home country?

The same question can be asked of the American man and woman met by Colón in Galway in 1477. Did they remain in Ireland, leaving an American genetic heritage, or did they manage to return home?

Sometime in the early European contact period, prior to English colonization, the Sewee people of coastal South Carolina set out in a boat to reportedly visit England. The vessel was apparently outfitted with sails, but unfortunately they were seized by an English ship out in the Atlantic and sold as slaves. This was perhaps during the period, prior to 1620, in which several English vessels captured Americans both along the New England coast and along the Rappahannock River in Virginia, transporting them as slaves to Europe. In any case, the fact that the Sewee set out on the Gulf Stream to visit England is a rather interesting confirmation of the possibility of intentional voyages to Europe by early Americans.[50]

We can be confident from all these examples of Americans reaching European waters or the Azores Islands that there must have been a large number of unrecorded visits both before and during this period.

In connection with this discussion, mention should be made of certain American traditions that point towards travel by sea to other lands. Modern Maya teachers and spiritual elders sometimes indicate that in ancient times Mayas traveled to other parts of the world, including India and Egypt. A more ancient tradition relates to one Votan, a culture-hero of Chiapas, who is said to have been sent by divine authority to divide up the land among the Americans and who introduced other aspects of later cultures. The oldest source (ca. 1690s-1702) states that Votan witnessed the Tower of Babel and was a grandson of Noah, but this is clearly a post-Conquest addition, I would think (facilitated, doubtless, by the fact that the oldest source is from a Dominican who became Bishop of Chiapas and Soconusco in 1683).

Later additions to the Votan story, a century or more later, have him stemming from a land called Valun Votan, actually "la Isla de Havanna which in the figurative language of the Snakes is Valunvotan." Votan claimed to be a Snake (Culebra) and a "Chivim." Supposedly he conducted seven families from Valun Votan "to this continent." Subsequently, he made four voyages to Chivim, also visiting Spain, Rome (when the "great house of God" was being built), passing "the houses of the thirteen Snakes." He did this, apparently, by following a road that his brother Snakes had bored in the earth. It is also said that Votan visited a very old city, where he witnessed the ruins, presumably, of the Tower of Babel.

Unfortunately, the Votan material is so fragmentary and so mixed with ideas of a post-Conquest nature that it is impossible to know what the original belief might have been. But there does seem to be a tradition of overseas travel to Europe, or at least, to Caribbean islands and the land of the Snakes. Interestingly, the Lenápe people of North America in their epic Walam Olum speak of the Snake Land. The Lenápe Snake Land may have been connected with the Great Serpent Mound of Ohio.[51]

The traditions of the Quiche of Guatemala point toward a migration from the Veracruz-Tabasco region. In this context, three chiefs' sons resolved on a return journey to the "East," across a sea, to where their fathers had led them from Tollan (Veracruz). They went to request certain insignia of royal authority from a Lord Nacxit. This "sea" was perhaps the Laguna de Terminos of Tabasco, in my judgment, and not the Gulf of Mexico or the Caribbean. Their original crossing of the sea was by means of stones piled up in the sand as the waters divided.[52]

The Mandan people of present-day North Dakota are said to have had a tradition of going out upon the ocean and perhaps visiting Europe. I have not been able to find any written evidence of the latter, but recorded Mandan stories do refer to visiting the mouth of a major river (the Mississippi presumably) and of going out upon the ocean and visiting another land. One account states that the Mandan

> were in the habit of going to an island in the ocean off the mouth of a river to gather ma-tä-ba-ho [beaked shells of many colors]. For the journey they used a boat by the name of I-di-he [Self-Going]. . . . This boat carried twelve persons and no more. . . . When they reached the ocean they were confronted by a great whirlpool. . . . So they kept on the journey until they came to a part of the ocean where the waves were rough. . . . Upon the island there were inhabitants under a chief named Ma-na-ge [or Ma-ni-ke].

This account is said to be very similar to one recorded in the 1830s. Another version, from 1929, states: "The Mandan people originated at the mouth of this river way down at the ocean."[53] Unfortunately, it has been many centuries since ancient native traditions might have been recorded from nations residing along most coastal areas.

In any case, the impact of visits to Europe may indeed be very great, embracing such diverse areas as genetic influences, the introduction of American plants, the possible introduction of drugs such as nicotine and cocaine, philosophical and cultural ideas, and even the spread of disease vectors.

The disease of syphilis is a case in point. As many readers are aware, syphilis attacked the Spanish, Italian, and French armies in Italy in the 1490s in a very virulent form. At first, no one blamed Americans for this outbreak and, in fact, the Spaniards soon called the malady *galico* or the French disease. Nonetheless, by the middle of the sixteenth century several Spanish writers began to identify the Caribbean region as the source for the contagion, although none of the earliest reports mentioned the disease. In more recent times, some archaeologists and non-native historians have joined the chorus, the former seeing in some skeletal remains signs of syphilitic infection, the latter simply echoing Spanish writers.[54]

For my own part, I rather doubted the pre-1492 presence of the disease in America for several reasons: (1) its total absence in the reports of all early diaries that I have examined from North America as well as the Caribbean, (2) the seemingly complete lack of fear on the part of white persons about having intercourse with American women (or men), (3) no descriptions of infected individuals known to me, at early contact, (4) the fact that Baja and Upper Californian natives were highly susceptible to the disease after contact, with less resistance then evidenced by Spaniards, and (5) the massive death rates of Americans after contact with Spaniards, throughout the Caribbean, Mesoamerica, and South America, indicating susceptibility to more than one disease vector that was new to America.

In researching my book *Africans and Native Americans* I discovered a note of Pedro Mártir de Anglería from April 1488 in which he refers to syphilis, which he states is called *bubas* in Spain and *Galico* in Italy. The combination of the terms *Galico* and *bubas* makes it certain that he was referring to syphilis and not to some other disease.[55]

Thus three years before Colón sailed west, syphilis was present in Spain. Now we know that syphilis was epidemic in at least some parts of England long before 1492. The port of Hull possessed an Augustinian priory that has been investigated archaeologically. Sixty percent of the skeletons unearthed have revealed signs of acute syphilitic infection, dating between 1300 and 1420, principally in the 1340s to 1369. The destruction of bones, including skulls, forehead, legs, and so on, was much more severe than the kind of lesions found in America, thus suggesting perhaps that Americans possessed a much milder form of the disease if, indeed, it existed at all prior to Colón's voyage.

A very thorough German scholar, Heinrich Haeser, authored an extensive study of the epidemiology of syphilis, published in 1882. He maintained that it was an "Old World" disease in origin. More recently, researchers have uncovered skeletons in Italy with indications of syphilis, dating back to 600 BCE, and including many indications in Pompeii, the port city mentioned earlier. Did Americans visit one of the European ports, become infected by a mild form of syphilis and carry it back to America, or did Colón's crew bring it to the Caribbean and spread its virulent form by means of their sexual exploitation of American women? It is possible that genetic research will one day tell us whether syphilis had its roots in Africa, Eurasia, or America. Until then, however, we must lean toward a Euro-African origin, but with the pre-contact American skeletal remains as a possible sign of ancient contact.[56]

In light of the evidence presented in this and earlier chapters, it is possible to suggest the following scenarios: (1) that the disease had an American origin but that it was carried to Europe by early American visitors, in the meantime dying out or becoming very mild in America until after the Spaniards introduced a new, more virulent strain (which might have hybridized with the surviving American variety); (2) that the disease had a Euro-African origin but was introduced by the Norse after 900 CE, primarily in the eastern part of North America (which could help to explain the abandonment of numerous large urban areas after 1200–1450 CE), but became less virulent after population dispersal; (3) that American visitors to Britain brought the disease back to America, at an early date; (4) that the American skeletons studied show the effects of a different, but perhaps related, disease. It should be noted that the abandonment of urban areas, as noted, could have been due to the bubonic plague (or other disease) being introduced by the Norse, the plague as a result of rattus rattus (European rats) and fleas arriving in the holds and supplies of Norse vessels. Since the plague reached Norway and probably Iceland, such a scenario is possible.

Further research will be necessary to answer some of these questions, but one thing is certain: agency can no longer be denied to Americans.

6.

The Inuit Route
to Europe

THE DUTCH COMMUNITY of Zierikzee has had a tradition that in 849 CE one Zierik arrived by sea to found the city. The local people also have believed for some time that he arrived in an Inuit kayak from Greenland, a kayak long on display in the Community Museum. This tradition was in existence as early as the seventeenth century, when an author stated that he no longer believed the story. By the eighteenth century Zierik's alleged kayak was already hanging in place, although current opinion is that the kayak only dates from that same century. Nonetheless, it is a genuine West Greenland kayak.[1]

The Zierik story seems to be the first in a long series of incidents involving Inuit visits to Europe or the finding of alleged Inuit harpoon heads in Scotland and Ireland. It is a very compelling subject, because of its inherently interesting, romantic, and also tragic elements, and also because of serious questions about whether northeastern American boats, whether of the Beothuk-Newfoundland, umiak, or kayak types, were capable of remaining afloat for a long enough period to reach Iceland, the Faeroes, and other islands of Europe.

Before dealing with this question, however, we should note that the advocates of St. Brendan's alleged voyages westward from Ireland have never seemed to have any doubts about the ability of Irish curraghs covered with hides to remain at sea for long periods. Similarly, E. F. Greenman and other anthropologists who have advocated ancient European voyages to America seem to believe that skin-covered craft could make the trip even in the virtually impossible east-to-west direction (possibly drying out the craft on convenient ice floes).[2]

The East Greenland Coast, September 1987, showing the mouth of a glacier and numerous ice floes. Photograph by Jack D. Forbes.

But first, I would like to suggest that the widespread reports of the existence of "mer-men" and "mer-women" (sea-men or sea-women) in northwestern Europe be considered as possible evidence of early Inuit or other American arrivals. Early descriptions of Inuits in their kayaks seem to suggest the appearance of a "fish-man" or a "finn-man" because the navigator is enclosed in skins that are actually part of the craft, and sailor and craft would appear to viewers to be one and the same. In addi-

An ice river reaching the sea on the East Greenland coast, September 14, 1985.
Photograph by Jack D. Forbes.

Where a river of ice meets the sea. East Greenland, September 14, 1985.
Photograph by Jack D. Forbes.

Inner fiords on the East Greenland coast, September 14, 1985. Photograph by
Jack D. Forbes.

tion, Inuit navigators were capable of great feats of seamanship, including
turning the craft upside down, apparently. Thus, for practical purposes,
sailor and kayak were a single sea-creature.[3]

There are many mer-person stories. For example, in 1187 it is recorded
that a "man-fish" was kept for six months in Orforde Castle in Suffolk,
England. Radulphus de Coggeshale wrote: "In the time of King Henry I
. . . the fishermen took in their nets a wild man, having the human shape
complete, with hair on his head, a long and picked beard, and a great deal
of shaggy hair on his breats; but he stole away to sea privately, and was
never seen afterwards."[4] In 1430 after a storm an alleged "wild woman"

"Kayakers" in the open sea, East Greenland, a sketch made by Fridtjof Nansen and finished by Th. Holmboe. From Fridtjof Nansen, *The First Crossing of Greenland,* trans. Hubert Majendie Gepp, London: Longmans, Green, 1892, 426.

came through a dike near Edam, Holland, and lived for many years in Haarlem. She reportedly learned to spin but never learned to speak the local language. The woman (called a "nimphe" or "Féme marine") was rescued by some young women of Edam who were passing by Purmerend in a boat. The woman eventually returned to her "first and natural element."[5]

Erich Pontopiddan, in 1751, makes reference to many examples of "mermen" seen by Norwegians as well as to several seen on the coast of Iceland, as reported earlier by the historian Torfaeus. The details are too meager, however, to determine if these "mer-men" were Inuits in their kayaks.[6]

In the early part of the 1500s, probably between 1517 and 1537, or in 1535 as one source asserts, a "sea-man" was captured along the North Sea coast of Yorkshire at the little village of Skengrave (Skinningrave). An "ancient manuscript," being a long letter about antiquities in the region written by one "H. Tr—" and sent to Sir Thomas Chaloner the naturalist (who died in 1615), is the original source for our information. The letter is probably dated 1597 and refers to the event as occurring some "60 to 80

"And as the wave breaks [they] throw themselves into its very jaws," a sketch made by Fridtjof Nansen in East Greenland, and finished by A. Bloch. From Fridtjof Nansen, *The First Crossing of Greenland,* trans. Hubert Majendie Gepp, London: Longmans, Green, 1892, 427.

or more years before." The letter was seen by William Camden prior to his editing of the 1607 Latin edition of *Britannia,* his encyclopedic survey of Britain. The letter of "H. Tr—" asserts:

> Old men that would be loathe to have their credit crakt . . . reporte confidently that 60 years since or perhaps 80 or more[,] a sea-man was taken by the fishers of that place . . . where duringe many weeks they kepte in an olde house giving him rawe fishe to eate, for all other food he refused[;] instead of voice he shreaked, and shewed a curteous to such as flocked farre and neare to visyte him. Fayr maydes were welcomest guests to his harbour, whom he would behold with a very earnest countenance. . . . One day . . . he privily stole out of doores and ere he could be overtaken recovered the sea, whereinto he plunged himself; yet as one that would not unmannerly depart without taking of his leave, from the middle upwards he raysed his shoulders often above the waves and making signs of acknowledging his

good entertainment to such as beheld him on the shore as they interpreted it[.] After a pretty while he dived down and appeared no more.[7]

This description would seem to clearly refer to an Inuit man departing in his kayak, with the image of having head and shoulders above the waves reflecting precisely the position of a kayaker departing through the surf. As we shall see, the description relates well to those of later Inuit visitors in the Orkneys and elsewhere.

At this point mention should be made of alleged Inuit harpoon heads found on beaches in Ireland and Scotland. In 1927 a head, said to be the "Thule type 2" was found on the shore of Mullin Bay, Tara, County Down. It was in very worn condition and was "no newcomer to the beach." The authors of the report argue that it was very unlikely to have been carried by a seal or walrus and that it is "absolutely certain that it is of Archaic Eskimo origin." They surmise that the harpoon head probably dated from "before the end of the 12th century or 13th," or 1200–1300 CE, and perhaps was brought to Ireland by a Norseman or by a Norwegian expedition to Ireland.[8]

Two Inuit-like harpoon heads have also been found on beaches in Scotland, both along the coast north of Aberdeen. The first was found near Collieston, Slains, before 1876 and the second at Cruden Bay. The former has four barbs on each side, about six centimeters long, with five holes and a notch at the base for attachment. It is worn but not too severely. It lay in sandy ground and the upper side "is quite polished." The second is a much simpler point, very worn and, at present, it has no barbs. But like

Much-worn harpoon point found at Cruden Bay, Aberdeenshire, Scotland. See *Eskimo Kayaks in Aberdeen,* a leaflet of the Marischal Museum, Aberdeen, Scotland. Photo © University of Aberdeen. Reproduced by permission.

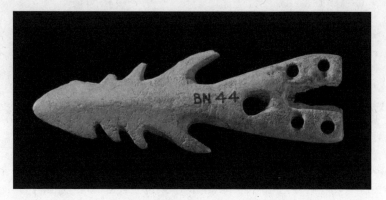

A harpoon head found on the coast of Aberdeenshire near Collieston, Slains, before 1876. © Trustees of the National Museums of Scotland.

the first it has five holes near the base. A fourth bone harpoon, donated to the National Museum of Antiquities of Scotland (CA 88) but now in the Royal Scottish Museum, could also have been found in Scotland, but no provenance is known.

I have sent photographs of the two Scottish harpoons to archaeologists specializing in Arctic North America. No one recognized them as belonging to a specific period or place, although the holes drilled in the base of both specimens is a Thule period characteristic primarily. The smaller head has been so worn down, or modified and worn down, as to be unclassifiable. The barbs on the larger harpoon seem strange and not typically Thule. Thus, without hands-on expert evaluation, little can be said as to their age or provenance.[9]

The presence of Inuit-like harpoon heads along the beaches of Ireland and perhaps Scotland suggests direct contact with these areas by Americans, presumably at an early date (e.g., in the 1200s or earlier). Did the Americans reach British waters by means of navigation from the Greenland area, or were they taken to British shores by Norse, Icelandic, or Greenlandic vessels (perhaps being utilized as hunters to supply flesh for ship crews)?

The latter possibility presents itself because it is known that Norsemen captured two Inuit youngsters in the 1000s and took them to Iceland and, probably, Norway. Similarly, Inuit kayaks and perhaps umiaks, along with living persons, were apparently sent to Norway in the 1400s and 1500s, as will be discussed below. On the other hand, evidence from Icelandic

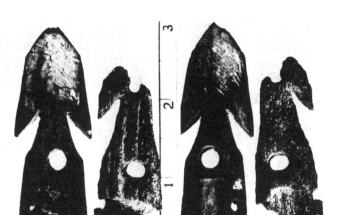

Comparison of the harpoon found at Tara, Ireland, with one from
Ellesmere Island, Canada (from E. E. Evans and C. F. C. Hawkes, "An
Eskimo Harpoon-Head from Tara Co. Down (?)," *Ulster Journal of
Archaeology,* third series, 3:2, July 1940.

and other scholars indicates that the Norse Icelanders and Greenlanders
failed to adopt Inuit cultural traits and, in fact, that no Inuit artifacts have
ever been found in Iceland (or in the Faeroe Islands) in an archaeological context (at least since the alleged American-type microblade of ca.
9000 BP).[10]

Oslo professor Christian Keller suggested to me in correspondence
that "very few—if any—technological traits seem to have been copied
from one culture to the other. This may have several explanations, of
which the most important may have been ideological. After the Norse
population became Christians, trade and other involvement with pagans
was prohibited, and even Inuit items such as harpoon heads may have
been considered 'tools of the Devil.'"[11]

Professor Sveinbjorn Rafnsson of the University of Iceland wrote to me:
"Harpoons are not known in Icelandic cultural history except for spears
. . . made of iron." Similarly, Professor Thomas McGovern has been quoted
as saying that the Norse Greenlanders "never learned to use harpoons."
Also, they failed to adopt skin clothing and skin boats. No harpoons

or points have been found in Norse sites in Greenland (although Norse materials are found in Inuit sites and an arrow point was found in a Norse site, presumably coming from the American mainland).[12] However, it should be noted that Inuits may have removed useful items, including harpoon points, from Norse sites after the Norse were gone (or were assimilated). It is known that Inuits were collectors of found objects, from the previous Dorset and other American cultures, as well as from the Euro-Greenlanders.[13]

Adding to the mystery of ancient American-Norse contacts is a wonderful little carved walrus, of walrus tusk ivory, found in Bergen, Norway, during excavations on the site of an ancient house. It was among the deepest finds, "right down in the very foundations," and much deeper apparently than "a burnt layer, which lay under the remains of the fire of 1413." Bergen was founded just before 1100 and Fridtjof Nansen states that the carving "may be of the twelfth, or at the latest, of the thirteenth, century."[14]

The walrus carving fits in nicely with descriptions of Dorset tusk carving of the pre–1000 CE period. As Jørgen Meldgaard has written, "The last Dorset people [in Greenland] are famous for their rich production of carvings in tusk, bone, and wood. In the Thule District they left behind a pair of excellent specimens of their art: two human figures carved in walrus tusk."[15] It would appear that the Thule Inuit culture that succeeded the Dorset (after 1000–1100 or so), was not so likely to produce fine objects. "As in the west, decorative elaboration was restricted, and the small carvings of human beings . . . were often plain and crude, although impressively carved or engraved objects do occur sporadically."[16] Of course, a beautiful object such as the walrus carving would have been valued and saved by Thule people, as well as by Norwegians. Thus our essential problem is how this thousand-year-old object came to be buried beneath a Bergen house.

The historian Pontoppidan tells us that during the reign of King Olaf a fisherman at Hordeland, in the later Bergen area, brought a "mer-man" to the king. The "mer-man" is said to have "sung an unmusical song to King Hiorlief [Olaf]."[17] There are several Olafs in Norwegian history, but the most famous is the one who reigned in the 1020s, and this fits in well with the possible age of the little walrus. Could it be that a Dorset or Thule sea-hunter carried the object to Norway? As in the case of the harpoon heads of nearby Scotland and Ireland, we cannot offer a certain explanation; but we are led to two possible conclusions: either the Norse were a lot more active in interacting with Americans than we have hitherto been led to believe by many Icelandic and Norwegian scholars, or Americans were finding their way to Europe with some continuing regularity.

In either event, it is likely that Americans were the ones carrying the harpoons and walrus ivory to Europe, either as kidnapped victims, as friendly emissaries, as helpers, or as independent voyagers. The latter possibility is subject, however, to the question as to whether Inuit skin-boats could make the journey. Before dealing with that issue, though, it is important to point out that Inuit sea-hunting technology with toggled harpoon heads may well have been ancestral to the development of similar technology in certain areas of western Europe at a later date. We have already noted the presence of toggled harpoon technology in Labrador, North America, as early as 7,500 years ago. This same type of technology shows up again in the Canadian Arctic and in the Imakpik-Alaska region some 4,000 years ago and continues on, with some breaks in the record, until modern times.

Toggled harpoon technology is, in my opinion, highly specialized and complex, considering that we are speaking not of a forked spear with a fixed shaft or a barbed point on a shaft, but rather of an advanced tool with many separable parts that allow a barbed point to become imbedded in a seal, walrus, whale, or other victim. The point separates from the shaft but remains connected to the hunter by means of a tough line. In the toggled system the point is attached in such a way that it turns in the animal's flesh, becoming transverse and more likely to hold, even under extreme pressure. Such a system is necessary for the hunting of large sea mammals such as walrus and whales, but is also useful for hunting certain seal species that may only be exposed at blow-holes in the ice.

In any case, the hunting of whales and other large and powerful sea game (such as walrus and, in the ancient Red Earth culture, swordfish) is apparently older in North America than anywhere else in the world. Robert Heizer, in his history of whaling, noted that Europe had not yielded any "prehistoric evidence of the hunting of whales in ancient times" except in the far north of Norway (presumably among the Sami of Finnmark). Heizer tells us that whaling had existed in Norway from 417 CE and later spread southward to the French coast. In circa 875 one hears of whaling near North Cape (of later Norway) and also off the coast of Flanders. By the 1100s or 1200s whaling had spread to the Bay of Biscay, with major Basque participation. Heizer is of the opinion that the toggling harpoon probably spread from Norway's north to the Basques.[18]

It is significant then that the most ancient toggling harpoon system in the world was found in Labrador, dated about 7500 BP. It may be that the long-held vision of every cultural innovation moving from Siberia to Alaska and then across Canada to Greenland and Labrador is in error and that some important traits may have originated in eastern North America. If so, then we might argue for a spread of large sea mammal hunting technology across the North Atlantic from the latter region, following the Gulf Stream and North Atlantic Drift to the coasts of Finnmark. As noted earlier, an American turtle has been found as far east as the Murmansk area, traveling to north Russia (Karelia) along the drift.

Heizer was of the opinion that "connection between Eskimo and Scandinavian cultures is a generally accepted fact" with "the intermediate links as yet unfound."[19] Perhaps the links are to be found in American contacts across the North Atlantic. In this respect, mention should be made of a Greenland chronicle in verse, written in circa 1600 by Claudius Christopherson, a Dane. In his chronicle, probably derived from an earlier source, it is stated that some "Armenians" were blown by a great storm into the Northern Ocean, landing in Greenland. From there they passed into Norway, where "they inhabited the rocks along the Hyperborean [Arctic] Sea." Isaac de la Peyrère termed this a fable, but perhaps the "Armenians" were "Americans."[20]

We know that Americans were being kidnapped as early as 1007–1010 and probably taken to Europe. It is conceivable that Norse contacts with Greenland or Newfoundland could have occurred as early as the 700s or 835, judging from references to Greenland in European documents. (But it must be noted that Greenland was for a long while conceived of as a vague land mass stretching from northern Norway through Spitsbergen to American Greenland. Thus early references to Greenland could refer to the northern point of Scandinavia).[21]

In connection also with kidnapping, we should note that Viking raiding of other countries began in the 800s, focused at first on Britain and Ireland. By 844, Vikings raided as far as Asturias, Lisbon, Cadiz, Sevilla, and Cordova, targeting both Christians and Muslims. In the 860s raiders went as far as Morocco, carrying off many "Blue-men" (Blacks or Browns) as captives to Ireland. (In the attempted settlement of Vinland-Newfoundland at a later date a "Turk" [Tyrkir] was present, perhaps referring to a Muslim from either Africa or Iberia, since the term Turk was used generally for Muslims by the Dutch and others).[22]

The Norse and Danes were actively engaged in the captive trade, enslaving numbers of Irish and Scots as well as Iberians, Africans, and other nationalities. This trade in captives had a genetic impact upon the later settler populations in the Orkneys, Faeroes, Iceland, and other islands occupied by the Norse, as well as upon those who eventually traveled to Greenland and Vinland. Of greater significance to us, however, is the very real possibility that Norse raiders depopulated part of Greenland and also seized Americans in Newfoundland and Labrador. Fridtjof Nansen states: "I have myself seen on the east coast of Greenland how the Eskimo take to their heels and leave their dwellings on the unexpected appearance of strangers, and this has been the common experience of other travelers in former and recent times." Danes who reached Greenland in the early seventeenth century found that the Inuit of western Greenland "were much more timid and mistrustful than the others [of northeast Greenland], for they had no sooner received their exchange [in barter] from the Danes, than they fled to their boats as if they had robbed them and were being pursued."[23]

When Eric the Red and his men reached Greenland they found dwellings, tools, and partial boats belonging to the same kind of people "who also live in Wineland, and who are the same as those the [Norse] Greenlanders call Skraelings." This statement, written in circa 1130 by Are Frode, seems to confirm, according to Nansen, that the Skraelingers (those who wear skin clothes) were still living in southwestern Greenland in the tenth century. Nansen also points out that one of the fjords in the "Eastern Settlement" of the Norse had an Inuit-like name, affording "strong evidence, not only that there were Eskimo in the Eastern Settlement when the Icelanders established themselves there, but also that they had intercourse with them." If such is the case, the subsequent disappearance of Americans from southern Greenland could be due to aggression and raids for captives. In any event, we may theorize that Americans could have been carried to Europe in the two centuries before circa 1010.[24]

Thus, when we consider the appearance of Americans in Europe, from the 900s onward, we have to consider the possibility that kidnapping may have been a major source of such persons. Some may have been seized with their kayaks or other boats, as we know to have been the case from the 1400s onward. Others still might have escaped and manufactured new kayaks from materials collected in Europe, although the bulk of kayaks preserved seem to have been made in Greenland, save one in Britain reportedly made with a European pine framework. European pine, however, could have drifted to Greenland shores and been used there.[25]

Well enough, but there is still the important question of whether Greenlanders and other Americans might have navigated skin-covered craft to Iceland and beyond. Interestingly, some commentators have been absolutely certain that they have known the answer. For example, W. S. Laughlin stated: "Kayaks and umiaks cannot be left in the water many days without damage to the skins; they must be removed, dried, and oiled. Depending upon its load, condition of the sea, and conditions of the skins, an umiak may be rendered unusable in nine or ten hours of travel." Laughlin went on to assert that "Eskimos have not crossed Danmark Strait between Greenland and Iceland, they have not crossed Davis Straight between Greenland and Canada."[26]

Such assertions, as we shall see, are surprising in view of several thousand years of possibilities. In any case, Knud Rasmussen, a firsthand observer, reports that the Inuit of Angmagssalik (upper South–East Greenland) used to journey in umiaks around the southern tip (Cape Farewell) to the west coast to secure iron and to barter. This was observed as early as 1752, when a group from the Angmagssalik area wintered south of Julianehaab. Generally, they secured supplies en route and often didn't beach their umiaks, but moored the vessels in the water. They didn't need to dry them out. In 1762 some East Greenlanders came to the west coast from so far up the east coast that they were called "Northerners" by the other east coast visitors.

I propose to review here some of the maritime exploits of East Greenlanders with umiaks and later kayaks, in order to shed further light on their intrepid seamanship and frequent journeys. Rasmussen learned of an Angmagssalik folktale about one Uiarteq and his wife, who "traveled about the country, namely from Angmagssalik southward, then up the west coast [of Greenland], where they passed the winter, and on to the northern end of the land; from there, along a steep coast, where they ran a swift tide, to a large fjord, where there were no seals but many white whales and narwhales; from there, farther on to the hero Kaisasik, who lived not far north of Angmagssalik," thus returning home from the north. This tale "implies that the East Greenlanders conceive of their land as an island."[27]

The incredible feat of circumnavigating Greenland suggests the kind of people who could travel vast distances for purposes of exploration, a tradition certainly suggested also by the movements of Thule ancestors from Alaska to Greenland.

The East Greenlanders became true "iron-age" people. They not only learned how to use iron but also used blacksmithing techniques, such as making the iron red-hot enough to drill needle holes, as in the making of needles from nails. This use of iron was a major motive for travel to the west coast, apparently, but iron could also be obtained from the drift wreckage and timbers brought to the east coast by the Greenland Current and winds.

In early times, the easterners journeyed to Pamiagdluk, Narssaq or, rarely, to Nanortalik. They never wintered on the west coast, but usually returned to places such as Nanuseq to spend the winter on their way home. They would travel "almost without nights" (without resting). They simply "drew into the shore and merely covered themselves over. Sometimes they would drag the umiak onto the beach, turn it upside down and sleep under it. Often, however, they did not take time for that but slept in the boat, which they moored by means of a seal-thong to a rock or anything else handy." Before the 1830s the umiaks went to Nanortalik to barter but sometimes they waited at Nunagssuk while the kayaks went on to trade at Nanortalik. Often at Nunagssuk the easterners met people from the west coast who had come hunting in umiaks to the east coast. Whole families made such trips. "Old Rosine," an easterner, is quoted as saying: "Yes, in the old days people could travel and they traveled far."

One 1752 diary records that some East Greenlanders when coming south had to go past Puissortoq Glacier but they couldn't go around it as normal. "So they had to shoot in under the stretch of this ice mountain which was like a roof and vault over them. In the evening they could not lie to, but contrary to all usual practice had to 'overnight' in the boat with all their baggage, which they moored to the ice."

After the Danes had established stations in West Greenland they desired to visit the easterners. Hans Egede "indicated the manner in which it was to be achieved for the first time, viz. in Eskimo umiaks along the coast inside the ice-belt." It remained for W. A. Graah to accomplish that, using Inuits, umiaks and kayaks, in the 1828–31 period. While on the east coast Graah eventually ran out of European (Qavdlunâq) food and began to decline. Hurriedly, he and his umiaks made their way back south to Nunagssuk, north of Prince Christian Sound. He could go no further, but he sent his kayak men on ahead all the way around the Cape to Narssaq (Frederiksdal) to get Qavdlunâq food at the trading station. They "traveled night and day . . . without resting on the way." After getting ships' biscuits and other Danish food, they returned to Narssaq "after only a very short rest," saving his life it seems. Graah's expedition illustrates the navigability of umiaks and also the ability of kayaks to negotiate the difficult waters around the south tip of Greenland, Kap Farvel (Cape Farewell).

As to the durability of umiaks, we can also cite from Knud Rasmussen information about Kialineq, far to the north of Angmagssalik, where five or six umiak crews wintered in 1919–20. The route north was dangerous: "usually there is not even room to draw an umiak ashore; it has to remain moored in the water. . . . It is only when they reach the site of their winter quarters that the Eskimos take their umiaks ashore."[28]

It is certainly a lot farther from Angmagssalik to the west coast of Greenland than it is to Iceland. It is true that the Greenland Current running southwesterly from Spitsbergen brings a great deal of ice in early summer and would make crossing to Iceland perhaps harder than heading towards Cape Farewell, but the Angmagssalik people knew how to return north after their visits, thus illustrating great navigational ability in difficult polar waters.

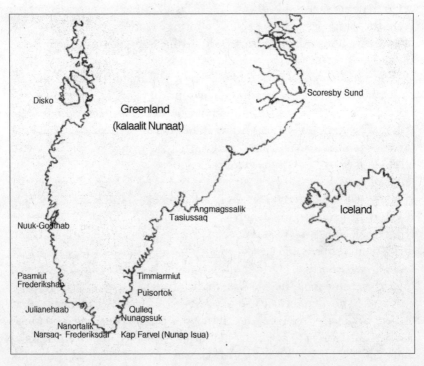

Map of the Greenland area, showing the relationship of Angmagssalik and Scoresby Sund to both Iceland and southwest Greenland. Map by Jack D. Forbes.

The fact that no Inuit remains have been found on Iceland in modern times can be partly explained by the changing coastal sea levels as well as by human activity and the extreme volcanism of the island. It should be noted that no evidence of Irish monks has ever been found on Iceland, in spite of documentary evidence of their having lived there through the late 800s.[29]

It is (by my calculation) 250 miles from the Greenland coast to Iceland, then 240 to the Faeroes, less than 200 from there to Shetland, then only 50 miles to Orkney. American peoples of the Sarqaq and Dorset cultures were living off and on in the Angmagssalik and probably Scoresby Sund districts of East Greenland from perhaps 2000 BCE onward. After 900 CE the incoming Thule culture people may have peacefully mixed with Dorset people in the Angmagssalik area.[30] In any case, the settlement of East Greenland areas required the use of umiaks (larger skin boats) since people had to travel from area to area by means of the sea. From Scoresby Sund to Iceland is about 300 miles, from Angmagssalik about 350 miles. In contrast, it seems to be about 650 miles from Julianehaab on the west coast around Cape Farewell to the Angmagssalik region. Thus we have evidence that umiaks could have stayed afloat long enough to reach Iceland, the Faeroes, and Britain, with intermediate stops at each place for drying and re-greasing. (Figures given by Ian Whitaker are 180 miles from Greenland to Northwest Iceland, then 275 miles from Southeast Iceland to the Faeroes, and 185 miles to Shetland, or 200 to the Orkneys).

The above distances may, however, have been different prior to 1456. The Norse sagas and Old Norse sailing directions mention a group of rocks or a skerry lying about halfway between Iceland and Greenland. This was "Gundebiurne Skeer," or "Gunnbiorn's skerries." Contemporary maps of Greenland have placed this locale directly on the coast of East Greenland, but such a location does not reflect earlier beliefs about their location. In any case, the Johann Ruysch map of 1508 shows Iceland and Greenland and places a small island between the two (a bit closer to Iceland), about which it states that it was consumed (burned up) in 1456: "Insula hec in anno domini 1456 fuit totaliter co[m]busta." This map is extremely important for incorporating the findings of Gaboti's (Cabot's) visits to northeast America as well as Portuguese and Basque information. For example, it is the first to use the term "Terranova" for Newfoundland and to use "Baccalauras" (Bacalaos) for an island nearby. It also notes that high up on the East Greenland coast "the ship's compass does not act."

How did Ruysch, a German, learn of a volcanic eruption west of Iceland in 1456? In any case, his map was so "up to date" that we must grant great respect to such information. A mountain peak island west of Iceland would have given Inuit navigators a place to rest perhaps, thus shortening the crossing from 180 to 300 miles to about half that number, a very manageable distance, it would seem, during the mildest period of mid-summer.[31]

Dutch scholar Gert Nooter visited Greenland in 1968. The Angmagssalik East Greenlanders told him that their kayaks could remain in the water for more than forty-eight hours "if the hides are new and well-greased." Kayak journeys did not usually last more than twelve hours "but older hunters tell of much longer voyages they made when they were young." Nooter received the impression, however, that the Greenlanders "considered the distance, the high waves, and lack of sufficient food . . . to be insuperable difficulties." Nooter found the East Greenland kayaks to be "superbly constructed" but "they certainly are not made for voyages over the open sea." Whitaker, on the other hand, calculated that a kayaker could have made the required distances if he could make from four to six nautical miles per hour for two days (48 x 4 = 192, 48 x 6 = 288) and of course, know the best route.[32]

Fridtjof Nansen, in the book about his east-to-west ski-crossing of interior Greenland in 1888, shows a number of photographs of kayakers out in very rough seas and managing large waves much like surfboard riders. Very old Inuit stories feature often the themes of: "Strong and mighty men, first-rate seal-hunters. No equals in kayaking far out to sea in all weathers. Thickness of their kayak paddles." There are old stories of one Giviok crossing the sea in his kayak "for Akilinek" (Akilineq means the "whole opposite country," while aki-leg means "right opposite"). During his voyage he passed through "sea-lice" that devoured his throwing stick, made a narrow passage between two opening and closing icebergs, and eventually came to a place of cannibals. Also an Angakok (medicine-man) and two brothers-in-law drifted upon the ice to Akilinek (the opposite country) and it is said that "travelers to Akilinek gave their boat a double coating."

The use of the term "Akilinek" is extremely important because a dictionary of the West Greenland language gives the definition: "*akilineq*, country on the other side; the coast of North America (on the other side of the Davis Strait), Labrador. Akilinermiut, the Eskimos of Labrador." This surely indicates that West Greenlanders knew of Labrador and Baffin Island, and were crossing Davis Strait in native skin boats. If so, then they could cross Denmark Strait also.[33]

We learn also from Knud Rasmussen that the kayak men at Igdluarssuit were the best in East Greenland "for they are compelled to go out hunting on the sea, always with a wind blowing, particularly from the northwest and southwest, whence the gales are very violent." "Field ice" coming down from the north and spreading southward along the coast, brought with it "driftwood, sometimes wreckage too, with nails and iron." It arrives in November or December and freezes far out to sea. Nonetheless, "the rule is that as long as there is no wind the field ice never hinders kayak hunting, though umiak rowing is impossible."

There is one story of two kayakers who were caught out by the winter ice and could not reach the shore. For days they labored continuously, carrying their kayaks over the massed ice, being carried, meantime to the southwest. Their kayaks became damaged, but one of them still managed to climb the peak of Orssuluviaq after reaching the shore, and then paddled his kayak to Tasiussaq after coming down. Such stories show the toughness of the Greenland kayaks and the ability of experienced persons to cope with extremely dangerous conditions.[34]

Most European writers have not considered that umiaks (larger skin boats) might have been used for such journeys, or that a kayak might have been carried within an umiak. This is because most modern (post-1500) encounters in Europe feature kayakers and kayaks.

David MacRitchie, one of the early writers who attempted to explain kayakers in Europe, tells us that "it is obvious that if the crossing was ever made it must have been by deliberate design . . . when Eskimo intend spending a night or two at sea it is their custom to go in pairs, and at night they lash their kayaks together, thus giving them the stability of a raft." He thinks that a "direct crossing" from Labrador to Scotland would be impossible; but a voyage initiated in Greenland, with stops in Iceland, the Faeroes, Shetland, and Orkney "would be comparatively short." It would still have to be deliberate. "A theory simpler still would be that of an involuntary voyage eastward, as prisoner on board a European ship."

Several other writers feel that an Inuit crossing to Europe was impossible, including William C. Sturtevant and David Beers Quinn, Dale Idiens, and Ejnar Mikkelsen. Some deal with the difficult question of how Inuits came to be in the North Sea, accompanied usually or often by a full array of hunting and survival equipment, by arguing that their kidnap-

pers (Dutch whalers or other European vessels) somehow were driven to
set them free upon reaching European waters. It is, however, simply an
imaginative argument to presume such actions when releases could have
easily been made in Greenland or Labrador waters rather than close to
Europe. In short, there is no evidence for such releases, with equipment,
by vessel crews.[35]

In the early 1600s, a Greenlander held captive in Europe escaped in his
kayak, and was recaptured thirty or forty leagues out at sea. His captors
told him by signs that he would never have known where to find Greenland. "He answered by signs, that he should have followed the coast of
Norway to a certain point, whence he would have crossed, and have been
guided by the stars to his country."[36] This suggests that the Greenlander
knew that if he went high enough up the Norway coast he could then
strike out for the Greenland Current or use favorable winds to reach his
home (a route somewhat similar to the old Norse route to Greenland).

Robert Grenier writes: "Years ago . . . in St. John's, Newfoundland, I
stumbled on this fragile looking skin craft at one of the far docks. Here
was Tim Severin's replica of St. Brendan's boat, beaten and dirtied by the
long voyage, but proud and defiant like a conqueror. This tiny leather craft
had vanquished some of the most hostile waters in the world." The 1970s
voyage to which he refers was made in an oxhide boat, tanned in oak bark,
and smeared with wool grease. Called *Brendan,* the ship had a watertight
hull, with 20,000 stitches of flaxthread, and was 8' x 36' overall. The hull
"improved in cold water," with the skin becoming saturated with seawater
"weeping a continual fine 'dew' on its inner surface," and the increasingly
cold conditions made the oxhide "stiffer and stronger."

Using wind power, the *Brendan* left the Aran Islands of Ireland, going
on to the Faeroes. They left the Faeroes on July 3, with gale force winds
helping them reach Iceland on July 17 (400 miles from the Faeroes, 1,000
miles from Ireland). Thus the oxhide survived two weeks in the ocean, but
three weeks of southwest winds and the season of autumn gales forced
the *Brendan* to remain in Iceland until the following year.

The next year the *Brendan* headed west, towards Newfoundland via the
south end of Greenland. The journey did not prove that an Irish oxhide
boat could have reached America, since they had to be rescued from a sea
of pack ice by a Faeroese fishing boat and also got fresh provisions from
a U.S. Navy ship. The *Brendan* continued to have trouble with icebergs
and eventually the hull was torn by two chunks of ice coming together.
The leak was repaired, but the accumulation of water was too much for

the crew and the assistance of a pump had to be obtained. Nonetheless, the *Brendan* finally moored in Newfoundland after six weeks at sea.[37]

The voyage of the *Brendan* seems to prove that skin boats can endure for a long period in cold, northern waters, if greased. On the other hand, the voyage shows that a *westward* voyage is very difficult even when destinations are clearly known. Such a journey might have been easier before the 1200s (when the quantity of ice began to greatly increase in the North Atlantic) or if pursued later in the summer (but the ability to pick up sporadic winds blowing westerly would be a must for any sailing vessel, as noted in chapter 2).

According to Konrad Maurer, referring to the "Islenzkir Annálar" as his source, in the year 1189 fourteen men sailed from Greenland to Iceland in a "Schiff" (boat) that was nailed together with wooden pins and bound (*gebunden*) with animal sinew. Another source states that the "captain" was one Asmundus Kastandratzius and the ship landed safely at Breidafjord in Iceland. In 1190 he left Iceland, but was not heard from again. P. De Roo believed that he was an Inuit because the Norse had "seaworthy ships." In any event, the craft was obviously not a wooden ship, but perhaps an umiak roughly the size of the *Brendan*.[38]

Paul Gaffarel had no doubt that Inuits could have been blown to Europe, citing (as noted previously) a storm that allegedly took the Marquis de la Roche from Sable Islands (Canada) in a small boat to France within a few days. In the early 1000s a group of Norse were sailing near Labrador when a storm carried them all the way eastward to Ireland, where they were shipwrecked and enslaved. Similarly, in 1347 a small boat, manned by Norsemen and/or Inuits, was driven by a storm from Markland (Labrador) to Iceland. They had no anchor and had seventeen or eighteen men on board. Thus one can readily see the power of eastward-driving storms, coupled with the probable combination of the Labrador Current and Gulf Stream. In connection with storms, Peyrère notes that in 1271 a strong northwest wind carried ice floes to Iceland "laden with . . . bears and so much wood" that sailors later explored to the northwest but found only ice.

The Inuits of Kialineq in East Greenland tell a story of how, during a time of privation, they took their six umiaks out on to the ocean, "one of the umiaks going on ahead and arduously breaking a way through the ice . . . a man had to stand in the bow of this boat to break the ice." They then climbed onto an ice floe of firm ice that was then blown far from land, out to the ocean to the east. They drifted far out to sea, but in this case they were able to return to shore after the southwest wind subsided and an opening in the ice developed. Nonetheless: "they were obliged to remain long on the floe."[39] Could other groups have been carried far from Greenland in a similar manner?

More recently, Richard Cooper writes that "An Atlantic crossing in a kayak . . . seems less inexplicable in the light of modern one-man crossings in small boats . . . the shortest route is the one which the Eskimo kayaks presumably used: 275 miles from Greenland to Iceland, 180 miles from Iceland to the Faeroes; 200 miles from the Faeroes to the Orkneys: a total of only 655 miles in the open ocean."[40]

Will Nordby, an authority on modern sea kayaking, notes that "bearded seal and female sea lion skins were preferred because they resisted saltwater soaking best and were normally without scars." He states also that "if a hull were damaged at sea, a sealskin float, or sponson, was used to support the kayak while repairs were made. In calm seas, a good hide could remain in the water for two weeks before being dried and re-oiled. Storm conditions required the treatment to be done within six days." A properly maintained kayak skin could last a year. Modern sea kayaks are made of fabricated materials, but they have been used for many long-distance voyages, such as one from Seattle to Ketchikan and back, with high winds, rain, and stormy seas being encountered.

Recently Jon Turk and his wife Chris were kayaking in the Beaufort Sea, Canada, in an area of icebergs when a wind came up blowing against the direction of the tide. The icebergs began to crash about with very choppy seas. The Turks climbed up on a berg with their kayak, jumped from pan to pan and finally reached the shore safely. Undoubtedly Inuit kayakers were even more adept at such feats.[41]

In summary, I believe that we can say that skin boats can endure long enough to cross from America to Europe but that the Europe to America direction is much less likely because of the danger posed by contrary winds and currents. In any case, successful navigation would depend upon an intimate knowledge of such things as the location of polar stars, the flight patterns of land birds, and/or the foreknowledge of the location of Iceland, the Faeroes, and other islands. Having said that, however, the question of whether any of the kayaks seen in European waters actually were rowed from Greenland is not resolved. As we shall see, some of the kayaks seen in the Orkney Islands may have been coming from Norway and perhaps were rowed by Inuits who had adapted to living in European waters. Conversely, they may have been attempting to use a route that took them to Norway, as mentioned above.

Before reviewing the arrivals of Inuits in Europe, it is well to review briefly the succession of American cultures that evolved in Arctic Canada, Greenland, and nearby areas after the period of the Red Earth culture discussed earlier. Developments in the north seem to be highly correlated with warming periods, when people tended to push northward following the musk ox or caribous, and periods of cooler temperatures in which some areas seem to have been abandoned. Our concern should be with maritime-oriented cultures, since only they could have produced boats capable of reaching Europe. The Independence I people of Greenland settled in the extreme north but gradually spread down the east coast at least as far as Scoresby Sund (which might indicate some form of navigation). This was a relatively warm period, around 2400–2100 BCE, with higher sea-levels than at present. The Independence II culture of Greenland possessed harpoons and seal hunting technology and was focused in northeast Greenland. It existed during a period of milder climate, around 1100–700 BCE, after a cold period had interrupted settlement in Greenland. At the same time, the Sarqaq, the first culture focused on west Greenland, gradually spread by sea around the south tip (Cape Farewell) to Angmagssalik and probably Scoresby Sund. The Sarqaq culture is dated from 2000 BCE to perhaps 900 BCE. The Sarqaq people possessed harpoons but from the heads found they do not appear to have had toggled harpoons. The umiak was probably present for navigation. People of the Dorset I culture succeeded the Sarqaq around the beginning of the CE period, and they occupied much the same areas as far as the Angmagssalik district on the southeast coast. They were followed, after a break, by Dorset II people, who seem to have occupied a smaller area.

We are at a loss to know what people might have left villages seen by the Norse in the 900s in southwestern Greenland. At that period, or soon after, people of the Thule culture were moving into north Greenland. Jorgen Meldgard tells us: "The Dorset people, small families dragging their small sledges, little by little withdrew east. Some may still have been in North Greenland when the new [Thule] people crossed Smith Sound, others moved south, as we have heard, across Melville Bugt to West Greenland, which was empty of people, and some groups apparently went through the north of Greenland to East Greenland."

A few centuries later, Meldgard suggests, the new Thule people probably arrived in East Greenland and it might be that the Thule and Dorset peoples mixed there. "The specific character of the Angmagssalik Eskimos, such as certain traits in their rich and distinctive art, might be explained by such a cultural meeting."[42] Robert McGhee also tells us that after 1000–1200 CE "small remnant Dorset populations may still have inhabited other areas of Greenland," such as the east coast, and he cites a story from Floemanna Saga as evidence for Norse contact. It seems that a Norse ship became trapped in ice along the east coast for three years around 1000 CE. The Norse came upon two strange figures cutting up a sea mammal, which they seized from the two. Later the same strange persons returned a small boat that had disappeared.[43]

The mixture of Thule Inuit people with Dorset or other pre-Thule people is attested to also by a statement of Kaj Birket-Smith to the effect that in Greenland "it is well known that one may often, from a purely physiognomic point of view, distinguish between two types, an 'Indian' and a 'mongoloid' one."[44] Don Dumond states that the Dorset people, as heirs of the Arctic Small Tool Tradition "were not Eskimo linguistically."[45] This could explain the mixture of physical types seen by Birket-Smith and also the frequent confusion among writers as to whether the people met by the Norse in Newfoundland and Labrador were "Indians" or "Eskimos." Actually, of course, all Native North Americans are equally "Indian" in terms of nomenclature, since all live in "New India" or "the Indies." (At the same time, of course, none are really Indians, that name belonging to old India in Asia. It is my understanding that Inuit and non-Inuit physical types have also mixed in parts of northern Canada and in Kodiak, Alaska, regions). An author of 1751 refers to Eskimos as "other Indians" and "Indians." Apparently they became non-Indians (in name only) somewhat later.[46]

To the west of Greenland, in Labrador and Newfoundland, the situation is somewhat confused historically. The common notion was that the Dorset tradition gradually evolved from about 4000 BP, eventually expanding southward in Labrador and to Newfoundland, where it survived for some one thousand or more years, from about 500 BCE to nearly 1000 CE. The push south seems to have corresponded with a colder period, in which the Dorset-style culture was able to find suitable environments in new areas. The cool period lasted until about 400 CE, with a warming period especially seen from 900 (or earlier) to 1200 CE. This warming period brought the Norse to the region from Iceland and the Thule whaling culture east and south from the central Canadian Arctic, it seems.

About 1000 CE (or perhaps slightly earlier) the Dorset way of life began to disappear from the Arctic and Newfoundland, but there is some confusion about whether it survived for another five hundred years or so in northern Labrador and Ungava (now northern Quebec) or whether it suffered a rather sudden demise everywhere. Some authorities believe that the Thule culture bearers replaced Dorset people, with perhaps some type of conflict or competitive engagement, while Algonkian and Beothuk people replaced them in parts of southern Labrador and Newfoundland.

Robert W. Park has, however, advanced the idea that the Dorset population could have suffered a "catastrophic collapse" a century or two prior to Thule occupation, some time around 1000 CE. By the 1300s, Thule people had spread their culture to "every part of the Canadian Arctic and Greenland formerly occupied by the Dorset" and the Thule people became the ancestors of modern Inuits, according to Park.[47]

Although no archaeologist has suggested it, I would propose that the Dorset "collapse" (if there was one) was due to European contact. Patricia Sutherland is reported in an article in *Science* to believe that Norse contacts could have commenced as early as the seventh or eighth centuries (because of the dating of Arctic Hare yarn samples, supposedly spun only by Europeans) and could have reached well up into the Baffin Island area. There are many American sites in that region with bits and pieces of Norse or other European goods dating from later centuries, but the assumption that only the Europeans engaged in trade and that only they made voyages for such purposes is doubtful in my view. Inuit people, as already noted, made trading journeys in umiaks and they could have distributed goods (such as pieces of metal) of European origin.[48]

Dorset people seem to have become metal-users by about 800 CE, while the Thule people from 1100 to 1450 on Somerset Island used a great deal of iron. Up to 46 percent of tools in a whaling-focused dwelling seem to have had metal elements. The sources of the iron and copper seem to have been meteoric and local, as well as traded from Europeans. European-derived copper was traded as far as a Dorset site of the 1100s on the east coast of Hudson Bay. As noted earlier, East Greenlanders were able to obtain iron from wreckage brought on the east coast ice.[49]

The American desire for metal, from circa 800, could, of course, help to explain intentional journeys both to new Norse settlements in south Greenland, and beyond to Iceland and Europe. In any case, there would seem to be no need to extend to the Norse settlers the *exclusive* role of voyagers and traders. Both Dorsets and Thule people could well have been active seekers rather than passive recipients. As to the apparent "collapse" of Dorset culture, I would like to propose that European impacts may have been a factor, either in terms of slave raiding or, more likely, the spread of new diseases to Americans. Reports indicated that Inuits and Newfoundlanders taken to Europe in the sixteenth and seventeenth centuries tended to die quickly, either from exposure to new diseases or to new diets, or both. It is stated in the sagas that an epidemic killed many Norse Greenlanders soon after their colony was established. We do not know the nature of their illness but they had been in contact with Americans on Newfoundland and elsewhere. Many later writers suggest that the "Black Death" (bubonic plague) spread in the mid-fourteenth century from Bergen, Norway (where it killed many people) to Iceland and Greenland. If true, the plague could have been spread with infected rats to Markland (Labrador) and elsewhere. Recently, a dead European brown rat was found in the hold of a sunken Basque ship at Newfoundland. We know that the bubonic plague eventually reached America and spread among rodents across the entire continent, but the date of its arrival is unknown. Its appearance in circa 1348–49 and subsequent spread across the continent could help to explain the abandonment of major American cities (such as Cahokia) in the subsequent centuries.[50]

There is some doubt whether the plague actually reached Iceland, but in any case, it could have been carried directly from Bergen to Greenland. Smallpox is another possible culprit. In the 1730s this disease hit Iceland very hard and in 1733 it spread to Greenland, with other epidemics following. There is no reason to suppose that the Norse of the 800s to 1000s were not also capable of spreading diseases to Americans lacking in any immunity.[51] The Thule people might have been less exposed, prior to the 1200s or later, due to their greater distance from Norse settlements and visitors. But the Dorsets, farther south, and the Newfoundlanders in general, would have borne the brunt of new infectious diseases, it would seem. Robert McGhee believes that Norse-American "contacts probably had minimal influence on the aboriginal peoples of the area." I certainly cannot prove the contrary, but the rapid disappearance of the Dorset culture suggests otherwise. Moreover, the sexual propensities of European males (especially in the time periods under discussion) would suggest that any contacts could have involved sexual relations as well as trade, warfare, and the exchange of pathogens for up to four hundred years.[52]

We do not know when Europeans first reached Greenland's waters.

Irish monks and their supporters, presumably using skin boats, reached the Faeroe Islands from northern Scotland, presumably in the 720s. Norse pirates caused them to abandon their sheep and return south by the 820s. Later they also settled on Iceland, but again withdrew after non-Christian Norse settlers arrived. The journeys of the Irish monks are significant, since they can serve as further arguments for the navigability of skin-covered watercraft (although some could have used an occasional wooden boat). In any case, Frisians were also very early leaders in European marine voyaging, during the seventh and eighth centuries, trading between Scandinavia and Britain. The Frisians were set back by a defeat from the Franks in 734, and in 810 a fleet of two hundred Danish ships ravaged the Frisian coast and islands. Nonetheless, there is a report of Frisians sailing to the Davis Strait-Greenland area in the 1020s. They were cast on the rocks and took refuge on the coast. They allegedly saw some "miserable looking huts hollowed out in the ground, and around these cabins heaps of iron ore, in which a quantity of gold and silver was shining. . . . But as they returned to their vessels, they saw coming out from these covered holes deformed men as hideous as devels, with bows and strings and large dogs following them." One Frisian was killed while the others escaped. No mention is made of Frisian contacts with Norse Greenland settlers, nor do we know if the Frisians continued to frequent American waters. Also, the story may be fanciful.[53]

Interestingly, the atlas of Andrés Bianco (1436) shows an island of "Stocafixa" located in the position of Newfoundland. "Stocafixa" is an Italianized version of a west Teutonic name for the dried codfish, presumably Dutch or Frisian. The use of this term by Bianco indicates that his information came from a Frisian or Holland-Dutch source (although "Stockfish" was later borrowed by the English). In any case, we have very strong support for the idea that the Frisians, or their close neighbors, may have maintained some contact with American waters.[54] But from the eighth century onward, it is the Norse and their Celtic and other slaves or relations who dominate the waters of northeastern America. It is said that there are Inuit traditions of the Norse appearing in Greenland in the 700s, during the Dorset period, which would mean that Dorset oral tradition became incorporated in the later Thule oral history of northwest Greenland.[55]

We are on more certain ground when dealing with the Icelandic sagas, which relate the early Norse visits to Greenland in the late 800s or 900s and then the settlement by Erik the Red in the 985–86 period. However, there are also several references to "Groenlandorum" and "Groenland-osque" in papal documents of 834–35 and a decree of Emperor Louis (834) mentions Groenlandorum along with Denmark, Sweden, Norway, the Faeroes, Iceland, "Scrifindorum" (home of the Sami), Helsinglandrum (Finland?), and other northern and eastern nations.[56] The Greenland of 834–35 may refer to the region from northern Norway to Spitsbergen, an area that was also called by that name, a practice that has led to confusion for historians.

As noted earlier, the Norse settlement in southwest Greenland seems to have been made at Dorset village sites, already abandoned according to some modern writers (but perhaps abandoned because of the Norse). The latter, as mentioned previously, were active raiders during this period, and they do not seem to have hesitated about using armed force to take possessions, territory, and captives from others, be they Scots, Irish, French, Iberians, or North Africans. As discussed previously, the Norse may have met Americans in East Greenland and may have also seen kayakers. Hans Egede cites a chronicle with tales of "marine monsters" that were seen "upon the coast of Greenland." One was described "as showing itself breast high above the waves. It resembled the human form in the neck, head, visage, nose, and mouth, except that the head was more than usually elevated, and terminating in a point. It had wide shoulders, at the end of which were two stumps of arms, without any hands. The body tapered downwards, but it was never visible below the middle."[57] This seems to be a near-perfect description of a kayaker and would suggest that the latter were seen in the water before they were seen coming ashore. (But it also could refer to kayakers seen near Iceland, since the source was an Icelandic one.) In circa 1075 Adam of Bremen refers to the "Greenlanders" as pirates, a curious reference because it seems unlikely that the Norse settlers, already at least partially Christianized according to Adam, would be attacking ships. Moreover, would he be referring to Norse settlers as "Greenlanders" so soon after their settlement? The reference, then, may be to Americans or, possibly, to Sami, Finns, Karelians, or other non-Christian peoples of northern Scandinavia.[58]

If the sagas are correct, the Norse visitors to Vinland and Labrador murdered some Americans by surprise attack and kidnapped two young boys, thus very possibly stimulating unrecorded reprisals. In any event, the story of the Norse in America, although fascinating, need not be reviewed here except insofar as it relates to Americans reaching Iceland and Europe. In this connection it is very significant that Bishop Gisli Oddsson (recorded in Latin in ca. 1637), states that around 1342 "the inhabitants of Greenland of their own will abandoned the true faith and the Christian religion . . . and went over to the peoples of America [*ad Americae populos se converterunt*]."[59] This would indicate that a group of Norse went over to the Americans and became Americanized, a significant process that would perhaps also mean that certain Norse ideas about navigation might have become at least for a time part of the Inuit, Beothuk, or Algonkian cultures. It should be noted that this occurred during the height of the very cold years of the fourteenth century.

We have already noted that in 1347 a boat, without an anchor, arrived in Iceland, driven by a storm from the waters between Greenland and Labrador. It had seventeen or eighteen men on board, and all writers have assumed that they were Norse. Now, however, we can suggest that the passengers might well have been Americans or Norse-American mixed-bloods; or this voyage could represent part of the evacuation of Greenland by Norse settlers and their resettlement among Americans in Labrador or Newfoundland.[60]

During this very same period, 1342 to 1370, the Western Settlement of the Norse was found to be empty of people, but with some livestock still alive. This would seem to confirm that Norse settlers had departed, perhaps voluntarily, since there was no evidence seen of an armed assault. By 1370 the settlement was said to be under American control.[61]

There are contradictory beliefs about whether the basic Inuit-Norse relationship after circa 1250 was one of hostility, one of peaceful interaction, or a little of both. But it is clear that Inuit people did come to live in and around Norse settlements and that some of their relationships were reciprocal, or could have involved racial intermixture. For example, in northwest Greenland, at Unanak Fjord, there is a tradition of a fight between Norsemen and Americans. The Norse "had pursued some little girls who had been out to fetch water. These girls came running home and shouted, 'They are attacking us!'" The Inuit people hid at first but "the Norsemen managed to get hold of some of them and maltreated them." Finally the Inuits lured the Norsemen out onto slippery ice and killed them all.[62]

This story suggests that the European men were trying to either rape the girls or to kidnap them, or both. A somewhat different form of interaction took place in 1385–86, when Bjorn Einarson Josalafari is said to have stayed for two years in the Eriksfjord district of south Greenland. While there he rescued "two trolls, a young boy and his sister, from a rock which was washed over by the sea at high tide." The siblings took an "oath of allegiance to him" and from that time "he did not lack provisions, for they were experienced in all kinds of hunting and fishing." This reciprocal relationship was severed when Bjorn sailed to Iceland and the Inuit siblings committed suicide when they were refused passage with him. There is also the story of Bjorn Thorleifson, who allegedly was wrecked on the coast of Greenland and rescued by two "trolls" (ca. 1450).[63]

It is also reported that in 1379 the "Skraelings" attacked the eastern settlement in South Greenland, killing eighteen persons and carrying off two boys and a woman. And the Inuits tell a story of an Inuit woman who went to live among the Norse but who created troubles between the two groups and was subsequently dragged to death by the Americans. Writers frequently quote a papal bull of 1448 indicating that some thirty years earlier the "heathen" attacked the settlers of Greenland, destroyed churches, and captured the inhabitants. Subsequently some of the latter were able to return and rebuild. However, this story probably refers to a Karelian-Finnish-Russian attack on Norse settlers in northern Norway ("Greenland") rather than to American Greenland, according to Christian Keller. Archaeology has failed to confirm Inuit violence against the settlers.[64]

What finally happened to the Norse settlers in America is still debated. Thomas H. McGovern, a noted authority, argues that ideological conservatism prevented them (or most of them) from adapting to the Inuit way of life and that this contributed to their finally dying out. Others have argued that pirates, perhaps Basque or English, might have carried many off or wiped them out. If the latter is true, then it is possible that Inuits and Newfoundlanders might also have been kidnapped by the raiders, as we shall see.[65]

I believe, though, that many Norse joined the Americans, became Americanized, and moved to Labrador and Newfoundland, at least in part. And actually there is evidence to suggest that they or their descendants were captured and carried off to Portugal as slaves and to England as curiosities. This evidence, consisting in physical descriptions of some of the captives, will be presented below as we discuss the general topic of kidnapped Americans arriving in Europe.

In connection with the movement of Norse-Americans to Labrador and then to Newfoundland, there is evidence of continuing Inuit trading expeditions to Newfoundland, as noted by the first missionaries to Labrador and other sources. Later, some Beothuk and Labrador individuals were described as being not very racially distinct from the English, once they were in European clothing and living conditions.[66]

As regards northeastern America, the year 1492 has virtually no significance whatsoever. The abduction of Americans commenced by at least 1007–10, when Thorfinn Karlsefoni captured two young Labrador boys and took them to Greenland, where they were reportedly Christianized. Subsequently, Karlsefoni traveled to Norway and then returned west to Iceland. We are not told specifically that his two captives were taken to Europe, but it seems likely given that they were his personal prisoners.[67]

During the 1200s and 1300s there are certainly many instances where American individuals might have been carried to Iceland or Norway, either from west or East Greenland or, as in 1347, perhaps from Labrador. But it seems clear that the presence of "trolls" or "Skraelings" were seldom recorded, even as mention of Irish, Scots, or other non-Norse persons seems scant after circa 1000. In any case, Olaus Magnus writes that in 1505 he saw two leather boats of the Greenland pirates captured by King Hakon and hung in the cathedral at Aslö (Oslo). The alleged pirates had the ability to go underwater and could supposedly bore holes in the bottoms of wooden ships. The event must have occurred in the time of one of the Hakons, who lived in the 1300s.

A similar account is given by Claudius Clavus Swart, who writes in the 1420s of having seen "pygmies" (as he terms the Inuits) "whom I have seen after they were taken at sea in a little hide-boat, which is now hanging in the cathedral at Nidaros; there is likewise a long vessel of hides, which was also once taken with such Pygmies in it." Thus, by the 1420s a kayak and an umiak were hanging in Trondheim's cathedral and, presumably, Americans had been captured with them and brought to Norway. Were these the same boats captured by King Hakon? If so, they survived for over a century. Hakon IV reigned from 1355 to 1380 and perhaps the boats were moved from Trondheim (Nidaros) to Oslo before 1505.[68] Or is it possible that both cities possessed American boats in their cathedrals? (It should be noted that the church at Nidaros burned many times, and also that kayaks were later displayed in churches in the Netherlands and Orkneys. Perhaps the hanging of such boats in churches represented the triumph of Christians over traditional religions, or perhaps the church was merely serving as a civic center of sorts, where "curiosities" could be displayed).

During the fifteenth century, Basques, Bretons, and Englishmen began to frequent northern waters as far as Iceland. In later years claims were made of ships reaching the Newfoundland and Greenland regions before 1492, following cod and whales, but the first documented visit after that of the "Stocafixa Island" visitors of circa 1436, was an expedition reportedly sent to Greenland in 1472–76 by Christian I of Denmark, at the request of his relative King Alfonso of Portugal. The expedition included Didrik Pining (a German or Norwegian), Hans Pothorst (a Dane), Joao Vaz Corte-Real (Portuguese), and Johannes Skolp (Scolvus), a Norwegian said to be familiar with the route to Greenland.

It is thought that they reached the Angmagssalik area, where they were allegedly attacked by "enemies" in small boats. Much more likely is their attempt to kidnap Americans, since the Portuguese were already involved in the slave trade elsewhere and Olaus Magnus later termed Pining and Pothorst "villains and pirates." Olaus Magnus reports that the Native Greenlanders lived in houses of whalebones, thus indicating that he actually had heard or seen authentic reports from the area before 1555.[69]

During the 1480s and 1490s the Portuguese, English, Basques, and others were actively seeking to reach lands or islands in northeastern America, doubtless prompted, in my opinion, by the presence of Inuits or Beothuks already seen in Europe, as well as by the boats seen floating in the Azores, as noted earlier. In any case, one Joao Fernandes claimed to have reached Greenland (called "the land of the lavrador" or Labrador in his honor) around 1492. It may well be that Fernandes captured Inuits or other Americans on his voyage, since a 1494 report from Lisbon stated that the Portuguese king possessed *pretos* (blacks or dark people) "of various colors," including reddish or copperish (*acobreados*) people. These were likely Americans, perhaps from Greenland or Newfoundland, since I have not seen evidence of Columbus selling Caribbean captives to the Portuguese crown.[70]

Soon thereafter, the Italian Giovanni Gaboti (John Cabot) arrived in England and was issued a patent to discover new lands of "heathens," together with crews of Bristol men familiar with northern waters. Gaboti sailed in 1497 to the Newfoundland region. In 1498 he sailed west again, sighting first the east coast of Greenland (called Labrador) and then he followed along the west coast for an unknown distance before reaching present-day Labrador.

Along the Labrador coast Gaboti did some bartering with Americans and may have abducted three or more persons. It is known that three men, "taken in the newfounde Iland," were presented to King Henry VII, but it is not clear whether they were presented in 1498–99, 1501–2, or the following year. In any event, two years after their capture (or presentation) a writer saw them dressed "after the manner of Englishmen in Westminster pallace" ("the King's Court at Westminster") and "I could not discerne [them] from Englishemen, till I was learned what they were" (or "could not be discerned from Englishmen").[71]

In 1501 Henry VII issued new patents of discovery to Richard Warde and others of Bristol, with Joao Fernandes and others of the Azores. They apparently reached Newfoundland, but whether they abducted any Americans is unclear. In any case, other Portuguese from the Azores were also intent on exploiting the human and other resources of northeast America. In 1499 Joao Fernandes returned to Portugal and obtained approval from King Manoel to conquer islands in the region, but he seems to have allowed Gaspar Corte-Real of the Azores to take over the project. The latter set sail from Lisbon in the summer of 1500, going north to East Greenland via the Azores. After being blocked by icebergs, they turned to the west coast, contacting Inuits just north of 63°, near Godthaabfjord. The latter were described as being like the Americans of Brazil except that they were "white" ("alvos" or "colore candido") but that they became darker with age ("baços" or "infuscatur"). They were described as "great archers," who resembled "os Lapos" or Sami in their ways of living. We must suppose that Corte-Real was able to kidnap some younger Inuits, for how else could he have known of their "white" color when young?

Corte-Real returned to Lisbon in Autumn 1500, confident that he had, like Gaboti, reached the coast of Asia. In May 1501 he set out again with three vessels but could not reach Greenland because of drift-ice packs. Instead, they explored Davis Strait and sighted Labrador, cruising southward past Hamilton Inlet and into St. Lewis Sound. Proceeding up one of the riverine openings, they came upon a group of Americans, of whom they quickly seized some sixty persons, forcibly stowing them in the holds of two ships. In September, after exploring southward to Newfoundland, Corte-Real sent the two slave ships on to Lisbon while he headed south (to a deserved death, it would appear). The captives reached Lisbon sometime between the eighth and eleventh of October.[72]

Thus the Portuguese initiated a slave trade from northeast America, very similar to that initiated by Columbus after 1492 from the Caribbean and by the Portuguese from Brazil after 1501. One thing especially interesting about the Americans seized by Gaboti and Corte-Real is the clear suggestion they included persons of European and American mixture.

It has already been noted that two of the three men seized by Gaboti looked like Englishmen after two years in England, and also that Corte-Real felt that young Inuits were "white." The fifty to fifty-seven Americans who reached Lisbon alive in 1501 were described as being taller than the Portuguese, with long hair worn "in curls." They wore tattoo marks. "Their eyes are greenish [presque verte]." The women captives had "most beautiful bodies, and rather pleasant faces. The colour of these women may be said to be more white than otherwise, but the men are considerably darker." They were also said to resemble "the Indiens, or the Tziganes [Gypsies]."[73]

The Americans, according to Pietro Pasqualigo, an observer: "apportèrent un tronçon de' épée dorée, certainement fabriquée en Italie, et un des enfants portait aux oreilles deux petits disques ó'argent comme on en confectionnait alors à Venise." Thus the Americans possessed a broken sword, of probable Italian origin, and one of the children had in its ears small disks or beads such as those made in Venice. These items could have been left in the Labrador region by Gaboti or others, but they could also, along with the curly hair and skin colors, point towards a connection with the former Norse-Celtic settlers of Greenland (who doubtless had obtained trade goods from various parts of Europe at different times). It is ironic, then, that the likely descendants of European and American mixture, along with other Americans, seem to have become among the early victims of the period that precedes what white historians have termed the "Age of Enlightenment."

King Manoel was reportedly delighted with the captives: "che seranno per excellentia da fatiga: I gli meglior schiavi se habia hauti sin hora." That is, they would be excellent for labor; and the best slaves who have been seen up to now.[74]

In May 1502 Miguel Corte-Real set sail with three ships from Lisbon. They reached Newfoundland and split up, in order to search southwards for Gaspar, and northwards, most likely to secure more victims. Late in August two of the ships met off of Newfoundland but Miguel's vessel was lost, like that of his brother the year before. Finally, two ships returned to Portugal, one at least carrying a "pay-load" of more captives. David Beers Quinn tells us that the captain "sent a ship with certain men and women whom he found in the said land" to Portugal. King Manoel sent out two other vessels in 1503, reportedly to search for the Corte-Real brothers, but apparently more victims may have been gathered in the nets of these vendors of human flesh, since captives from "Terranova" (the common name for the Newfoundland region) show up widely in Iberia and even South America from the 1490s through 1650.[75]

A German publication of the seventeenth century produced a partial dictionary of Greenland Inuit words. Significantly, the word for "Schiff" (ship) was recorded as *nau,* most likely a borrowing from Portuguese *nao.* This word does not appear in a more modern Inuit dictionary but, nonetheless, it would seem to indicate that the Portuguese maintained extensive contacts with Inuits of Greenland, most of which are unrecorded. Given the Portuguese search for human captives, such contact would not auger well for Greenlanders, whether of full American or part-European ancestry. The Portuguese (and other Mediterranean peoples) made no distinctions of color in their thirst for human "commodities." Perhaps their voyages provided the final blow to any Norse remaining in southwest Greenland and also were responsible for the gradual disappearance of Inuits from parts of the Labrador coast and the decline of the Beothuks of Newfoundland.[76]

There is definite evidence that the Beothuk people retreated from the southern and eastern sections of Newfoundland, concentrating their reduced population in northern areas on Notre Dame Bay and in the watersheds of Exploits River. Slave-raiding by the Portuguese, as well as seizures made by the British and other Europeans may have been to blame. Sebastian Gaboti (Cabot) in 1508–9, for example, carried off people from "Bacallaos," probably referring to Newfoundland. By the 1580s an Englishman noted that "in the South parts [of Newfoundland] we found no inhabitants, which by all likely-hood, have abandoned these coasts, the same being so much frequented by Christians; but in the North are savages altogether harmless."[77]

As we shall see, Americans were being removed from many regions in the late fifteenth and early sixteenth centuries and many of them ended their lives in Europe and the Mediterranean littoral.

7.

Native Americans Crossing the Atlantic after 1493

THE STORY OF AMERICANS reaching Europe greatly intensifies after 1492, when literally tens of thousands are kidnapped and carried across the Atlantic below the decks of Spanish, Portuguese, and other vessels. Hundreds or perhaps thousands of others traveled "above-deck" as diplomats, curiosities, allies, converts, and entertainers. Considerable attention has been given to the latter categories, while the victims of the captive trade have received far less examination in spite of their much greater numbers and probably significant demographic impacts upon Portugal and Spain in particular.

Carolyn Thomas Foreman in her study of *Indians Abroad* devoted attention to the captive trade in Americans, as did I in my book *Africans and Native Americans*. In Chapters 1 and 2 of the latter book, the arrival of Americans as captives in Europe, North Africa, and Africa is reviewed in considerable detail, so much so that it seems unnecessary to present essentially the same information here. Readers are invited to read *Africans and Native Americans* if they wish to review a detailed discussion of American involuntary immigrants to Europe.

Here, however, it is necessary to emphasize that the many thousands of Americans who reached Portugal, Spain, and other European countries must have had a decided genetic impact, since it is clear from the records that they produced descendants. We can document their presence in cities such as Valencia, Sevilla, and Lisbon especially, but it is more difficult to know how many were resold to the Baltic and other sections of Europe. I believe that we can be sure that Americans were traded widely in the

Mediterranean region, not only in areas possessed at times by Spain (such as southern Italy and locations in North Africa) but also wherever Spanish, Portuguese, Genoese, Tuscan, and Venetian merchants plied their commerce. It would seem especially likely that Americans might have been trans-shipped to Sicily and Naples during Spanish domination of that region. But since many or all Americans would have been classified as non-Christians, they also might have fallen into the hands of Iberian Jewish and Muslim merchants and become part of the North African-Middle Eastern-Ottoman captive trade, especially during times of relative peace between Portugal and Spain on the one hand, and Muslim and Greek Orthodox regions on the other.

The "Low Countries" (Belgium and the Netherlands), along with other parts of Europe, became associated with Spain during the Hapsburg ascendancy. It seems likely that Antwerp might well have become a place where American captives would have been resold and from whence they might be transferred to other Hapsburg domains. Significantly, Antwerp figures in the lives of Sir Thomas More, author of *Utopia,* and other pre-"Enlightenment" figures.

The period from 1493 into the early 1500s would most likely be the period of the heaviest shipment of Americans to Spain. We do not have records of every vessel's cargoes, but it can be estimated conservatively that up to eight hundred captives were transported each year from 1494 for about ten years. The total that we can document is in the range of four thousand from 1493 through 1503, but the records are very incomplete, and eight thousand is a more likely figure.

Gradually, the shipment of Caribbean Americans to Spain probably declined due to the great labor needs developed in Haiti and Cuba, as the indigenous population was decimated by disease, exploitation, and slaughter. But we do know that Americans continued to be taken to Spain from the Caribbean region and Mexico all during the sixteenth century, and especially in the first half of that century. Slave records in Sevilla, Valencia, and the Canary Islands attest to many new arrivals from the Caribbean and Mexico in the years through 1600.

Nonetheless, we can suppose that even the shipment of alleged "Caribs" with a "C" branded on their faces probably declined due to the Caribbean internal labor market. On the other hand, the Portuguese expansion in Brazil resulted in a new source of slaves after 1501, not only for Portugal itself but also for resale elsewhere in Iberia and Europe in general. Also, as noted, slaves from Terranova (Newfoundland) were received in 1650, with many being sent to Peru. These Terranovans, like the Brazilians, came to Spain in Portuguese ships.

After 1542 efforts were made by Spain to restrict the enslavement of Americans (except for alleged "Caribs," and persons from rebel or enemy groups, such as Mapuches and, later, Apaches, Yavapais, and other frontier tribes). Some Americans may have been liberated from captivity in Sevilla in 1549, but such persons had to ask for their freedom and probably mixed-race children would not have been eligible, especially if the mother were African or Muslim. Benzoni tells us in his day (ca. 1550s) that American captives were being traded in Spain for wine, flour, biscuits, and other merchandise, even including women made pregnant by their Spanish captors.[1]

During the sixteenth and early seventeenth centuries, Spain was home to from one hundred thousand to three hundred thousand captives. If a mere 10 percent of these were American, that would yield a total of ten thousand to thirty thousand, a quite possible number given the continuing importation of Brazilians from the early 1500s (and continuing into the eighteenth century). In 1516, for example, eighty-eight "negros" (eighty-five of whom were Americans from Brazil) were imported into Valencia. In the period from 1569 to 1620, of listed slaves in Valencia, twenty-two were specifically from Brazil (las Indias de Portugal). This number compares well in significance with twelve from Cabo Verde (some of whom could have been American or part-American), twenty-three from Sao Tomé, and twenty-three from Angola.[2]

American captives in Spain were of both sexes, and usually young. As mentioned above, some women were pregnant upon arrival, while other women are mentioned specifically as having children or infants with them. Females are common, it would seem, and many appear to have married Spaniards, as is reported especially for the towns of Ayamonte and Gibraleón (located near the Portuguese border). Nonetheless, there are cases where males seem to be more common, as in Las Palmas (Canary Islands), where seventeen Americans were sold between 1537 and 1600, of whom fourteen were males from age six to forty-eight (and at least five were from Brazil). A *cacique* from Mexico is specifically mentioned, along with one Agustín Inglés (Augustine English?), condemned for a "sexual perversion" (perhaps the latter male was from an English-speaking region, hence his name). As late as circa 1650 three female American slaves were donated to a nun living in a monastery in Spain.[3]

The lives of Americans in Spain probably varied considerably. Many women doubtless served as domestic labor or as concubines or wives for Spaniards. Males sometimes were assigned to the galleys. One Benjamin fled from his owner, a dyer of Sevilla, and was subsequently jailed. Another American was condemned to the galleys for committing a robbery.[4]

The people of color of Sevilla were allowed to organize their own communal lives, centered, it would appear, around the section of the city called Triana. To a degree, at least, they were allowed to regulate their own marriages, celebrations, and social life under the supervision of an African governor of royal ancestry. They were also able to organize fraternal groups (through the Roman Catholic Church) for burials, funerals, and so forth. Thus, although they were captives and their labor was prescribed, they also were able to gradually merge into the proletariat of Spain and probably into the "Gitano" (Gypsy") grouping (the Caló-speaking population). I personally have met Gitanos in Spain (and Portugal) who appeared to me to have American facial characteristics.[5]

The Americans in rural areas probably were engaged in agricultural labor or, in small towns, in various trades. They lived in a Spain where hundreds of thousands of Muslims were forced to abandon their homes for exile in North Africa, while other Muslims were eventually forced to become Christianized. Surviving Jews were all forced to be "New Christians." Nonetheless, many rural regions and proletarian urban areas must have been rich in diversity, with African and American attitudes towards life, sexuality, and spirituality having an impact beyond the eyes of church and government. One custom that appeared was that of the use of tobacco for smoking, a habit that eventually spread to a large percentage of Spaniards of all classes.[6]

Large numbers of captives in Spain and Portugal were Muslims of Spanish, Wolof, Berber, or Arab origin. Spanish officialdom seems to have been highly suspicious of all non-whites in Spain who had become *ladino* (Spanish speaking or, literally, "latino") and attempted to prevent their passage to the Americas out of fear of spreading dangerous ideas to the Native Americans there (such as Islamic or Judaic ideas). The fear was that persons of color might have been "contaminated" in Spain by contact with Muslims, Jews, or people of color who had imbibed "subversive" ideas. In any case, it would be interesting to know how Americans from such diverse areas as Brazil (mostly Guaraní-Carijó probably), Borinquen, Haiti, Cuba, the Bahamas, Florida, Mexico, and the Venezuela-Colombia coast interacted with each other and with Muslims and Africans of very diverse backgrounds.

Portugal launched a vigorous trade in human captives along the west coast of Africa before 1500. This was soon supplemented by the sale of Americans from Newfoundland and Brazil. In 1502 a contract was given by the Crown to Fernao de Noronha to "trade in brazilwood and slaves" from Brazil. Six ships were to be sent to Brazil each year. In 1503 four ships at least carried slaves across the Atlantic, and this process continued at a steady pace. The Crown created twelve feudal domains in Brazil, each one of which was allowed to sell twenty-four slaves (one domain could sell forty-eight) each year to Portugal. Thus a total of 3,240 or more Americans could be legally sent to Lisbon up to 1549.

Not satisfied with sales to Portugal (and Africa), the Portuguese began quite early to attempt to sell Brazilians in the Spanish islands and in Spain itself. The Spanish Crown finally agreed in 1570 to the importation of Brazilians who had been enslaved first by other Americans (with what proof, we might wonder). In 1553 Ulrich Schmidl carried 209 Carijós to Lisbon and perhaps eighteen of them went on with him to Antwerp.

The enslavement of Brazilians was a continuing process, in both the south and in the Amazonian region. Between 1630 and 1650 alone, some one hundred thousand to two hundred thousand Americans from the Paraguay region were captured and sold to various places. As late as circa 1710 the Portuguese of the Piaui region were trading away three or four Americans for one African from Angola. A Jesuit estimated that "three million Indians were descended (as slaves) from the Rio Negro alone in the century up to 1750." This figure is perhaps exaggerated but, nonetheless, it indicates that very large numbers of Americans were available for resale to Europe, the Caribbean, Cabo Verde, and other areas. A law of 1755 prohibited the captivity of Americans in the female line. It not only ignored descendants of male Americans, but left many classes of semi-slaves still available for exploitation. In point of fact, the trade in indigenous slaves continued on in the region between the Amazon and Surinam into at least the middle of the nineteenth century.[7]

Many Americans ended up in Lisbon, the Algarve, and other sections of Portugal. References in records from Lisbon refer to American captives. In 1550 special places along the river were set aside both for Indian males and Indian females (along with other people of color) so that they could sell water to residences in the city. In 1591 a *confraria* (organization) existed for Indians living in Lisbon.[8]

One can find Portuguese living in the Algarve and elsewhere who still show evidence of American ancestry, in my judgment. But the Portuguese were also very vigorous in terms of seeking to sell Brazilians and Paraguayans in many other parts of the world. As we have seen, Spain was a major market, but many other areas were targets, including Caribbean islands, the Azores, and other places from which, eventually, persons of part-American descent could reach countries such as France, Belgium, the Netherlands, and so forth.

Not many American captives were ever sent directly to France, where slavery was generally illegal, but many individuals from Martinique, Guadeloupe, Haiti, and other French colonies did reach France in various capacities. Some of these may well have been of American or part-American ancestry (as is still common among those stemming from French Guiana). In 1654 a large number of Dutch, Portuguese Jews, and their American slaves abandoned Brazil and moved to Martinique and Guadeloupe. The Dutch (who had attempted to conquer Brazil) also sold Brazilian and Arawak captives to other French islands in this period. Some of these Brazilians were used as military auxiliaries. In 1656 a group helped to suppress an Angolan slave rebellion on Guadeloupe.

The French themselves also became slavers in Canada, Louisiana, and the Caribbean. Many Americans of the Pawnee, Apache, Chitimacha, and Natchez nations were enslaved or were purchased as captives from other tribes. Such slaves were known as "panis" or "paducahs" in the Mississippi Valley and Canada. Many, including especially Natchez people, ended their days as slaves on Haiti. In the 1750s a Spanish vessel freed three Americans from a French vessel, thus illustrating that they were being shipped at that date.[9]

The significance of the above is that when we read of Caribbean people of color, or other non-whites, living in France during the eighteenth and nineteenth centuries (as well as today) we must bear in mind that many such persons are doubtless descended from Americans of Brazil, Guiana, Surinam, the Mississippi Valley, and other areas, mixed often with people of African or European descent. It is, of course, common for writers to assume that French residents of color possess only African ancestry when, in fact, their ancestry from Martinique, Guadeloupe, or elsewhere might well be more complex than that.

There were some Americans actually sent to France as prisoners, including thirty-six Iroquois men who were assigned to the king's galleys in 1687. They suffered a great deal as galley-slaves but at least thirteen survivors were freed two years later and allowed to return home as a peace gesture to the Iroquois Confederacy.[10] Many other Americans reached

France periodically from 1508 to 1509 and forward, often being very well received, as will be discussed below.

Americans began to reach other areas of Europe, such as Antwerp, quite early. In the period from 1495 to 1502 Dutch and German vessels were already being used to deliver occasional slaves between Iberia and Algeria and Spain and the Canary Islands. Somewhat later, after the Dutch began their long period of warfare against the Spanish and Portuguese, Dutch warships and pirate vessels (called Pichilingues on the Pacific coast of America) frequently captured Iberian vessels loaded with captives and/or non-white crews. Some of these captives were taken to Europe while others were resold, as when a group of Spanish-surnamed persons were sold to the English in Virginia in 1619. Others were taken to New Amsterdam (New York) where many Maya captives from Campeche (and elsewhere) appear in the city records.

The Dutch allied themselves with many American nations, as in Brazil and New York-New Jersey, but, as noted, they also did not hesitate to deal in slaves in the seventeenth and later centuries. For example, in 1644 Esopus captives were sold from New Amsterdam to the Netherlands, Bermuda, and Curaçao (the latter becoming a great center for the captive trade). Generally, Americans were free upon arrival in Holland itself, and a large American community developed in Amsterdam (especially comprised of Brazilians).[11]

The English, like the French and Dutch, were somewhat slow to become fully involved in the trade in human flesh. Nonetheless, English vessels often were guilty of kidnapping Americans, especially after 1576–77, when Martin Frobisher kidnapped Inuits from Greenland. The most common target areas were New England and Virginia, especially after 1603. The numbers were usually small until 1614, when Captain Thomas Hunt secured twenty-four Americans and carried them to Málaga for sale. It is from this group that Tasquantum ("Squanto") later escaped, making his way to England and eventually back to Massachusetts.

After the settlement of Jamestown (1607), kidnapping from the Virginia area diminished, and various individuals were taken from time to time to Britain, including Matoaks (Pocahontas) and Uttamakomak ("Tomocomo"), reportedly her brother-in-law, along with almost a score of other Powhatan-Renápe people.

The English began capturing Spanish ships from the 1570s on. From these ships they acquired prisoners and crew members of American, African, and mixed races. Some of these people of color ended up in

Portsmouth and other English ports, becoming numerous enough that Elizabeth I in 1596 and 1601 ordered the departure of all "negars and blackamoores" from England, Wales, and Ireland. It would appear that many, who were servants, were resold to other countries.

Nonetheless, the numbers of non-whites, including Americans, seem to have steadily increased. In 1621 thirteen "Negroes or Indian people" (six women, seven males) were sold. In the 1688 to 1709 period there are reports of Indians running away in England, while from 1629 to 1695 they appear in plays and pageants, frequently representing "America."

The establishment of British colonies in North America and the Caribbean greatly accelerated the adoption of slavery by the English. Many thousands of Americans were either captured in warfare or purchased from allied tribes and sold to various regions, including Barbados, Jamaica, Providence Island, Spain, and North Africa. New England saw large numbers of Pequots, Narragansetts, and others sold in 1638 and in the period from 1676 to 1683 many went to Tangiers, Morocco. After 1670, South Carolina became a major exporter of slaves, depopulating Florida in the process. Virginia also authorized the export of Americans between 1660 and 1723.[12]

It cannot be said how many Americans reached Europe through English activities, but when one considers the sale of Americans to Bermuda, Barbados, Jamaica, and other colonies, and the eventual migration of large numbers of people from these islands to Britain (especially after World War II), one can assume that American ancestry has become somewhat common, although usually mixed with African or Caucasian. In addition, one needs to take into account Trinidad, Dominica, and other islands where Native Americans have survived to the present day and the widespread use of Miskito men on board English vessels and as providers of meat on Jamaica and elsewhere. Many North American tribesmen also served on whaling vessels and other ships that could well have put in at British ports. Finally, we can refer to Scots fur traders in Canada, reportedly sometimes returning to Scotland with their Cree or other American wives and mixed children.[13]

Now let us turn to discussing the many Americans who began to reach Europe as free visitors and not as captives. The first groups taken by Columbus to Lisbon and Palos and by Martin Alonso Pinzón to Galicia in 1493 may have been treated as free persons (although we actually know nothing about Pinzón's possible passengers). England began to receive free visitors from 1502 and France from 1508, while Holland and other areas cannot be precisely documented but were doubtless visited by Americans from 1566 on. Neighboring Germany apparently witnessed a visit by Brazilians and other Americans as part of a project of Holy Roman Emperor Maximilian I. A number of Tupinamba individuals were drawn as a part of a series of illustrations of a "triumph" ordered by this monarch. It would seem that they must have reached Germany from France. Albrecht Dürer drew a Brazilian in 1515, perhaps using the same models as Albrecht Altdorfer or Hans Burgkmair for sketches of 1512–16.[14]

As regards France, Captain de Gonneville of Honfleur sailed to Brazil in 1503, bringing back an American boy of fifteen who was the son of a Carijó leader. The boy was educated in France, married a French woman, and was still living there in 1583. During this period the French became rivals of the Portuguese in Brazil, allying themselves with the Carijós of the south, the Tamóios of Rio de Janeiro, and other groups north of Pernambuco. As a result of intermarriage some Tupinamba children began to be born with blonde hair and European features.

Naturally, numerous Brazilians and residents journeyed to France, including the Portuguese pioneer of Bahia, Caramuru (Diego Alvares). He and his wife Paraguazu were legally married in France in 1510, sponsored by the king and queen. Other Brazilians seen by Dürer and Burgkmair probably came from Rouen.

In 1550 a large number of Americans put on a great spectacle in Rouen for Henry II and Catherine de Medici. The writer Michel de Montaigne interviewed three Americans in Rouen in 1563. From the 1590s through the 1610s other Brazilians visited France, enough to worry the Jesuits of Portuguese Brazil about the possible influence of French Calvinism (then not yet suppressed in France).[15]

The French also began to bring Americans from Canada to France, initially by means of kidnapping, from the 1520s and 1530s. Later, allies reached Europe including Assacombuit, an Abnaki leader. He had long been involved in French efforts to oust the English from northeast America and Newfoundland. For his efforts, Assacombuit was knighted by Louis XIV (in 1706). He returned to his homeland in 1707, continuing to aid the French in attacking New England English settlements.[16]

The Low Countries, as indicated earlier, were involved in trade with the Portuguese quite early on and later were under Spanish domination. Antwerp in particular became a cosmopolitan port. It "was the reshipment point for goods from all over Northern Europe and a place where agents for Portuguese business houses made vast fortunes out of their monopolies in overseas goods." Albrecht Dürer journeyed to Antwerp in 1520–21, sending "Indian feathers" back to Nuremburg. Baltasar the Moor, perhaps an American from Brazil, was an early resident of Antwerp, along with other Americans and Africans. Dürer was able to see "Cortez' Aztec treasures, which happened to be on display in Flanders" in 1520.[17]

It is interesting to note that in 1515 Thomas More traveled to Antwerp, where he met various persons. It was here that he wrote his famous *Utopia,* a work supposedly based upon conversations with a Portuguese man who had been left in South America by Amerigo Vespucci (1504). It seems more than likely that More did speak with Portuguese individuals in Antwerp, and perhaps even with Brazilians there. In any event, his book *Utopia* became very important in the evolution of European social thought, coming as it did after several centuries of peasant revolts, laborer agitation, and other radical folk movements seeking a more just social order and a fairer distribution of goods.

In the meantime, radical Christian ideas were spreading in the Netherlands, eventually coalescing into organized Protestantism. The Spanish authorities began to persecute the Protestants, especially after Philip of Spain assumed control of the process in 1556. By 1567 the Dutch were in open revolt, with Zeeland and the port of Vlissingen as a key rebel area.[18]

As noted, Dutch warships soon (1560s-1609) began to be involved in capturing Spanish and Portuguese shipping, thus doubtless increasing greatly the numbers of Americans and other non-Europeans in Vlissingen and other Dutch ports. After the 1620s the Dutch involvement in Brazil brought large numbers of Brazilians to the Netherlands. By 1636, when the Irishman Bernard O'Brien arrived in Holland, he saw many Americans from Brazil in Dutch cities such as Rotterdam, Delft, and The Hague, and especially found many Americans in Amsterdam with their own "synagogue" (perhaps a Calvinist church, but some Brazilians could have embraced Judaism). "They gave him messages to take back to their relatives in Brazil."[19] In 1566–67 an Inuit woman and child were brought to Vlissingen from the Greenland-Labrador region. She was put on display in Antwerp, an area under Spanish control. More on this below.

Americans seem to have become an interesting part of Dutch urban life. A painting by Jan Steen, *Het huwelijkscontract,* has a likely Native American man included at the right hand side of the painting. Other Dutch and Flemish paintings of the "Golden Age" also include individuals of probable Indigenous American ancestry. Americans continued to live in

Holland during later centuries. For example, in the 1770s a boy named Weekee from the Surinam-Guyana border was living in Bergen-op-zoom. He had learned to be a cook and "something of a tailor." He later returned to South America.[20]

One should add that the Netherlands today is home to large numbers of persons of American race from Surinam (Caribs and Lokonos), as well as from Aruba and nearby islands. This is in addition to many mixed persons from the same regions.[21]

The northern countries, and especially Denmark, have been more affected perhaps by Inuit contacts with Europe. Since the Inuit story is somewhat distinct from the rest of America, I shall present it separately here, following from where we left off in chapter 6.

As discussed, there is strong evidence for Inuits from Greenland being kidnapped or otherwise carried to Norway long before 1492. It is very likely that the many European vessels reaching the Newfoundland and Greenland areas after 1500 were occasionally able to kidnap Inuits, although the somewhat vague use of the term "terra nova" (new land) after 1500 does not always allow us to distinguish Newfoundland Beothuks and Labrador or Cape Breton Algonkians from Inuits. In any case, between 1517 and 1537, as discussed, an Inuit kayaker apparently reached the coast of England north of York. This is very significant, because the North Sea became an area where many Inuit kayakers were subsequently to be seen.

Little is known of European traffic in the Greenland-Labrador region except as already discussed in connection with Portuguese activities. Basques seem to have been in the region from 1512, while other contacts may have occurred between then and the 1530s. López de Gómara, writing before 1552, has detailed knowledge of the Greenland Inuits, who are "valiant," he states, and "handsome men who navigate with boats covered over by leather, because of fear of the cold, and of fish [skins]." As noted, his information would appear to have come from Portuguese sources. During the same period (ca. 1532) Jacob Ziegler stated that the "Skraelings" used light boats of hide and attacked other ships. Ziegler, a Bavarian, probably got his data from Erik Axelsson Valkendorf, who had become Bishop of Nidaros in 1510, and who had collected information on Greenland.[22]

In 1539–41 ships from Hamburg are known to have reached Greenland. On August 9, 1539, after eighteen weeks at sea, one ship returned after having failed to find Iceland, reaching Greenland instead. Strong winds prevented any landing. In 1540 a man called Jon Greenlander reached Greenland on a German ship, apparently approaching one of the former Norse settlements. The ship came into a fjord with islands, some occupied by Inuits. The Germans were afraid to land and continued to another island, where they found the remains of a deceased man who "wore a hood" on his head and had clothes of "sealskin and frieze." A curved dagger, much worn, and a sheath were nearby. Was this man a last Norse, or, as the sealskin clothing might imply, an American or Norse-American mixed blood?

In 1541–42 a very large Hamburg vessel under captain Gert Mestemaker also reached Greenland but reportedly found no people. The scholar Paul Herrmann asked why a ship of the largest type was sent out. Surely a cargo was anticipated, but what kind? We might also wonder just who Jon Greenlander was, a Norse Greenlander himself, or of Inuit ancestry?[23]

Between 1550 and 1600 Basque whalers are said to have entered Davis Strait. They may be the source of Inuits kidnapped in the next few years, although pirates of many nations, including Algerians from North Africa, began operating in the Iceland and Faeroe region from the 1570s on. People were kidnapped in their attacks. During the sixteenth and seventeenth centuries Basque corsairs rivaled those of the Dutch along the coasts of the Atlantic, according to one source.[24]

By the 1560s it is clear that kidnappings from Inuit areas were continuing. As mentioned above, a woman and child were captured in 1566, reportedly by a French (Basque?) vessel at "Terra Nova," and taken to Vlissingen in Zeeland. Her husband had been reportedly killed. Subsequently the captives were exhibited in the Hague and in Spanish-controlled Antwerp with fliers being printed up for distribution in German-speaking areas. Their subsequent fate is not known, but given the turbulent condition of the Low Countries from the 1560s onward, it is not surprising that they disappear from view.[25] Given the helplessness of their position, it would not be surprising if the twenty-year-old woman was forced into a pregnancy, although death rates were high for Inuit captives (especially in England, it should be noted).

Such abductions could also be a partial explanation for men setting out to reach Europe in a kayak, in order to recover family members, wives, brothers, sisters, or close friends and hunting partners. For small Inuit communities, the loss of a skilled hunter or a wife and child would be keenly felt, in my judgment.

Within ten years the English also joined in the kidnapping of Americans from the Davis Strait area. Martin Frobisher led two expeditions to the Baffin Island region at the head of Davis Strait in 1576 and 1577. His first visit started out auspiciously, with trading proceeding well with Inuits who had come up in an umiak. But relations were tense, perhaps because of Frobisher's suspicions or perhaps because the Baffin Islanders had already been tricked by prior visitors. In any case, five of Frobisher's crew disobeyed orders, rowed out of sight, and disappeared, never to be seen again. Subsequently, Frobisher managed to meet up with a number of kayaks and an umiak containing twenty men. The Inuits refused to approach except for one, who was hauled on board by trickery, kayak and all with him. On August 25, Frobisher abandoned the area, sailing back to England, leaving the people of Cathay (of "Cathay or new land India"), also called "Tartars," alone for a time.

Frobisher's victim soon died "of a cold" in England after two weeks there, while the English captain quickly planned another journey to "Cathay" in 1577, principally to gather worthless ore (thought to contain gold). While trading with Inuit men, two Englishmen treacherously seized two American men. The latter broke loose, recovered their weapons, and fired arrows at the fleeing English. Frobisher himself was wounded in the buttocks, but a wrestler caught one of the Inuits, probably causing serious internal injuries, as we shall see.

Thereafter a group of Inuits were attacked in order to acquire more captives. Five or more Inuits were killed (several by drowning when eluding capture) and a European was wounded. Two women were captured. One who was elderly was suspected of being a devil or a witch and several sailors pulled off her lower clothes to see if she had cloven feet. The younger woman with her wounded child was abducted. The three captives were taken to Bristol and London in the fall, where the man gave demonstrations of his skills with kayak and weapons, but soon perished from his painful internal injuries. Shortly thereafter the mother and child also died.[26]

An English expedition of 1578 seeking to capture Americans was unable to make contact with any, "they being nowe growen more wary by their former losses." In the following year King Frederik II of Denmark-Norway dispatched an expedition to Greenland under the English navigator John Alday, but it was a failure. Nonetheless, the effort signaled the Danish-Norse desire to reestablish contact with the region and to thwart English and Dutch competition. In 1585–86 John Davis led two expeditions for the English to the Greenland area, reaching the Nuuk

(Godthab) region and seeing several bodies covered by a seal-skin and a cross. He also abducted an Inuit as hostage for the return of an anchor, but the American died at sea.[27]

In the meantime there is evidence a storm drove two kayaks (leather boats) ashore in Holland in 1577. Graf Moritz (Count Morice), a Dutch general, obtained the three Greenlanders called Calitgoch, his wife Egnocth, and child Nutiocth. Eventually some of the Inuit equipment ended up in the Museum of Ethnography in Munich, Germany, where it was described in a 1689 inventory. Strangely, however, these three Americans may be confused with those brought to England by Frobisher as noted above.[28] The three Americans are definitely identified in the Munich Museum's record as being from Greenland, and as being driven by a storm to the coast of Holland. An inventory of 1776 listed portraits of the "Sea-man" (Seesischer Mann) and his wife, along with two paddles and a leather boat. A picture of the latter was published by H. Stöcklein in 1911.[29]

The waters around Greenland and Labrador continued to be visited by Dutch vessels, and in 1602 and 1606 English ships reached the area, one English navigator losing his life at the hands of Labrador Americans in the latter year. Thereafter, the English concentrated official attention upon fruitless efforts to discover a "northwest passage" to Asia, from 1610 until 1632. In the meantime, Scandinavians, led by the Danish monarchy, sought to reestablish their position in the American Arctic. Many Americans were kidnapped, killed, or left without a hunter as a result.[30]

Admiral Gotske Lindenau, with the help of several Britons, took three vessels out in 1605. A Scots captain (John Cunningham) of one ship followed the old Icelandic strategy of sailing north and then turning southwest to avoid East Greenland's ice packs. They rounded Cape Farewell and entered Davis Strait, finding good harbors and Inuits eager to trade but very "timid and mistrustful," doubtless due to prior kidnappings. Cunningham nonetheless was able to capture four Americans, one of whom was beaten to death with musket butts as he tried to resist. After intimidating other Inuits with musket and cannon fire, the Europeans weighed anchor and sailed to Denmark.

Meanwhile, Lindenau had continued in a northeast direction to a part of East Greenland where Europeans had probably not been for many years. The East Greenlanders jumped into their kayaks and went to visit the Danish vessel. Eager to trade, the Americans offered skins of "dogs, bears, and seals" along with walrus ivory. They were especially eager for any articles of iron or steel "for they like them above everything, and would give . . . whatever they most prized, their bows, arrows, boats, and oars; and when they have nothing more to give they stripped themselves and gave their shirts."

The Danes remained three days off the coast, returning the Americans' friendship by kidnapping two men "who made so many efforts to free themselves . . . and to jump into the sea, that they found it necessary to bind them." The Americans on shore "uttered horrible cries" but were frightened off by cannon fire. The stupidly brutish behavior of the Europeans in North American waters thus continued unabated.

According to Isaac de la Peyrère, writing in the 1640s, the three Americans from West Greenland were "much better made and more civilized" than the two from East Greenland and had "different clothes, language, and manners." This might indicate that the isolated East Greenlanders were still speaking the Dorset language or, at the very least, a distinctive dialect of Inuit. In any case, they reached Copenhagen, where an effort was made to understand their languages or dialects, but to no avail.[31]

In 1606 Lindenau led another expedition (or should we call it a "raid"?), this time to West Greenland. He took with him the three previously captured Inuits from that area. "The poor creatures manifested unspeakable joy at their return to their country; but one . . . died of illness, and was thrown overboard." Four vessels reached Greenland, but Lindenau was forced repeatedly to move from bay to bay due to American hostility and mistrust. The latter kept up with the Danish ships, using kayaks apparently. Finally, the Danes "surprised at different times six of the savages, with their boats . . . and carried them on board." A foolish Danish soldier went ashore at one point and was promptly killed by the Greenlanders.

It should be noted that writer Peyrère always refers to the Americans as "savages" in spite of the behavior of the Danes as aggressors and kidnappers. In 1607 the king of Denmark sent out a third expedition with two large vessels under Karsten Richkardsten, using some Icelandic and Norwegian sailors. Apparently they approached East Greenland and were blocked by huge ice floes from reaching land.

After these voyages Peyrère tells us that nine Americans remained in Denmark. Those who could "seized their little boats and oars and put out to sea to try the passage." A storm cast them upon the coast and they were taken back to Copenhagen, to be guarded more closely. Four died, with five remaining to put on a maritime show for the visit of an ambassador from Spain, a rather typical use made of captive Inuits in Europe. One prisoner was put to work diving for pearls and died of exposure. His friend, disconsolate because of the death of his companion, managed to get possession of a kayak and set out to sea. He was captured, however, thirty or forty leagues out to sea, as he sought to travel north along the coast of Norway and thence westward, guided by stars, to Greenland. He soon died.

Fortunately, two Inuits who escaped in kayaks could not be overtaken by the Danes and their fate is unknown. Perhaps they are among the Greenlanders who were seen in European waters between 1613 and 1625, as shall be noted below. Or, hopefully, they managed to return home to wives and families.

A fourth expedition in 1612 to Davis Strait resulted in the death of Captain James Hall at the hands of Inuits. One of the English pilots noted that "every one [of the Inuits], both man and woman, has a boat covered with seal's skin, close sewed, that no water can enter them."[32]

In circa 1613 a small kayak, with a framework of bone, was found in the North Sea with a deceased Inuit in it. The kayak was taken to Hull, England. In 1625 a Greenlander gave a demonstration of his skill in a kayak on an ornamental lake near The Hague, Netherlands. This indicates either that one of the Danish captives reached Holland or, more likely, that the Dutch were also continuing to kidnap Inuits in this period.[33] In 1656 a Vlissingen vessel captained by Nicolaas Tunes penetrated to the north end of Davis Strait, but I do not know if any Inuits were abducted. Tunes is known to have brought to Holland a large collection of kayaks and clothing.[34]

Meanwhile, the Danes resumed their raids on Greenland. In 1636 King Christian IV granted a charter to the "Greenland Company" that obligated them to annually kidnap a pair of young Americans, between sixteen and twenty years, so that the latter could be taught Danish and be converted to Lutheranism. Peyrère tells us that two Inuits were kidnapped; however, upon being set loose after the ship went out to sea, the captives jumped into the water to swim to freedom. Whether they were able to make it to shore is not known. Adam Olearius reported that other captives were taken to Denmark, where they lived for twelve years. Strangely, however, Peyrère doesn't seem to have met them in the mid-1640s, so perhaps they had escaped or perished.[35]

When Frederick III became king in 1648 he revived interest in Greenland commerce and raiding. Four years later a monopoly was granted to one Henrik Müller for thirty years. Several voyages were made to Greenland waters, on the third of which six Americans were seized after they had been induced to come on board for trading. One boy escaped, an old woman was released, and four captives were taken out to sea. A man, Ihiob, died on the voyage, while three women Küneling (a mother of two children), Kabelau ("Codfish," a woman of twenty-five), and Sigoko, a girl of thirteen, were first taken to Bergen, Norway, where a drawing or portrait was made that included Ihiob before he died en route to Copenhagen. Adam Olearius, keeper of the ethnological collections for the Duke of Holstein-Gotlorp, was able to study the women for some time. Allegedly, they were to be converted to Lutheranism, taught Danish, and returned to Greenland, but that did not happen. Instead they died of fever in Copenhagen.[36]

After the 1650s the Danes turned away from Greenland expeditions for about seventy years, leaving the waters of Davis Strait and the Spitsbergen area in the hands of Dutch and English whalers and explorers. In 1663 a Dutch ship seized a kayaker in the former area. The kayak eventually ended up in Amsterdam in a display where the kayak contained a "figure made of wood and dressed in the same fur clothing he wore" when found. What happened to the American is not specified. But it is clear that Dutch whalers were kidnapping so many Inuits that in 1720 the Dutch government issued a decree establishing severe penalties for the molesting and kidnapping of the inhabitants of Davis Strait.[37] The Danish Crown issued comparable decrees in 1732, 1758, and 1776, designed to avoid the cost of repatriating Greenlanders brought to Denmark from the small Danish colony established there in the 1720s. Nonetheless, Inuits did arrive in Copenhagen from 1724 on, and this has continued right up to the present day, as Greenland gradually developed as a Danish colony and, more recently, as a self-governing associated area.[38]

It is impossible to estimate how many Americans have been brought to Europe from the Inuit regions, precisely because the vast majority of whalers and other vessels reaching the area left no records behind. It is also difficult to know the impact of continued European-American interaction. No doubt, the manufacture of goods and the acquisition of ivory desired by European traders must have distorted indigenous economics, even as many communities or households lost hunters to European raids and kidnappings. Could diseases also have been introduced in these years (as was the case with smallpox in the early eighteenth century)? Perhaps many of the abandoned community sites seen in later years, as along the East Greenland coast, were due to such influences.

In any case, we should conclude this topic by referring to the sightings of kayakers in North Sea waters, between the 1660s (perhaps) and the early 1700s. David MacRitchie found a record from the Orkney Islands, stating that on May 26, 1661, a collection was taken up to help care for "ane poore Yetland [i.e., Shetland] man whom God had wonderfully preserved into a storme at sea into his litill boate, and taken in by one vessell finding him upon the seas." MacRitchie argued that the little boat was probably a kayak because a true Shetlander would not be out in a storm so far from home in any small craft. A kayak later housed in the church at Burray Island could have been this one, he suggests as well.[39]

Sometime prior to his death in 1688 the Reverend James Wallace, a minister at Kirkwall in the Orkney Islands, wrote a description of the region, published posthumously in 1693.

> Sometime about this Country are seen these men which are called *Finnmen*. In the year 1682, one was seen sometime sailing, some time Rowing up and down in his little Boat at the south end of the Isle of Eda, most of the people of the Isle flocked to see him and when they adventured to put out a Boat with men to see if they could apprehend him, he presently fled away most swiftly. And in the Year 1684, another was seen from Westra, and for a while after they got few or no fishes; for they have this Remark here, that these *Finnmen* drive away the fishes from the place to which they come.

He then continues by making this key observation: "These *Finnmen* seem to be some of these people that dwell about the *Fretum Davis,* a full account of which may be seen in natural & moral History of the *Antilles,* Chap. 18 [The work of Charles de Rochefort, attributed to Louis de Poincy]." He adds that "one of their boats sent from *Orkney* to *Edinburgh* is to be seen in the Physicians hall with the Oar and Dart he makes use of for killing Fish."[40] In 1696 the Orkney kayak was transferred from Physicians Hall to the University of Edinburgh, with an entry noting that "the oars of the boat and the shirt of the barbarous man that was in the boat" were already at the university. This would seem to be the same kayak referred to by Wallace. Since he died in 1688, we must assume that the kayak was obtained originally in the 1680s. But what happened to the "barbarous" American? (This kayak could not be identified in the 1930s.)

In a 1700 reprint of Wallace's work, his son added that the kayak was "catched in Orkney" and "was sent from thence to Edinburgh," to the Physicians Hall. The younger Wallace believed that the Inuits (called Finnmen) were driven by storms from home. "They have this advantage that be the seas never so boisterous, their boats being made of fish skins are so contrived that he can never sink but it is like a sea-gull swimming on top of the water. His shirt he has is so fastened to the boat that no water can come into his boat to do him damage, except when he pleases to untie it, which he never does but to ease nature or when he comes ashore."[41]

The use of the phrase "fishskins" to refer to seal or walrus hides is worth noting, because the name applied to the Americans in Orkney waters, "Finnmen," apparently referred to the idea that they were fish-like and that they possessed fins. This would be an apt way to refer to the Americans in their kayaks, because at that moment they would appear to be fish or, as discussed earlier, mer-men or mer-maids. As we shall see, the Americans may have also been referred to as "finny-folk" in Orkney-Shetland folklore. Some writers have confused fish "finns" with the terms used for Suomi and Sami peoples in some Nordic languages, for example, *fenni, kven,* and *Finn.* But the Orkney and Shetland islanders had largely lost their previous Norse speech and were mostly English-speakers in the seventeenth century.

The younger Wallace also wrote that another kayak was located in the church of the small island of Burra or Burray in the year 1700. It is clear that the Orkneys and Shetlands were being visited by many Inuits in this period. A minister, John Brand, went to the Orkney region in 1700, and he learned "there are frequently *Fin-men* seen here upon the coasts, as one about a year ago on Stronia, and another within these few Months on *Westra,* a Gentleman with many others in the isles looking on him nigh to the shore, but when any endeavour to apprehend them, they flee most swiftly; which is very strange, that one Man sitting in his little boat, should come some hundred of leagues, from their own coasts, as they reckon *Finland* to be from Orkney." Brand thus confuses the kayakers with Scandinavians. He continues:

> It may be thought wonderfull how they live all that time, and are able to keep the Sea so long. His Boat is made of Seal skins, or some kind of Leather, he also hath a coat of Leather upon him, and he sitteth on the middle of his boat, with a little Oar in his hand, Fishing with his Lines: And when in a storm he seeth the high surge of a wave approaching, he hath a way of sinking his Boat, till the Wave pass over, least thereby he should be overturned. The Fishers here observe that these *Finmen* or *Finland-Men,* by their coming drive away the Fishes from the Coasts. One of their Boats is kept as a Rarity in the Physicians Hall at Edinburgh.[42]

Brand was also unaware of the transfer of the kayak to the university. In addition, he notes the existence of witches and wizards in the islands, "but not so many" as in Iceland, Lapland, and "other places to the north of Zetland." A "Brouny" or "evil Spirit so called" once served a family, but the spirit had gone away after a ceremony was abandoned, notes Brand. More significantly, Brand wrote that timber and shipwrecks came ashore in the Shetlands "which is brought here by the Ebb from *Norway,* or other places lying to the east of Zetland."[43] (This is interesting because most such debris probably came from the Gulf Stream.)

During the same general period a kayaker appeared in the North Sea, probably close to the mouth of the River Don, according to one source, or farther out at sea according to another. By one writer the kayaker was called "an Indian man" and his craft was termed a "canoe." He was brought alive to Aberdeen but died soon after. "He is supposed to have come from the Labrador coast, and to have lost his way at sea. The canoe is covered with fish-skins, curiously stretched upon slight timbers, very securely joined together." The Inuit had all of his equipment with him, including oar, spear, harpoon, birdspear, and throwing stick. The kayak and tools were preserved in the "Common hall" of Marischal College, now part of the University of Aberdeen. The wood was examined by W. Dawson, a lecturer on forestry, who determined that it was *pinus silvestris,* a tree found in northern Europe. Such wood commonly drifts to the east coast of Greenland and, according to William Clark Souter, "up the West Coast of Greenland" as well.

The kayak is a relatively long one, eighteen feet (or 213 inches). It seems to have come from East Greenland (although Birket-Smith felt otherwise). In any case, one Rev. Mr. Gastrell has written that he saw it in 1760 at King's College in Old Aberdeen and that it "was driven into the Don with a man in it who was all over hairy . . . he lived but three days." The date was circa 1728. By the time Francis Douglas wrote (1782) the kayak had been moved to Marischal College and the date had been pushed back to "about the beginning of the century."[44] Having the hairy side of his clothing on the outside would be unusual, but could indicate proximity to landing and no fear of waves, or the description could be in error.

The presence of Inuits in Scottish waters between circa 1661 and circa 1728 has been explained (see chapter 6) by some writers with the theory that whaling crews were allowing them to leave the latter's ships with all of their gear. But this explanation breaks down when one notes that no penalties for abductions existed prior to 1720, and that only for Dutch vessels. Souter notes that "it was a custom to bring home, as curiosities, natives of various places and exhibit them." He goes on to state that "the custom of bringing to this country, for a season on board whalers, Yakies or Eskimos, is well known and remembered." But all of his examples were from later years.

Souter also notes that a Dutch friend, one Professor van der Hoeve of Leiden, "assures me that there is no tradition in Holland of any Eskimos being brought there by any of the many whalers," an assertion directly contradicted by Dr. Gert Nooter and other evidence.[45] In any case, it seems unlikely that whalers would give liberty to captives carried across the Atlantic, without trying to gain profit from exhibiting them or selling their kayaks and tools as curiosities. Also, the appearance of the Finn-folk in Orcadian-Shetland waters is apparently too ancient to be explained by whaling.

Many writers, in referring to the folklore of the Orkney and Shetland islands, make reference to traditions that suggest that Inuits in their kayaks had long been a feature of island life. Related traditions from the Gaelic coastal regions of Ireland and Scotland are also worth mentioning. A key folklore element common to the above regions is the idea that selkies (large seals) or other sea-creatures (finfolk) had the ability to remove their outer skin garments and to become a human being, or to put on a skin and use it as a boat or flotation device in the ocean. Isn't this precisely what Inuit men and women kayakers do? They take off their skins (and fins) and become human in appearance. They put on their skins and kayak and become sea creatures!

The beliefs described by nineteenth-century and modern writers cannot, of course, explain at what date Gaelic and Pictish peoples came to believe that sea-creatures could shed skins and come ashore as humans, or that such creatures could marry ordinary people and produce children. In the Orkney and Shetland islands the Pictish people apparently were subordinated to Norse rule and their language disappeared, being replaced by Norn, a Germanic dialect, and then later by Scots English. Nonetheless, it would appear that Celtic-Pictish ideas survived within the population. In Shetland it would appear that selkie-people and finny-folk were confused, whereas in the Orkneys the two were treated as separate. Not knowing where the sea-people come from, some imagined a homeland beneath the waves, while others (outsiders?) imagined that the strangers came from Norway or Finland and were actual humans.

There also seems to be a tradition in the islands of visitors who were dark-visaged and who served as medicine-people, curers, or wizards. These people are confused with, or are regarded as one and the same with, the kayakers, apparently. They have been assigned magical qualities in the folk tradition, including the ability to row their boats at high speeds. Although some have tried to connect these Finn-people with Norway, information available fails to support any seagoing by Sami (Lapp) people south of Bergen and, in any case, the Sami and the people of Finland could hardly be referred to as dark skinned. The Sami and Finns whom I have met have been virtually all blondes, the former in Finnmark itself.[46]

In short, I am suggesting that Inuits had long been in contact with the region, long enough to influence important elements of local folklore. The Inuit harpoon heads of allegedly Thule date and provenance found in Ireland and Scotland, although the latter not certain as to origin or date, and the other evidence cited in chapter 6, together tend to support such an argument.

I have brought this narrative up to the year 1700 and somewhat beyond in the case of the enslavement of Americans. In general, the character of American visits to Europe changed during the eighteenth century, becoming somewhat less coercive and more along the lines of diplomacy, entertainment, education, and work.

Carolyn Thomas Foreman in *Indians Abroad* and Christian Feest and other authors in *Indians and Europe* provide many examples of other Native Americans who visited Europe after 1700 and, in the case of Feest, who are still traveling to Europe. Many have arrived to be performers, from Aztec-Mexican jugglers brought by Cortez in the 1520s, to Buffalo Bill's troupes of the Victorian era, to modern Ecuadorian Quichua and Bolivian Aymará musicians playing along Swiss and Dutch streets. Others have arrived as ambassadors from their nations, such as the famous visit of the Creek leader Tomochichi leading a delegation to Britain in 1733–34, which included a Yuchi spokesperson, Umphichi, as well.[47]

More recently, indigenous delegations have visited the League of Nations and the United Nations in Geneva, seeking international recognition for the rights of small nations around the world. Others have spoken at universities and in meetings all over Europe and as far east as Moscow, while still others have conducted ceremonies, taught courses, and given lectures ranging from the political to the historical and spiritual.

The Bertrand Russell Tribunal on the Rights of the Indians of the Americas, held in Rotterdam in 1980, was especially important in bringing together Indigenous Americans from many countries, including Canada, Mexico, the United States, Guatemala, Ecuador, Peru, Bolivia, Brazil, and Surinam. But each year other delegations travel in Europe, seeking support on a broad range of issues.

I was invited to serve as a consultant to the jury at the Bertrand Russell Tribunal and was able to meet delegates from all over the Americas, as well as persons of Native American and mixed ancestries living in Holland. In 1981 my wife and I were able to attend the indigenous meetings at the United Nations in Geneva as participants and later to visit universities in Switzerland. During the year I lectured at universities and other venues in Britain, Belgium, Germany, and other countries, and organized the first modern Native American conference in Britain in May 1982 at the University of Warwick. Delegates from the continent as well as Britain were part of the program, including Mapuche refugees from Chile.[48]

In earlier times, Native Americans visited Europe to study for the Christian ministry or priesthood. Now they are more likely to be teaching Europeans about native philosophy! But not all who went to Europe were on peaceful missions. Sakaweston, an Algonkian from New England, was captured by the English in 1611 and was taken to England, where he remained many years. Subsequently he reportedly served as a soldier in the wars of Bohemia, perhaps being the first of many to serve in the wars of Europe. Others doubtless served in the French armies of Napoleon, stemming from Martinique, Guadeloupe, and other French colonies. Later many Native Americans served in World War I and World War II with both Canadian and U.S. forces. In the latter case, some persons of Native American ancestry were forced to serve in "colored" units because of part-African ancestry.

Clearly, then, many countries of Europe have been visited by substantial numbers of persons of Indigenous American race, in whole or in part, after 1493. Spain and Portugal undoubtedly received the greater numbers by far, in the sixteenth and seventeenth centuries, but France, the Netherlands, and Britain saw many as well. Modern times have seen all of western Europe equally affected as numerous Mexicans, Puerto Ricans, Ecuadorians, and others of indigenous ancestry have gone to study or live in Spain and many other countries.

The impact of Native America continues to accelerate with each passing year, as indigenous peoples the world over gain new respect, increased self-awareness, and acquire increased means for influencing global values. It may well be that the earth-based values of indigenous peoples will reeducate people from more materialistic societies and thereby help to save our planetary home from the human-made disasters threatening all of us.[49]

Notes

Introduction

1. Francis Bacon, "The New Atlantis," in Charles W. Eliot, *The Harvard Classics* (New York: P. F. Collier, 1909), 3:156–59.

Chapter 1: Americans across the Atlantic

1. I will use both Colombo and Colón as last names for Christoforo or Christoferens, dubbed Columbus (a latinized form) in the United States. I will start out with Columbus to give familiarity to English-speaking readers, then go to the Genoese "Colombo," and finally his mature "Colón." See Rivière, *Christopher Columbus,* for a short study of Columbus's career.

2. Aeneas Sylvius, as reproduced in d'Ailly, *Ymago Mundi* (1930), 3:743.

3. René Marie de la Poix de Fréminville, a.k.a Jean Merrien, *Christophe Colomb* (1955), 80. His works will be cited under Jean Merrien.

4. Edmond Buron translation, in d'Ailly, *Ymago Mundi,* 3:743.

5. Morison, *Journals,* 22. In Morison's *Admiral of the Ocean Sea,* 33, a slightly different translation is presented, with "two boats adrift."

6. Cristobal Colón, *Textos y Documentos,* 9.

7. P. G. W. Glare, ed., *Oxford Latin Dictionary;* Lewis and Short, *A Latin Dictionary;* and Morison, *Admiral,* 1:33. I also wish to acknowledge the consultation and valuable suggestions of Professor David Traill of Spanish and Classics, University of California, Davis.

8. Ispizúa, *Historia* (1922), 2:229.

9. Morison, *Admiral,* 1:15, 29–32, 33–34; d'Ailly, *Ymago Mundi,* 1:10.

10. Morison, *Admiral,* 1:31.

11. Morison, *Journals,* 401.

12. Morison, *Admiral,* 1:45–46, 85–86.

13. Ispizúa, *Historia* (1922), 2:201–2, 218–19, 226; Winsor, *Christopher Columbus,* 7, 121; Morison, *Admiral,* 2:47; d'Ailly, *Ymago Mundi,* 1:29–33; Winsor, *Narrative and*

Critical History, 2:30–32; Jorrin, *Los Autografos Ineditos,* 5–16; see also C. Ugurgieri della Beardenga, *Pio II Picolomini;* Arbolí y Fernando and de la Rosa y López, *Biblioteca Colombina.*

14. "The Journal of Friar William of Rubruck, 1253–1255," in Komnoff, ed., *Contemporaries,* 119; Ispizúa, *Historia* (1922), 2:238.

15. Morison, *Journals,* 13–14.

16. Morison, *Admiral,* 2:86–92, 100–101. Behaim's map is on 88–89.

17. d'Ailly, *Ymago Mundi,* 1:249, 259–63, 304–6; 2:426–27; 3:660–61; Morison, *Journals,* 22; d'Ailly, *Imago Mundi, with Annotations,* 18B, 21B; Ispizúa, *Historia* (1922), 2:242–43, 245.

18. d'Ailly, *Ymago Mundi,* 3:743–48.

19. Ibid., 3:743, 746–47.

20. Christopher Columbus, *Diario of Christopher Columbus' First Voyage to America, 1492–1493,* 62–63, 90–91, 96–97, 146–47, 158–59, 164–65, 340–41, henceforth cited as Columbus, *Diario;* Morison, *Journals,* 74, 75n; and "The Journal of Friar Odoric, 1318–1330," in Komnoff, *Contemporaries,* 229–30, where he says that "the first city of India which I came to is called Ceuskalon [Canton]." After that he came to Zayton.

21. Letter of Christophe Colomb to Santangel, in Harrisse, ed., *Christophe Colomb,* vol. 1, pt. 6, 420–35; and Letters of Colón to Santangel and Sánchez, in Díaz-Alejo and Gil, eds., *América y el Viejo Mundo,* 132–37, 141–55.

22. Columbus, *Diario,* 53, 108–9, 111, 113, 115, 119, 124–25, 127, 129, 145, 177, 217, 273, 285, 307.

23. Columbus letter to Santangel, in Harrisse, *Christophe Colomb,* 420–21, 429.

24. Morison, *Journals,* 223, 225n.

25. d'Ailly, *Ymago Mundi,* 3:742.

26. Morison, *Journals,* 379.

27. Ispizúa, *Historia* (1922), 2:239; Fite and Freeman, *Book of Old Maps,* 15; Morison, *Journals,* 375–79.

28. Fite and Freeman, 14–16.

29. Ispizúa, *Historia* (1922), 2:241, 277.

30. Ibid., 2:211; Fite and Freeman, 18–19; and Díaz-Alejo and Gil, map 115a. Some European writers continued to regard the Chinese as Indians for some time. See, for example, John Isaac Pontanus, in Pinkerton, ed., *General Collection,* 128.

31. Fiske, *Dutch and Quaker Colonies,* 1:60–61.

Chapter 2: The Gulf Stream and Galway

1. Brochado, *Descobrimento do Altantico,* 43ff.

2. William B. Carpenter, "The Atlantic Ocean," *Werner Encyclopaedia* (Akron: Werner, 1908), 3:17–19; Gaskell, *Gulf Stream,* 12–15; Stommel, *Gulf Stream,* 23, 33, 51.

3. Stommel, *Gulf Stream,* 1–2, 4.

4. Carpenter, "Atlantic," 19.

5. Gaskell, *Gulf Stream,* 16–17, 120ff. See also MacLeish, *Gulf Stream,* 220, 226.

6. Stommel, *Gulf Stream,* 23.

7. Ibid., 32, 173.

8. Gaskell, *Gulf Stream,* 115–17, 122–23.

9. MacLeish, *Gulf Stream,* 210, 226. Some seeds cannot sprout when exposed to saltwater, but some may sprout after long periods if protected by mud or by a very hard shell. I recall reports on the recovery of the *Atocha* in newspapers of June 28, 1987, or thereabouts.

10. Gaskell, *Gulf Stream,* 120; Pontoppidan, *Natural History,* 1:156; Wallace, *Description of the Isles of Orkney,* 14, 17, 19; Scott, "Drift Timber," 151, quoting from Thomas Pennant, *A Tour of Scotland* (London: White, 1790), 2:266; Martin, *Descriptions of the Western Islands of Scotland* (1703), as cited in Thomson, *People of the Sea,* 38–39.

11. Gaskell, *Gulf Stream,* 120–22.

12. Scott, "Drift Timber," 151–52.

13. Humboldt, *Examen Critique,* 246–47, 250, 254; Humboldt, *Views of Nature,* 122–25; Paul Gaffarel, *Étude sur les Rapports,* 84–85; Morison, *Admiral,* 1:82–83.

14. Humboldt, *Views of Nature,* 122–23; Scott, "Drift Timber," 151–52.

15. Scott, "Drift Timber," 151.

16. Merrien, *Christopher Columbus,* 64–65; Merrien, *Lonely Voyagers,* 37–38, 264.

17. Jane Gottesman, "French Rower Expected to Reach Land Today," *San Francisco Chronicle,* November 21, 1991: A8. Also, a crossing from Boston to Gibraltar in 1903 in a nineteen-foot rowboat required only one hundred days. Two Norwegians rowed a boat from New York to LeHavre in sixty-two days, starting on June 6, 1896. See Hyde, *Ancient Greek Mariners,* 162n. See also Nelson, "Exotic Drift Fruits and Seeds," 148, 152.

18. Merrien, *La Vie Quotidienne,* 75; Magnusson and Pálsson, *Vinland Sagas,* 103–4.

19. Gad, *History of Greenland,* 1:52, 55, 60, 88; Jones, *Norse Atlantic Saga,* 96–97; Morison, *European Discovery,* 59.

20. Morison, *Admiral,* 1:84.

21. Cornell, *World Cruising Routes,* 62–66, 71, 84, 89–90.

22. Aimé Humbert, "A European Sojourn in Japan," in Bates, ed., *Illustrated Travels,* 190; Forbes, *Native Americans of California and Nevada,* 29.

23. Robinson, *Stones of Aran,* 28–29, 42–43, 53–54, 179–80, 262–63.

24. Hardiman, *History of . . . Galway,* 2, 4, 6n, 34, 70; O'Sullivan, *Old Galway,* 38, 46; Westropp, "Early Italian Maps," 373, 376; Quinn, *Atlantean,* 19, 39.

25. Westropp, "Early Italian Maps," 385, 399–400, XXXI, Section C, maps.

26. Postcard of "St. Nicholas' Collegiate Church," and "Welcome To: St. Nicholas Collegiate Church, Galway." No date for either, but acquired in 1989.

27. Westropp, "Brasil and the Legendary Islands," 248.

28. O'Sullivan, *Old Galway,* 46n; Morison, *Admiral,* 1:190–92, 197–99; Gould y Quincy, "Nueva Lista," 85 (1924) to 92 (1928), especially 85 (1), 34–39, and (2), 145–59, as cited in Morison above.

29. Colón, *Textos y Documentos,* 230–34.

30. Simmons et al., "Diego Blood Group," 406–7. It should be noted that some scholars read this as a "Mongoloid" blood marker, but that interpretation is questionable given the actual distribution and character of the antigen; for example, see Mourant et al., *Distribution of Human Blood Groups,* 604–14; and Tills et al., *Distribution of the Human Blood Group,* 142–44.

31. Robinson, *Stones of Aran,* many sections; Quinn, *Atlantean,* 18, 64, 147; Jacobs, "Coos Narrative," 45–51.

Chapter 3: Seagoing Americans

1. See Boxer, *Portuguese Seaborne Empire,* and Boxer, *Race Relations.*

2. Smith, "Heir to Columbus," 14, and Thompson, *Maya History and Religion,* 7, 127, 158.

3. Las Casas, *Historia,* 67; and Humboldt, *Views of Nature,* 123.

4. Ferdinand Hernando Colón, *Life of the Admiral,* 231–32; Morison, *Journals,* 327.

5. Morison, *Journals,* 236; Morison, *Admiral,* 2:273n.

6. Colón to Santangel, in Harrise, *Christophe Colomb,* 426–28; also in Jane, *Voyages,* 261–62. See also Bernaldez, *Memorias del Reinado,* 275; and Morison, *Journals,* 184.

7. Columbus, *Diario,* 69, Jane, *Voyages,* 150.

8. Columbus, *Diario,* 189, 193.

9. *Ibid.,* 231, 237, 291; Jane, *Voyages,* 276; Las Casas, *Historia,* 2:12.

10. Las Casas, *Historia,* 2:19; Jane, *Voyages,* 213; Columbus, *Diario,* 267, 341.

11. Columbus, *Diario,* 187, 193.

12. Ibid., 115; Juan Carlos Orihuela and Martha Cajias, personal interview, March and July 1993. "Huara" seems to be the term used for mat-sails, rather than *vela.*

13. Las Casas, *Historia,* 1:352–53.

14. Colón, *Life of the Admiral,* 135, 231–32; Columbus, *Diario,* 259, 267. Doran et al., "A 7,290 Year Old Bottle Gourd," 354, 356.

15. Morison, *Journals,* 180, 185; Harrisse, *Christophe Colomb,* 431; Columbus, *Diario,* 315, 331, 335, 339, 341; Colón, *Life of the Admiral,* 88; Las Casas, *Historia,* 1:307–8.

16. Colón, *Life of the Admiral,* 111.

17. Bernaldez, *Memorias,* in Jane, *Voyages,* 316, 320.

18. Las Casas, *Historia,* 1:325.

19. Colón, *Life of the Admiral,* 111–12, 118–19, 170. Colón gave the Haitians "metal basins" in 1493, but these were perhaps of a cheap metal and not of iron.

20. Ibid., 169–73.

21. Ibid., 172. See also Las Casas, *Historia,* 1:409.

22. Colón, *Life of the Admiral,* 171; Morison, *Admiral,* 2:159.

23. Bernaldez, *Memorias,* in Jane, *Voyages,* 313.

24. Columbus, *Diario,* 190, 115, 119; Jane, *Voyages,* 164.

25. Morison, *Journals,* 67; Jane, *Voyages,* 150.

26. Mártir de Angleria, *Decadas,* 2:589–91.

27. López de Gomara, *Historia General . . . y vida de Hernan Cortes,* 59–60.

28. Ballard, *Yuchi Green Corn,* 54; Loven, *Origins,* 66–67. Crane, "An Historical Note," 332; Crane, *Southern Frontier,* 12, 13.

29. Columbus, *Diario,* 315; Jane, *Voyages,* 164, 229; Morison, *Journals,* 222; Loven, *Origins,* 62–63.

30. Jane, *Voyages,* 287; Las Casas, *Historia,* 2:35, 352; Morison, *Admiral,* 2:279; Colón, *Life of the Admiral,* 113.

31. Colón, *Life of the Admiral,* 88, 112–13, 154–55, 231–32, 237; Columbus, *Diario,* 331; Morison; *Admiral,* 155, 265, 273n, 335, 342; Jane, *Voyages,* 318. The "Island Caribs," Garifuna or Karifuna and other names, actually speak an Arawak language. See Hulme and Whitehead, *Wild Majesty,* for a discussion of Carib culture over the centuries, and Hulme, *Colonial Encounters,* especially 13–87.

32. Columbus, *Diario,* 121; Loven, *Origins,* 58–60.

33. Bernal Díaz del Castillo, *Historia Verdadera,* 62; Wagner, *Discovery of New Spain,* 67, 81, 89, 96–97; Loven, *Origins,* 58–59.

34. Loven, *Origins,* 468–73, 567–68, 595, 656.

35. Mártir de Angelería, *Decadas,* 2:589–90.

36. Loven, *Origins,* 417, 419.

37. Benzoni, *Historia,* xi; Doctor Layfield, "Description of Dominica," in Purchas, ed., *Purchas His Pilgrimes,* 16:52.

38. Charles Leigh, "Voyage to Guiana," in Purchas, *Purchas His Pilgrimes,* 16:312, 320–21.

39. John Stoneman, "The Voyage of M. Henry Challons," in Purchas, *Purchas His Pilgrimage,* 19:284–85.

40. Vázquez de Espinosa, *Compendium and Description,* 66.

41. Fernandez de Oviedo, *De la Natural Historia,* 157–58. William H. Sears, "Seaborne Contacts Between Early Cultures in Lower Southeastern United States and Middle Through South America," in Benson, ed., *The Sea,* 2.

42. Charles de Rochefort, *History of the Caribby-Islands,* 306, 313, 319, 320–21, 324.

43. Jean Baptiste DuTertre, as cited in McKusick, "Aboriginal Canoes," 6; Vázquez de Espinosa, *Compendium and Description,* 64–72.

44. Johannes Wilbert, "Navigators of the Winter Sun," in Benson, *The Sea,* 15, 17–19, 21, 27, 39.

45. Wagner, *Discovery of New Spain,* 62–63, 75, 83, 85, 97.

46. López de Gómara, *Historia de la Conquista de Mexicos,* 25.

47. Díaz del Castillo, *Historia Verdadera,* 45–46, 57, 102.

48. Thompson, "Canoes and Navigation," 71.

49. Thompson, "Canoes and Navigation," 69, 72–74. Schele and Freidel, *Forest of Kings,* 98, 100, 351, 434n.

50. Thompson, *Maya History,* 128, 131, 157; Scholes and Roys, *Maya Chontal,* 29; Arthur G. Miller, "The Maya and the Sea," in Benson, *The Sea,* 99. For archaeology of coastal sites in Belize, see McKillop, *In Search of Maya Sea Traders.*

51. Jeremy A. Sabloff, "Old Myths, New Myths," in Benson, *The Sea,* 72, 74–77, 83; Thompson, *Maya History,* 11, 13–14, 44–46, 90–91, 128–30, 152; Miller, "Maya and the Sea," in Benson, *The Sea,* 73; Scholes and Roys, *Maya Chontal,* 3–4, 29–34, 82–83, 86, 244.

52. Miller, "Maya and the Sea," in Benson, *The Sea,* 98–99, 100–107, 127, 129–30; Thompson, *Maya History,* 15, 131, 189; Scholes and Roys, *Maya Chontal,* 2.

53. Sabloff, "Old Myths, New Myths," in Benson, *The Sea,* 76–77; Thompson, *Maya History,* 4, 91, 129.

54. Thompson, *Maya History,* 128, 131, 157; Scholes and Roys, *Maya Chontal,* 29.

55. Ciudad Real and de San Juan, *Relación Breve,* 375–76; Thompson, "Canoes and Navigation," 72; Thompson, *Maya History,* 134.

56. Edwards, "Possibilities of Pre-Columbian," 3–10; Friederici, *Schiffahrt,* 73–74; Benzoni, *Historia,* 55–56.

57. Fernández de Oviedo, *De la Natural Historia,* 158.

58. Friederici, *Schiffahrt,* 75–76; McKusick, "Aboriginal Canoes"; John Stoneman, "The Voyage of Henry Challons," in *Purchas His Pilgrimes,* 19:284–93; Hulme and Whitehead, *Wild Majesty,* 70.

59. Rochefort, *History of the Carriby-Islands,* 319–20.

60. Morales Padrón, *Canarias,* 45.

61. Payne, *History of the New World,* 2:394n; Nelson, "Geography of the Balsa," 159–60, 172; Barrère, *Nouvelle Relation,* 130–35.

62. Saco, *Historia de la Esclavitud de los Indios,* 169–70.

63. Court de Gebelin, *Monde Primitif,* 534.

64. Lawson, *History of North Carolina,* 7.

65. Murphy, *Voyage of Verrazano,* 175, 180; Hoffman, *Cabot to Cartier,* 108, 110; Lindeström, *Geographica Americae,* 237–38.

66. Williams, *Key Into the Language of America,* 108–11. Beck, *American Indian*

as a Sea-Fighter, 12, 30, 49, has information on the use of sails in the New England area.

67. E. Winslow, "Good News from New England," in *Purchas His Pilgrimes,* 19:392; Beck, *American Indian,* 14, 16–17.

68. Sturtevant, "Significance of Ethnological Similarities," 27.

69. Pigafetta, *Primer Viaje,* 41; Staden, *Vera Historia,* 132.

70. Leite, ed., *Monumenta Brasiliae,* 4:131–32, 244.

71. Loven, *Origins,* 63.

72. "Occurrents in Newfoundland," in *Purchas His Pilgrimes,* 19:422–23; see also "John Guy's Narrative," in Howley, *The Beothuks,* 17; and Marshall, *Beothuk Bark Canoes,* 11, 14, 20.

73. Richard Whitbourne, in *Purchas His Pilgrimes,* 19:438, and Marshall, *Beothuk Bark Canoes,* 14.

74. Eusebius, *Chronicon,* folio 174–75; Murphy, *Voyage of Verrazano,* 62; Biard, *Relation de la Nouvelle France,* 39; "Relatione di Giovanni Verrazano," in Ramusio, *Navigationi et Viaggi,* 3:422.

75. Bembo, "Rerum Venetarum Historiae" or "Istoria Veniziana," in *Opere del Cardinale,* 1:188.

76. Rose et al., *Cambridge History,* 6:18; and "The First Americans in Europe," *Atlantic Monthly,* July 1892, 70:417, 140.

77. Greenman, "The Upper Palaeolithic and the New World," 411–18, 53, 87.

78. See Forbes, "The Urban Tradition among Native Americans," in Lobo and Peters, *American Indians and the Urban Experience,* 5–25, and Brain, "The Great Mound Robbery," 18–25.

79. Sears, "Seaborne Contacts," in Benson, *The Sea,* 4, 6, 8, 11, 12, 14; Sabloff, "Old Myths, New Myths," in Benson, *The Sea,* 82, 93.

80. Girard, *Esotericism of the Popul Vuh,* 97–98, 103, 109–10.

81. Allison C. Paulsen, "Patterns of Maritime Trade between South Coastal Ecuador and Western Mesoamerica, 1500 BC–AD 100," in Benson, *The Sea,* 143, 152–53, 155.

82. Vázquez de Espinosa, *Compendium,* sections 1000, 1008, 1188, 1218, 1384, 1420, 1435, 1541, 1561, 1752, 1775, 1791.

83. Nelson, "Geography of the Balsa," 157ff.

84. Ibid., 169–71.

85. Fox Tree, "How Native People . . . Sailing Ships Discovered Europe and Other Lands Before 1492," photocopied brochure, ca. 1990.

Chapter 4: Ancient Travelers and Migrations

1. Dillehay, *Settlement of the Americas,* has much information on this topic. Also see Wright, "First Americans," 53–54. For examples of some earlier ideas about

American antiquity see, for example, Nadaillac, *Prehistoric America,* especially 42–45. Also see Müller, *America,* 222–23; and Cremo and Thompson, *Forbidden Archaeology,* xxviii, 18, 20, 36, 197ff., 339, 396–97, 439ff., 970ff.

2. But see Dillehay, *Settlement,* 11–12, 269, for excellent discussion of these issues; also Müller, *America,* 170–71, 186, 198, 201, 214, 227–28.

3. Forbes, *Atlas,* for maps of movements; Forbes et al., eds., *Handbook of Native American Studies,* 19ff., and 27–33, 40, 42, 49–52, 54ff.

4. Forbes, *Apache, Navaho, and Spaniard* (1994), vii–xxiii; Forbes, *Apache, Navaho, and Spaniard* (1960), xx–xxi.

5. Imakpik (the first "k" as in Scottish "loch") is the Yupik Eskimo name for the sea separating Alaska from Siberia.

6. Dillehay, *Settlement,* 244, 282, for brief discussions of "back migrations"; Müller, *America,* 25–26, 220–21; Menon, "More than a Pointy Rock," 10.

7. Dillehay, *Settlement,* 61; Metzer, "Pleistocene Peopling," 157–61; Goodman, *American Genesis,* 55.

8. "ʙᴘ" means "before the present." Discussion of early projectile points occurs in Dillehay, *Settlement,* 5–6; see also Wright, "First Americans," 53–54, and Mewhinney, *Manual,* 18–23, 87–93.

9. Kunzig, "Erectus Afloat," 80; d'Agnese, "Not Out of Africa," 54–56; Cremo and Thompson, *Forbidden Archaeology,* xxxiv; Müller, *America,* 175–78; Thompson, *To the American Indian,* 83; Chen et al., "Antiquity of Homo Sapiens," 55–56; Klein, "Problem of Modern Human Origins," in Nitecki, *Origins;* Stringer, "Emergence of Modern Humans," 98–104; Wilson and Cann, "Recent African Genesis," 68–73, and Thorne and Wolpoff, "Multiregional Evolution," 76–83; and Stone, "Testing New Theory," 63. Ibarra Grosso, in *Los Hombres Barbados,* 16–17, believes that Neandertals reached America.

10. Cremo and Thompson, *Forbidden Archaeology,* 209, 287, 291ff., 311–12, 353ff., 365–67, 413, 826–28; Dillehay, *Settlement,* xix, 5–6, 32, 215–16, 235–36, 269; Shutler Jr., ed., *Early Man,* many sections but especially 11, 43–45, 191–95; Dixon, *Quest for the Origins,* 4–7, 116–33; Holden, "Tooling Around," 1268; Waters et al., "Diring Yuriakh," 1281–83; West, "Migrations," 158–66; Greenberg et al., "Settlement of the Americas," 477ff.; Greenberg, "A *CA* Book Review" of *Language in the Americas,*" 647ff.; Mithun, "Studies of North American Indian Languages," 309–25; Patterson, *America's Past,* 15–25. Crawford, *Origins of Native Americans,* adds an analysis of genetic data to the question of American origins. See 22–30 especially.

11. Dillehay, *Settlement,* discusses some of these early, disputed sites, but not all. See xix, 10–12, 190–94, 242–45; Cremo and Thompson, *Forbidden Archaeology,* xxx, 354–56.

12. There are those who believe that Homo Erectus was also "sapiens" and that modern humans left Africa perhaps two million years ago. See d'Agnese, "Not Out of Africa," 54–56; Shutler Jr., *Early Man,* 43–44.

13. Müller, *America,* 17–23, 25–27; Holden, "Tooling Around," 1268; Waters et al., "Diring Yuriakh," 1281–83; Gjessing, "Circumpolar Stone Age," 11, 64–66, 70.

14. Dillehay, *Settlement,* 56, 61, 65–67, 70. See Kurt Fladmark, "Times and Places," in Shutler Jr., *Early Man,* 13ff., for discussion of Arctic climates; Goodman, *American Genesis,* 50–51, 59–62.

15. Dillehay, *Settlement,* 65, 230; also d'Agnese, "Not Out of Africa," 54–56.

16. Dillehay, *Settlement,* 228, 236, 242–43, 286; Thor Heyerdahl, "Feasible Ocean Routes to and from the Americas in Pre-Columbian Times," 484–88; Wright, "First Americans," is especially guilty of fantastic statements about American physical types. See also Goodman, *American Genesis,* 175, 178. Ibarra Grosso, *Los Hombres Barbados,* provides evidence of beardedness from many American nations, as well as other divergent features.

17. Forbes, *The Indian in America's Past,* 4–5; Forbes, *Native Americans of California and Nevada,* 11; Forbes, *Afro-Americans in the Far West,* 5–7. Blood Type A of the ABO series is found in America, especially in North America. There is some evidence that groups A and B may have once existed in South America. See Llop and Rothhammer, "A Note on the Presence of Blood Groups A and B," 107–11. In the nineteenth century Nadaillac stated: "I do not attach as much importance as do some . . . to differences between bones, especially the bones of skulls. Too often we find beneath the same mound . . . brachycephalic and dolichocephalic skulls, skulls of the Caucasian, and skulls of almost Negroid types. All varieties from extreme longheads to rounded or nearly square heads have been found among undoubted Eskimo crania." Nadaillac, *Prehistoric America,* 194–95; Dillehay, *Settlement,* 235–36.

18. Dillehay, *Settlement,* 5, 68, 243; Wright, "First Americans," 61–62; Greenman, "Upper Paleolithic," 61–66; Müller, *America,* 33, 36–37, 182–85, 217, 224–26.

19. Wright, "First Americans," 54ff.; MacDonald, "Eastern North America," in Shutler Jr., *Early Man,* 105; Gjessing, "Circumpolar Stone Age," 69; Stuart, *Life in the Ice Age,* 56; Fernández-Armesto, *Before Columbus,* 166; Cornell, *World Cruising Routes,* 62–64, 71–84, 89–90; Mewhinney, *Manual,* 18–23.

20. Reinaga, *América India* 25–28, 34–38; Cremo and Thompson, *Forbidden Archaeology,* xxviii, 311–12.

21. d'Arbois de Jubainville, *Les Premiers Habitants* (1877), 11–17; d'Arbois de Jubainville, *Les Premiers Habitants* (1889), 16–47; De Roo, *History of America,* 162–67.

22. Beddoe, *Races of Great Britain,* 9–10, 13.

23. Goodman, *American Genesis,* 18–20, 66–67, 114–15, 161–66.

24. Ibid., 121–22, 127, 154.

25. Müller, *America,* 27, 33, 36–37, 182–85, 217, 222–23, 224–26; Fladmark, "Times and Places," in Shutler Jr., *Early Man,* 32–33.

26. Müller, *America,* 218–25; Collins, "The Arctic and Subarctic," in Jennings and Norbeck, eds., *Prehistoric Man,* 88–89.

27. Chen et al., "Antiquity of Homo Sapiens," 55–56.

28. "Ohio Artifacts," 14A; Wright, "First Americans," 57, 62; Dillehay, *Settlement,* 243.

29. See Forbes, *Africans and Native Americans,* especially early chapters.

30. Cremo and Thompson, *Forbidden Archaeology,* 199; Wright, "First Americans," 60; and Black, "Geology and Ancient Aleuts," 126. See Pennick, *Lost Lands,* for a discussion of changing coastlines, especially in Britain.

31. Kevin P. Smith to Jack D. Forbes, February 6, 2003 (e-mail letter); "Artifact in Iceland," 6–7; Black, "Geology and Ancient Aleuts," 126, 134; Wright, "First Americans," 60.

32. "Archaeologists Confirm Antiquity," 15B.

33. Tuck and McGhee, "Arctic Cultures in the Strait," 80, 89, 91; Fitzhugh, "A Maritime Archaic Sequence," 117, 133, 137.

34. Piggott, *Ancient Europe,* 30, 66n; Stuart, *Life in the Ice Age,* 50–57; Darvill, *Prehistoric Britain,* 49, 121; Ireland, *Ireland and the Irish,* 7–9.

35. MacLeish, *Gulf Stream,* 216–17.

36. Stuart, *Life in the Ice Age,* 8–9, 11.

37. Letter of José Carlos Valle Perez, Director, Museo de Pontevedra, to Jack D. Forbes, December 4, 1991; Fabregas Valcarce, "Dos Objetos," 83–90.

38. See chapter 2; also Scott, "Drift Timber," 151–52; Letter from Donald Moore to Jack D. Forbes, July 1, 1993, relative to American origin organic matter washed up in Cardigan Bay, Wales.

39. Evans, *Personality of Ireland,* 44–45, 115.

40. Johanna Nichols, "The First Four Discoveries of America: Linguistic Evidence," manuscript, "The First Americans, circa 20,000 BC," 24.

41. Among recent sources on the Diego system are Tills et al., *Distribution of the Human Blood Groups,* 142–44; Mourant et al., *Distribution of the Human Blood Groups,* 21, 604–14; Edwards-Moulds and Alperin, "Studies of the Diego Blood Group," *Transfusion* 26:3 (1986): 234–36; Bruce et al., "Band 3 Memphis Variant II," *Journal of Biological Chemistry* 269:23 (June 10, 1994): 16155–58 (a very technical but important article relating to a mutation that precedes the presence of the Diego antigen); Daniels, *Human Blood Groups,* 452–58; and Crawford, *Origins of Native Americans,* 103–4.

42. Letter of I. F. Young, Brisbane, Australia, to Jack D. Forbes, October 16, 1991.

43. See Heyerdahl, *Early Man,* 214–36.

44. Forbes, "Urban Tradition among Native Americans," in Lobo and Peters, *American Indians;* 5–25; Dillehay, *Settlement,* 289. Menon, "The Earthmovers," 30.

45. Timreck, editor and director, *The Mystery of the Lost Red Paint People* (Bullfrog

Films), with W. N. Goetzmann, 1987; Fitzhugh and Allen, "Secrets of the Lost Red Paint People," 71, 84.

46. Gjessing, "Circumpolar Stone Age," 64–65.

47. Ibid., 18, 65.

48. Quote from Tuck and McGhee, "Archaic Cultures," 80; Heizer, *Aboriginal Whaling,* 24, 93–96, 108, 142; Collins, "The Arctic and Subarctic," in Jennings and Norbeck, *Prehistoric Man,* 94, 96, 98, 100–101.

49. Piggott, *Ancient Europe,* 64.

50. Tuck and McGhee, "Archaic Cultures," 80, 89, 91; Fitzhugh, "Maritime Archaic Sequence," 133, 137; Wright, "First Americans," 61; Bradstreet and Davis, "Mid-Post-Glacial," 18–19; Tuck, "Northeastern Maritime Continuum," 140–41; "The First Americans," *Discover* 22:1 (January 2001): 52. See also Pennick, *Lost Lands,* for data on disappearing coastlines.

51. Snow, "The Passadumkeag Sequence," 58; Bourque, "Comments on the Late Archaic," 35, 41, 43.

52. Bourque, "Comments on the Late Archaic," 43.

53. Sanger, "Culture Change," 69–70, 72; Bradstreet and Davis, "Mid-Post-Glacial," 19; Tuck, "Northeastern Maritime Continuum," 142–45. Slightly different dates are in Tickell, "Climate and History," 27–29; Krishnamurthy et al., "Late Glacial Climate Record," 1565.

54. Tuck, "Northeastern Maritime Continuum," 142–43.

55. See Seán McGrail, "Pilotage and Navigation in the Times of St. Brendan," 25–27; David B. Quinn, "Atlantic Islands," 77, 86–87; Claude Evans, "Early Breton Voyages to Canada," 159, all in Ireland and Sheehy, eds., *Atlantic Visions;* and Ireland, *Ireland and the Irish,* 40; Westropp, "Brasil and the Legendary Islands," 223–40.

Chapter 5: From Iberia to the Baltic

1. See Forbes, *Columbus and Other Cannibals;* Beck et al., *Sacred Ways of Knowledge,* 102ff.; Forbes, "Nature and Culture," 103–24; Forbes, "Indigenous Americans," 283–300; Linderman, ed., *Pretty Shield,* 120–21; Grinnell, ed. *Pawnee Hero Stories,* 116–18.

2. Penhallwick, *Turtles off Cornwall,* 15.

3. Nelson, "Models for the Moment," 115; Letter of R. D. Penhallwick to Jack D. Forbes, June 7, 1993. See also Nelson, "Exotic Drift Fruits and Seeds," 147–86, for excellent coverage of all drift plants.

4. Penhallwick, *Turtles,* 23, 31–35, 41.

5. Ibid., 52–53, 61, 73–74.

6. "Magnetic Field Guides Turtles' Lives," *USA Today,* October 15, 2001, 8D.

7. Quotes from Hristov and Genovés, "Mesoamerican Evidence," 207–12; Wuthenau, *Terracotta Pottery,* 49ff., 51; Coe, *Lords of the Underworld,* 65; Gordon, *Before Columbus,* 179–87.

8. Posnansky, *Precursores de Colón,* 1–16; see also Posnansky, *Las Americas;* Cordry, *Mexican Masks,* 8–9, 34, 38; masks were also used in the Andean region, for mummy bundles and tombs. See Kauffmann-Doig, *Ancestors of the Incas,* 120–21.

9. Photograph by Paule Mexel Bertrand Desollier, N. 2289, published by Réunion des musées natiónaux, 1993 (postcard); Stephen C. Jett, "Nicotine and Cocaine in Egyptian Mummies and THC in Peruvian Mummies: A Review of the Evidence and of Scholarly Reaction," in Jett, *Precolumbiana.* The Americans might have been bringing hashish or marijuana back from the Mediterranean, while trading tobacco and cocaine to Egypt, since Jett claims that marijuana-type residues have been found in Peruvian mummies. See also Heaviside, *American Antiquities,* 7–12.

10. "Da Pompei, casa VII, 2, 6, Napoli MNN (Museo Nazionali di Napoli) 9058, Busti-ritratto due coniugi, probablimente *Terentius Neo* e la moglie. I sec. d.C," and Napoli MNN 10010, both in Cantarella, *Pompei,* 26, 162–63. Incidentally, an Irish visitor to the Creek Nation in 1828 witnessed a ball game of the La Crosse type. His description led an Irish writer to assert that the Irish game of "coman" was related to La Crosse. See "The Game of Coman," 95–96.

11. Notes of a visit to the Louvre, April 27, 1994, by the author. The bronze was earlier numbered "626."

12. "Réunion du 16. Mars 1859," 83–85; Henri Adrien Prevost de Longpérier, "Notice des Bronzes Antiques exposés," 143, as cited in Schiern, "*Une Enigme Ethnographique,*" 263–64. See also Gaffarel, *Histoire,* 171–72. Much of the same material is in Gaffarel's *Étude sur les Rapports.*

13. Gaffarel, *Histoire,* 172; De Ceuleneer, "Type d'Indien," as cited by Gaffarel, 172.

14. L. Gallois, Review of Paul Gaffarel's *Histoire,* 158; Ashe et al., *Quest for America,* 92; Winsor, ed., *Narrative and Critical History,* 1:26n.

15. Mela, *Works,* 77; Schiern, "Une Enigme Ethnographique," 246–47, 247n, 255; Ashe et al., *Quest for America,* 91n; Gaffarel, *Histoire,* 167–68, 170–71. For the Suevi as the "wandering people," see Muirhead, "Saxony," *Werner Encyclopedia,* 21:366–67; Todd, *Northern Barbarians,* 8–9, 11, 16, 22, 33–34.

16. Pliny, *Natural History,* 1:304–5; Schiern, "Une Enigme Ethnographique," 247, 249n; Gaffarel, *Histoire,* 168n. See also De Roo, *History,* 167–69, 600.

17. Ispizúa, *Historia . . . en las Edades,* 107–8, 150–51; Strabo, *Geography,* vol. 1, maps, v, xiii, xxv.

18. López de Gómara, *Historia General* (1979), 20–21.

19. Mela, *Works,* 74; Glob, *The Bog People,* 127, 141.

20. See chapter 1.

21. Aeneas Sylvius, *Historia Rerum,* 4; Aeneas Sylvius, *Asiae Europae,* 5; Mitchell, *The Laurels and the Tiara,* 137, 138n, 292; Aeneas Sylvius, *Opera Geographica,* 8–9; see also Ugurgieri della Beardenga, *Pio II Piccolomini.*

22. Sylvius, *Historia Rerum,* 4; Schiern, "Une Enigme Ethnographique," 285.

23. López de Gómara, *Historia General,* 21; Schiern, "Une Enigme Ethnographique," 288.

24. Gaffarel, *Histoire,* 170–71; Cornille Wytfliet, *Descriptionis Ptolemaicae augmentum,* as quoted in Gaffarel, *Histoire,* 171, 171n.

25. Wytfliet, *Histoire Universelle,* 125–26. Harald E. L. Prins does not believe that Americans could have crossed the Atlantic on their own. He conjectures that the Lubeck arrivals were carried on a Viking vessel, a theory that contradicts the language of the sources. See Prins, 177.

26. Galvano, *Discoveries,* 18.

27. W. R. Morfill, "Slavs," *Werner Encyclopedia,* 22:154–55; "Lubeck," in *Werner Encyclopedia,* 15:33–34; Hugh A. Webster, "Lapland," in *Werner Encyclopedia,* 14:307; Muirhead, "Saxony," in *Werner Encyclopedia,* 21:366–68; Burl, *Stonehenge People,* 130, 132–33, 155–56, 206–7, 210–19.

28. Gaffarel, *Histoire,* 11, 167–68, 170–71.

29. d'Ailly, *Ymago Mundi,* 1:232–33, 248–49; Winsor, *Narrative and Critical History,* 2:7, 30–32.

30. d'Ailly, *Ymago Mundi,* 1:260–63; Gaffarel, *Histoire,* 197–98.

31. d'Ailly, *Ymago Mundi,* 2:426–27.

32. Ibid., 3:742–43.

33. Ibid., 743–44.

34. Merrien, *Lonely Voyagers,* 25; Merrien, *Navigateurs Solitaires,* 37.

35. Merrien, *Christopher Columbus,* 60; and Merrien, *Christophe Colomb,* 80. Merrien's birth name was René-Marie A. M. de la Poix de Fréminville. He was born in 1905 and died in 1972 after a very active life as a yachtsman, historian, and student of all things pertaining to the sea. I have attempted to track down his notes and sources in the Bibliotèque Nationale without much success.

36. Pitt Rivers Museum accession lists; *Gloucester Journal,* May 19, 1883, vol. 6, 13, 15, 52 [Newspaper Cuttings Index and file, Gloucester City Library].

37. John Rhodes to Jack Forbes, August 30, 1991; McShane to Jack D. Forbes, November 1, 1991.

38. J. F. Rhodes to B. E. B. Fagg, December 5, 1967 (copy); B. Blackwood to J. F. Rhodes, December 18, 1967 (copy); J. F. Rhodes to B. E. B. Fagg, June 6, 1968 (copy); B. Blackwood to J. F. Rhodes, June 18, 1968 (copy).

39. City of Gloucester, Museums, Annual Report to the City Council, April 1, 1951 to March 31, 1952, 6–7; *Gloucester Journal,* July 7, 1951, v. 15, 314, Cuttings File, Gloucester Library.

40. "Mediaeval Pottery from Bull Lane, Gloucester," a copy of a single-sheet typed manuscript with one written correction, supplied by D. M. Rennie to Jack Forbes, October 25, 1993, as an enclosure to a letter.

41. D. M. Rennie to Jack Forbes, October 25, 1993.

42. Jack Forbes, notes of interview with D. M. Rennie, May 6, 1994, Oxford, England.

43. Interview with John F. Rhodes, Gloucester, May 1993; Rhodes to Flagg, December 5, 1967.

44. Interview with Rhodes; Cole, *Rental,* 21, 23; T. G. Hassall to Jack Forbes, August 6, 1992; *Cheltenham Examiner,* November 1861, v. 1, 263–65; *Gloucester Journal,* January 1, 1951, v. 15, 360; *Gloucester Journal,* August 28, 1948, v. 14, 496. Note that all newspaper pages and volumes refer to a "Newspaper Cuttings Index" and collection at the Gloucester City Library.

45. Linda Mowat to Jack Forbes, July 19, 1993. Four clay heads, apparently of Navajo origin, also resemble the Mexican masks of Gloucester. See Jett, "Ye'iis Lying Down," 138–49.

46. Purchas, *Purchas His Pilgrimes,* 16:106–7. See also the introduction to Hulme and Sherman, *"The Tempest,"* 8.

47. Cordry, *Mexican Masks,* 3, 86, 92, 92n; Lechuga and Sayer, *Mask Arts,* 7–8, 14–15.

48. The Gloucester City Museum has been the recipient of other American objects. The Hoskold Collection of Native slate heads from Catamarca, Argentina, was donated to the Cotteswold Naturalist's Field Club in 1892. Later it came to the Gloucester City Museum (1920s) and probably was passed on to the Pitt Rivers in the 1950s. *Proceedings of the Cotteswold Naturalist's Field Club,* 11:1895, 309.

49. Las Casas, *Historia de las Indias,* 1:67. See also Hernando Colón, *Vida del Almirante,* 51.

50. Lawson, *History of North Carolina,* 7.

51. Nicholson, *Topiltzin Quetzalcoatl,* 53:159–64; Bancroft, *Native Races,* 3:450–54; 5:159–65.

52. Nicholson, *Topiltzin Quetzalcoatl,* 173, 177; Tedlock, *Popol Vuh,* 54, 177, 199, 203–4. For an excellent discussion of the history of the Tula (Tollan) and its significance, see Brotherston, *Book of the Fourth World,* 156ff.

53. Beckwith, *Myths and Hunting Stories,* 4–5, 10, 12. See also Parks et al., *Earth Lodge Tales,* for shorter versions of Mandan stories.

54. López de Gómara, *Historia General,* 48–49; Morison, *Admiral,* 2:193–218; Crosby Jr., "The Early History of Syphilis," 218–27.

55. Mártir de Anglería, *Opus Epistolarum,* Epistle 68, 54; also Mártir de Anglería, *Opera,* Epistle 67, 327.

56. Haeser, *Lehrbuch*, 213–318; "The Syphilis Enigma," film produced by Christopher Salt and Georgiana Pye, Granada Productions, United Kingdom, and WNET, Boston, 2001. Broadcast by PBS in the United States.

Chapter 6: The Inuit Route to Europe

1. Gert Nooter, *Old Kayaks*, 6–7, 64–69.

2. See chapter 4.

3. Inuit visitors to Europe demonstrated such feats. See Brand, *Brief Description*, 51; Wallace, *Description*, 28; Honour, *New Golden Land*, 16; Nooter, *Old Kayaks*, 5; Egede, *Description*, xliii–xliv.

4. Camden, *Brittania* (1806), 2:156; Childrey, *Britannia Baconia*, 102.

5. Parival, *Las Délices*, 130; Baring-Gould, *Curious Myths*, 509; Bassett, *Legends and Superstitions*, 189.

6. Pontoppidan, *Natural History*, 2:186, 186n, 189–91.

7. Letter of H. Tr— to Sir Thomas Chaloner, Cottonian manuscript Julius F. VI. f431 (now ff453–462), British Library, London, translated by Winfried Schleiner and Laetitia Yaendal for the author; letter of David Griffiths, History Librarian, University of York, September 6, 1991; Graves, *History of Cleveland*, 34n, 369–70, 369n; Childrey, *Britannia Baconia*, 160; Young, *History* (1817), 2:485, 798n; Camden, *Britannia* (1594), 556; Camden, *Britannia* (1616), 586; Camden, *Britannia* (1806), 251; Stephen and Lee, eds., *Dictionary of National Biography*, 3:729–36; 9:456.

8. Evans and Hawkes, "An Eskimo Harpoon-head," 127–32.

9. Letter of Charles Hunt to David Clarke (copy), August 15, 1985; Letter of D. V. Clarke to Charles Hunt, August 19, 1985; Letter of Andrew Foxxon to Charles Hunt, August 29, 1985; Letter of Charles Hunt to Andrew Foxxon, September 10, 1985; Letter of Trevor Cowie to Jack D. Forbes, August 16, 1991; Letter of Charles Hunt to Jack Forbes, August 17, 1992; e-mail of Allen P. McCartney to Jack Forbes, December 20, 2002; Don E. Dumond to Jack Forbes, December 9, 2002; *Eskimo Kayaks in Aberdeen* (pamphlet prepared by Marischal Museum, University of Aberdeen, Scotland), 3–4; James Dalgarno, "Donations to the Museum and Library," 407.

10. Letter of Guðmundur Ólafsson, National Museum of Iceland, to Jack Forbes, November 28, 1991; Letter of Guðrun Sveinbjarnardóttir to Jack Forbes, October 30, 1991; Letter of Sveinbjorn Rafnsson, University of Iceland, to Jack Forbes, August 26, 1991; Christian Keller, Universitet i Oslo, to Jack Forbes, July 31, 1991; and Letter of Simún V. Arge, Føroya Fornminnissavn (Faeroe Museum), to Jack Forbes, September 12, 1991.

11. Christian Keller to Jack Forbes, July 31, 1991.

12. McGovern, "The Lost Norse Colony of Greenland," 16; and McGhee,

"Norse and Eskimos in Arctic Canada," 42, 45–49, both in Guralnick, ed., *Vikings in the West;* Svitil, "Greenland Viking Mystery," 29; Ingstad, *Westward to Vinland,* translated by Erik J. Friis, 40, 93.

13. Park, "The Dorset-Thule Succession," 210, 213.

14. Fridtjof Nansen, *In Northern Mists,* 2:80.

15. Meldgaard, "Prehistoric Cultures," 33.

16. Dumond, *Eskimos and Aleuts,* 141.

17. Pontoppidan, *Natural History,* 2:186.

18. Heizer, "Aboriginal Whaling," 34, 40, 93–96, 108, 142; Jenkins, *History of the Whale Fisheries,* 59–63; Sanderson, *Follow the Whale,* 133; Hacquebord and de Bok, *Spitsbergen,* 14.

19. Heizer, "Aboriginal Whaling," 24, 40, 95–96; Nansen, *In Northern Mists,* 2:213–15; Dumond, *Eskimos and Aleuts,* 63, 90, 101, 108, 118.

20. Lyschander, *Gronlandske Chronica* 1, 7; Peyrère, *Relation du Groenland,* 10; Peyrère, "Histoire du Groenland," 184; Keller, "The Eastern Settlement Reconsidered" (doctoral dissertation, University of Oslo, 1989), 66.

21. Pontanus, *Rerum Danicarium,* 96–98.

22. Sturlason, *Heimskringla,* 192; Bury, ed., *Cambridge Medieval History,* 3:7, 311–12, 315–20; Jones, *Norse Atlantic Saga,* 186–87; Morison, *European Discovery,* 56; Guralnick, *Vikings in the West,* 7; Forbes, *Africans and Native Americans,* 80.

23. Nelson Annandale, *The Faeroes and Iceland,* 8–11, 161–64; Nansen, *In Northern Mists,* 2:89; Peyrère, "Histoire de Groenland," 220.

24. Nansen, *In Northern Mists,* 2:77–79.

25. MacRitchie, "Kayak in North-Western Europe," 496–97.

26. W. S. Laughlin, comment, *Current Anthropology* 4:1 (February 1963): 78.

27. Ostermann, ed., *Knud Rasmussen's Posthumous Notes,* 43, 53, 53n.

28. Ibid., 4, 7n, 9, 9n, 33, 52–60, 53n, 60–62.

29. Winsor, *Narrative and Critical History,* 1:60; Letter of Guðmundur Ólafsson to Jack Forbes, November 28, 1991; Jones, *Norse Atlantic Saga,* 5–8; Letter of Thor Magnusson, Director, National Museum of Iceland, to Jack Forbes, May 3, 1989.

30. Meldgaard, "Prehistoric Cultures," 25, 28, 30–32, 34, 36.

31. Whitaker, "Scottish Kayaks" (1954), 99, 101–2, Biggar, "Voyages of the Cabots," 501–2, 540, 540n.

32. Nooter, *Old Kayaks,* 8–9, Whitaker, "Scottish Kayaks" (1954), 99, 101–2.

33. Rink, *Eskimo Tribes,* 86, 107, 113; Nansen, *Pa Ski Over,* photo section; Schultz-Lorentzen, *Dictionary,* 9.

34. Ostermann, *Knud Rasmussen's Notes,* 17, 24, 51–52.

35. MacRitchie, "The Kayak in North Western Europe," 496; Sturtevant and Quinn, "This New Prey: Eskimos in Europe in 1567, 1576, and 1577," 118n; and Dale

Idiens, "Eskimos in Scotland: c. 1682–1924," 163–64, both in Feest, ed., *Indians and Europe;* Mikkelsen, "Kajakmanden Fra Aberdeen," 55–56, 58.

36. Peyrère, "Histoire du Groenland," 226.

37. Grenier, "The Basque Whalers of Labrador," in Ireland, *Atlantic Visions,* 109; and Severin, "Voyage of Brendan," 772–90.

38. Maurer, *Island,* 15; and De Roo, *History,* 169, 169n.

39. Ostermann, *Knud Rasmussen's Notes,* 64–65; Peyrère, "Histoire du Groenland," 207; Gaffarel, "Histoire," 11; Jones, *Norse Atlantic Saga,* 96, 181; Jones, "Historical Evidence for Viking Voyages to the New World," in Guralnick, *Vikings in the West,* 10.

40. Cooper, "Eskimo Voyages," 20–21.

41. Nordby, "Sea Kayaks," 9, 11, 13; Turk, "Ocean Chaos," 41.

42. Meldgaard, "Prehistoric Cultures," 20–34; Dumond, *Eskimos and Aleuts,* 89, 97–98.

43. McGhee, "Norse and Eskimos in Arctic Canada," in Guralnick, *Vikings in the West,* 42.

44. Birket-Smith, *Ethnography,* 34.

45. Dumond, *Eskimos and Aleuts,* 154.

46. Jac. Baumgarten, *A General Account of the Continent of America* (1751), as cited in Pontopiddan, *Natural History,* 235. See also Harp Jr., *Cultural Affinities,* 9–10.

47. McGhee, "Norsemen and Eskimos," in Guralnick, *Vikings in the West,* 40; Dumond, *Eskimos and Aleuts,* 97, 98, 145; Meldgaard, "Prehistoric Cultures," 30–31; Morrison, "Dating Thule Culture," 66–67; Park, "Dorset-Thule Succession," 203–13; Maxwell, *Prehistory,* 251–52.

48. Pringle, "Hints of Frequent," 783, 785; Pringle, "New Respect," 766–67; McGhee, "Norsemen and Eskimos," in Guralnick, *Vikings in the West,* 45, 48.

49. Pringle, "New Respect," 766–77; McGhee, "Norsemen and Eskimos," in Guralnick, *Vikings in the West,* 42.

50. Grenier, "The Basque Whalers," in Ireland, *Atlantic Visions,* 122; Sturlason, *Heimskringla,* 195; Peyrère, "Histoire de Groenland," 230; Friederici, *Der Charakter,* 3:68. Gad, *History of Greenland* 1:49; Egede, *Description,* xlvi. The slave trade was outlawed by Denmark only in 1792, to end by 1802. See also Lindroth, *Faunal Connections,* 16, 21.

51. Birket-Smith, *Ethnography,* 35.

52. McGhee, "Norsemen and Eskimos," in Guralnick, *Vikings in the West,* 50.

53. Jones, "Historical Evidence," in Guralnick, *Vikings in the West,* 5–6; Bury, *Cambridge Medieval History,* 3:310, 315; Peyrère, "Histoire de Groenland," 207; Adam of Bremen, *History of the Archbishops,* 220–21; Egede, *Description,* xli, xlii.

54. Charles de la Roncière, *Histoire de la Marine,* 399.

55. Winsor, *Narrative and Critical History,* 1:61n.

56. Pontanus, *Rerum Danicarium,* 96–98; Winsor, *Narrative and Critical History,* 1:61; Egede, *Description,* xxi; Jones, "Historical Evidence," in Guralnick, *Vikings in the West,* 8; Friederici, *Der Charakter,* 3:48–49.

57. Egede, *Description,* xliii-xliv.

58. Adam of Bremen, *History of the Archbishops,* 218; Gad, *History of Greenland,* 1:53; Jones, "Historical Evidence," in Guralnick, *Vikings in the West,* 9.

59. Jones, "Historical Evidence," in Guralnick, *Vikings in the West,* 12; Winsor, *Narrative and Critical History,* 1:68.

60. Gaffarel, "Histoire," 11; Jones, *North Atlantic Saga,* 96; Jones, "Historical Evidence," in Guralnick, *Vikings in the West,* 10.

61. Fiske, *Discovery of America,* 224; McGovern, "The Lost Norse Colony of Greenland," in Guralnick, *Vikings in the West,* 19; Peyrère, "Histoire du Groenland," 192–93; McGhee, "Norsemen and Eskimos," in Guralnick, *Vikings in the West,* 44; Thalbitzer, *Phonetical Study,* 27–28, 35n.

62. Thalbitzer, *Phonetical Study,* 26–27.

63. Ibid., 28–29, 29n.

64. Ibid., 27–28; McGhee, "Norse and Eskimos," in Guralnick, *Vikings in the West,* 44; Winsor, *Narrative and Critical History,* 1:69; Gad, *History of Greenland,* 1:88, 173, 181; Kaalund, *Art of Greenland,* 176–78; Keller, "Eastern Settlement," 57–58; Olson and Bourne, eds., *The Northmen,* 71–72n; Birket-Smith, *Ethnography,* 7–8; Morison, *European Discovery,* 60.

65. Keller, "Eastern Settlement," 61, 102, Svital, "Greenland Viking Mystery," 38–39; McGovern, "The Lost Norse Colony," in Guralnick, *Vikings in the West,* 19; Morison, *European Discovery,* 61; Ingstad, *Westward to Vinland,* 23, 26.

66. Thalbitzer, *Phonetical Study,* 20, 20n, citing D. Grantz; *Histoire von Grön-land,* 2:313 (further publication information unavailable), and an early map of the region.

67. Gad, *History of Greenland,* 1:49; Nansen, *In Northern Mists,* 2:18–19; Morison, *European Discovery,* 56; Anderson et al., *Norse Discovery of America,* 327; Torfaeus, *History of Ancient Vinland,* 58.

68. MacRitchie, "Kayak in North-Western Europe," 505–6; Nansen, *In Northern Mists,* 2:269; Thalbitzer, *Phonetical Study,* 33; Birket-Smith, *Ethnography,* 8.

69. Morison, *European Discovery,* 37; Keller, "Eastern Settlement Reconsidered," 60, 65; Birket-Smith, *Ethnography,* 8; Biggar, "Voyages of the Cabots," 496, 542n; Gad, *History of Greenland,* 1:181; Magnus, *De Gentibus,* 48.

70. Biggar, "Voyages of the Cabots," 494, 532; Morison, *European Discovery,* 51, 95, 162; Harrisse, *Discovery of North America,* 13; Harrisse, *John Cabot,* 43. It is also claimed that French sailors reached Labrador in 1487. See Roncière, *Histoire,* 400n; Forbes, *Africans and Native Americans,* 21. There is a tradition of an English visit to Greenland in circa 1360. See Ingstad, *Westward to Vinland,* 89, 95.

71. Harrisse, *John Cabot,* 142–48; Morison, *European Discovery,* 66–67, 205; Biggar, "Voyages of the Cabots," 489n, 490, 554, 560; Harrisse, *Discovery of North America,* 38; David Beers Quinn, *England and the Discovery,* 118; Hoffman, *Cabot to Cartier,* 17.

72. Morison, *European Discovery,* 70, 216, 218, 219; Biggar, "Voyages of The Cabots," 564–85; Hoffman, *Cabot to Cartier,* 29; Foreman, *Indians Abroad,* 7.

73. Harrisse, *Découverte et Evolution,* 45; Hoffman, *Cabot to Cartier,* 29; Biggar, "Voyages of the Cabots," 580–81n.

74. Biggar, "Voyages of the Cabots," 585, 586n; Foreman, *Indians Abroad,* 7; Parry, ed., *European Reconnaissance,* 286–87; Harrisse, *Découverte,* 46; Ingstad, *Westward to Vinland,* 223–25.

75. Biggar, "Voyages of the Cabots," 587–89; Quinn, *England and the Discovery,* 117; Forbes, *Africans and Native Americans,* 21, 28–31.

76. Olearius, *Vermehrte Newe Beschreibung,* 171; Schultz-Lorentzen, *Dictionary,* 158–59. Significantly, López de Gómara, in the 1550s, gives the distance from Fayal (Azores) to Greenland, thus indicating Portuguese visits. He also says that the Inuits were "valiant" and "handsome people, navigating with ships covered above with skin." López de Gómara, *Historia General,* 22. It should also be noted that for many years the Portuguese considered Greenland and parts of northeast America to fall on their side of the line that the Papacy had drawn, separating the Spanish from Portuguese zones of conquest. Also see Morison, *European Discovery,* 72.

77. Marshall, *History and Ethnography,* 4, 14, 22; Howley, *The Beothuks,* 12.

Chapter 7: *Native Americans Crossing the Atlantic after 1493*

1. Forbes, *Africans and Native Americans,* 24, 28–34; Benzoni, *History of the New World* (1857), 11, 78.

2. Forbes, *Africans and Native Americans,* 43–45. See also Harrisse, *John Cabot,* 223–25, 422; Dominguez Ortiz, "La Esclavitud," 376.

3. Forbes, *Africans and Native Americans,* 33, 42–47.

4. Ibid., 42, 45, 47.

5. Ibid., 46

6. Reportedly, smoking is noticed in Sevilla in 1607; Forbes, *Africans and Native Americans,* 42. See also Dominguez Ortiz, "Esclavitud," 165–56.

7. Forbes, *Africans and Native Americans,* 58–59; Hemming, *Red Gold,* 264–65, 441–43; Verlinden, *L'Esclavage,* 1:837.

8. Forbes, *Africans and Native Americans,* 39–40; Brasio, *Os Pretos,* 75–82, 88–89, 111n; Pires de Lima, *Mouros,* 60–61; Saunders, *Social History,* 180n, 211n.

9. Forbes, *Africans and Native Americans,* 36, 51, 53–54.

10. Foreman, *Indians Abroad,* 32.

11. Forbes, *Africans and Native Americans,* 47–52; Gonsalves, *Tempo,* 219–20, 231–33, 263, 265; Stedman, *Narrative,* 2:324; Buve, "Traffic."

12. Forbes, *Africans and Native Americans,* 55–56; Foreman, *Indians Abroad,* 8, 14–24, 28; Sidney Lee, "Call of the West," 316–22; Friederici, *Der Charakter,* 3:208–11. O'Brien, "Memorial Autobiográfico," 103; Morales Padron, *Jamaica,* 430; Hemming, *Het Rode Goud,* 23; Shyllon, *Black People,* 6, 11, 122; Quinn, *England and Discovery,* 390, 403, 419–20, 428, 430; Southey, *History,* xxxvii; Leach, *Flintlock,* 225–26; Ure, *Prince Henry,* 72; Fryer, *Staying Power,* 27–31.

13. Forbes, *Africans and Native Americans,* 56–58.

14. Honour, *New Golden Land,* 14, 15, 29; William C. Sturtevant, "First Visual Images of Native America," in Chiapelli et al., *First Images,* 1:421–23. Also see Dickason, "The Traffic Was Two-Way," for more information. Harald E. L. Prins also provides interesting details about Americans arriving in Europe from 1493 through 1620. See Prins, 175–95.

15. Forbes, *Africans and Native Americans,* 53; Southey, *History,* 414, 422; Hemming, *Het Rode Goud,* 23, 25; Leite, *Novas Cartas,* 109; Staden, *True History,* 177n, 178n.

16. Foreman, *Indians Abroad,* 33.

17. Steck, *Dürer,* 107–8, 114, 132; Forbes, *Africans and Native Americans,* 48; Staden, *True History,* 120, 176n, 183n.

18. Chambers, *Thomas More,* 118, 123, 139–40; Wells, *Outline of History,* 770–73.

19. Hemming, *Red Gold,* 288; O'Brien, "Memorial Autobiográfico," 100–101.

20. Forbes, *Africans and Native Americans,* 51–52.

21. I was fortunate to meet many Lokonos and Caribs living in Holland in 1980 and again in 1983–84.

22. Keller, "Eastern Settlement," 61–62; Veyrin, *Les Basques,* 45; Sturtevant and Quinn, in Feest, *Indians and Europe,* 62–64; Nansen, *In Northern Mists,* 2:86; López de Gómara, *Historia General,* 22.

23. Herrmann, *Conquest by Man,* 258–59, 266; Lappenberg, *Hamburgische Chroniken,* 169, 187.

24. Birket-Smith, *Ethnography,* 15; Veyrin, *Les Basques,* 45–46; LaFarga Lozano, *Los Vascos,* 27–28; Sturtevant and Quinn, in Feest, *Indians and Europe,* 62–64; F. Y. Powell, "Iceland," *Werner Encyclopaedia,* 12:656.

25. Sturtevant and Quinn, in Feest, *Indians and Europe,* 61–62; Sturtevant, in Chiapelli, *First Images,* 1:438, 440; Peter Mason, "Ethnography of the Old World Mind," 552; Dickason, "Traffic Was Two-Way," 72. A Dutch source of 1578 may indicate that a man was also seen in 1566–67. See Nooter, *Old Kayaks,* 73.

26. Birket-Smith, "Earliest Eskimo Portraits," 5–13; Sturtevant and Quinn, in Feest, *Indians and Europe,* 72–81; Honour, *New Golden Land,* 16, 67–68.

27. Whitaker, "Scottish Kayaks Reconsidered," 43; Keller, "Eastern Settlements," 64.

28. Hans Plischke, "Eine Verschlagung von Eskimo," 125; Sturtevant and Quinn, in Feest, *Indians and Europe,* 85–86.

29. Stöcklein, "Naturgeschichtl.," 513–14; Hennig, *Terrae Incognitae,* 291.

30. Delpar, *The Discoverers,* 303–4;

31. Peyrère, "Histoire du Groenland," 218–21, 231; Friederici, *Der Charakter,* 3:71–72; Olearius, *Vermehrte,* 166.

32. MacRitchie, "Kayak in North-Western Europe," 502, 510; Peyrère, "Histoire du Groenland," 222–27; Friederici, *Der Charakter,* 3:73; Whitehead, "Earliest Extant Painting of Greenlanders," in Feest, *Indians and Europe,* 144. See also Dam-Mikkelsen and Lundbaek, *Etnografiske Genstande,* 3ff.

33. Nooter, *Old Kayaks,* 5; Souter, *Story of Our Kayak,* 11.

34. Nooter, *Old Kayaks,* 5, 64; MacRitchie, "Kayak in North-Western Europe," 498–99; Birket-Smith, "Ethnography," 9; Rochefort, *Histoire Naturelle,* 188–204.

35. Idiens, in Feest, *Indians and Europe,* 163; Olearius, *Vermerhte,* 166–67; Peyrère, "Histoire du Groenland," 229.

36. Olearius, *Vermerhte,* 167–72; Whitehead, in Feest, *Indians and Europe,* 144–45; Dam-Mikkelsen and Lundbaek, *Etnografiske,* 3ff.

37. Nooter, *Old Kayaks,* 6, 10.

38. Whitaker, "Scottish Kayaks," 43.

39. MacRitchie, "Kayak in North-Western Europe," 500–501.

40. Wallace, *Description,* 28–29.

41. MacRitchie, "Kayak in North-Western Europe," 497–99; Souter, *Story of Our Kayak,* 12, 14.

42. Brand, *Brief Description,* 17, 50–51.

43. Ibid., 35, 79–80, 110–12.

44. Douglas, *General Description,* 109, 114–15; Reid, *Illustrated Catalogue,* 51; Souter, *Story of Our Kayak,* 9, 11, 13–16; Whitaker, "Scottish Kayaks," 42; Idiens, in Feest, *Indians and Europe,* 171.

45. Souter, *Story of Our Kayak,* 17.

46. MacRitchie, "Kayak in North-Western Europe," 503–10; Whitaker, "Scottish Kayaks," 99–101; Marwick, *Folklore,* 14–15, 23, 25–29, 48; Bassett, *Legends and Superstitions,* 178–79; Dennison, "Orkney Folk-Lore: Sea Myths," 113–20; Dennison, "Orkney Folk-Lore: Selkie Folk," 171–73, 175; MacRitchie, *Fians, Fairies,* 30–35; Horace Beck, *Folklore,* 220–23; Thomson, *People of the Sea,* 146, 159; Nansen, *In Northern Mists,* 1:203–4, 211–12; Reidar Th. Christiansen, "Norwegian Research," 89, 89n; Schiern, "Une Enigme Ethnographique," 279–80.

47. Reese, "Red Indian Visit," 334–37; Foreman, *Indians Abroad,* 56–63, 82–85, 109–16.

48. See Forbes, *Africans and Native Americans,* 63; and Feest, *Indians and Europe,* 609–24. Feest presents a rather negative view of modern Native American visits to Europe. Sidney Lee, "The Call of the West," gives a great deal of information on early Native American visits to England, but with a very racist and anti-native, as well as ill-informed, perspective. Much better is Alden T. Vaughan's "Trinculo's Indian: American Natives in Shakespeare's England," in Hulme and Sherman, eds., *"The Tempest,"* 49–59.

49. Many scholars deal with the topic of the American influence upon Europe after 1492: examples are Brandon, *New Worlds for Old;* Crosby Jr., *The Columbian Exchange;* Hulme and Jordanova, eds., *The Enlightenment;* Brotherston, "Candide and Native America," in Hulme and Jordanova, eds., *The Enlightenment,* and Arciniegas, *America in Europe.*

Bibliography

Manuscripts and Unpublished Materials

City of Gloucester, Museums, Annual Report to the City Council, April 1, 1951 to March 31, 1952.

Eskimo Kayaks in Aberdeen (pamphlet prepared by Marischal Museum, University of Aberdeen, Scotland, no date).

Fox Tree, "How Native People . . . Sailing Ships Discovered Europe and Other Lands Before 1492," photocopied brochure, ca. 1990.

Letter of H. Tr— to Sir Thomas Chaloner, Cottonian manuscript Julius F. VI. f431 (now ff453–462), British Library, London. Translated by Winfried Schleiner and Laetitia Yaendal for the author.

"Mediaeval Pottery from Bull Lane, Gloucester." Copy of a single-sheet typed ms. supplied by D. M. Rennie to Jack D. Forbes, October 25, 1993, as an enclosure to a letter.

"The Mystery of the Lost Red Paint People." Film. T. W. Timreck, editor and director. Bullfrog Films, with W. N. Goetzmann, 1987.

Nichols, Johanna. "The First Four Discoveries of America: Linguistic Evidence." Presentation to Annual Meeting of the American Association for the Advancement of Science, February 16, 1998. Photocopy.

Pitt Rivers Museum accession lists. Pitt Rivers Museum, Oxford, England.

Interviews

Orihuela, Juan Carlos, and Martha Cajias, interview with, by Jack D. Forbes. March and July 1993.

Rennie, D. M., interview with, by Jack D. Forbes. May 6, 1994, Oxford, England.

Rhodes, John F., interview with, by Jack D. Forbes. May 1993, Gloucester, England.

Correspondence in the Author's Possession

Ange, Simún V., Føroya Fornminnissavn (Faeroe Museum), to Jack Forbes, September 12, 1991.

Blackwood, B., to J. F. Rhodes, June 18, 1968 (copy).

———, to J. F. Rhodes, December 18, 1967 (copy).

Clarke, D. V., to Charles Hunt, August 19, 1985 (copy).

Cowie, Trevor, to Jack D. Forbes, August 16, 1991.

Dumond, Don E., to Jack D. Forbes, December 9, 2002.

Foxxon, Andrew, to Charles Hunt, August 29, 1985 (copy).

Griffiths, David, History Librarian, University of York, to Jack D. Forbes, September 6, 1991.

Hassall, T. G., to Jack D. Forbes, August 6, 1992.

Hunt, Charles, to Andrew Foxxon, September 10, 1985 (copy).

———, to David Clarke, August 15, 1985 (copy).

———, to Jack D. Forbes, August 17, 1992.

Keller, Christian, Universitët i Oslo, to Jack D. Forbes, July 31, 1991.

Magnusson, Thor, Director, National Museum of Iceland, to Jack D. Forbes, May 3, 1989.

McCartney, Allen P., to Jack D. Forbes, December 20, 2002 (email).

McGhee, Robert, to Jack D. Forbes, n.d.

J. McShane to Jack D. Forbes, November 1, 1991.

Moore, Donald, to Jack D. Forbes, July 1, 1993.

Mowat, Linda, to Jack D. Forbes, July 19, 1993.

Ólafsson, Guðmundur, National Museum of Iceland, to Jack D. Forbes, November 28, 1991.

Penhallwick, R. D., to Jack D. Forbes, June 7, 1993.

Rennie, D. M., to Jack D. Forbes, October 25, 1993.

Rhodes, J. F., to B. E. B. Fagg, December 5, 1967 (copy).

———, to B. E. B. Fagg, June 6, 1968 (copy).

———, to Jack D. Forbes, August 30, 1991.

Siverts, Henning, University of Bergen, to Jack D. Forbes, August 24, 1991.

Smith, Kevin P., to Jack D. Forbes, February 6, 2003 (email).

Sommer-Larsen, Anne, University of Trondheim, to Jack D. Forbes, August 23, 1991.

Sveinbjarnardóttir, Guðrún, to Jack D. Forbes, October 30, 1991.

Sveinbjorn Rafnsson, University of Iceland, to Jack D. Forbes, August 26, 1991.

Svensson, Tom G., to Jack D. Forbes, May 8, 1989.

Valle Perez, José Carlos, Director, Museo de Pontevedra, to Jack D. Forbes, December 4, 1991.

Young, I. F., Brisbane, Australia, to Jack D. Forbes, October 16, 1991.

Photographs and Postcards

Photograph by Paule Mexel Bertrand Desollier, N. 2289, published by Réunion des musées natiónaux, 1993 (postcard).

"St. Nicholas' Collegiate Church" and "Welcome to St. Nicholas Collegiate Church, Galway," postcards. No dates; acquired 1989.

Newspapers

Note that all newspaper pages and volumes refer to a "Newspaper Cuttings Index" and collection at the Gloucester City Library.

Cheltenham Examiner, November 1861, v. 1.

Gloucester Journal
   May 19, 1883, v. 6, 13, 15, 52
   August 28, 1948, v. 14, 496
   January 1, 1951, v. 15, 360
   July 7, 1951, v. 15, 314.

Unpublished Dissertations

Heizer, Robert Fleming. "Aboriginal Whaling in the Old and New Worlds." Doctoral dissertation, University of California, Berkeley, 1941.

Keller, Christian. "The Eastern Settlement Reconsidered." Doctoral dissertation, University of Oslo, 1989.

Books and Articles

Acosta, Joseph de. *Historia Natural y Moral de las Indias.* México: Fondo de Cultura Económica, 1940.

————. *The Natural and Moral History of the Indies.* Translated by Edward Grimston. London: Hakluyt, 1880.

Adam of Bremen. *History of the Archbishops of Hamburg-Bremen.* Translated and edited by Francis J. Tschan. New York: Columbia University Press, 1959.

Alcedo, Antonio de. *The Geographical and Historical Dictionary of America and the West Indies.* Translated by G. A. Thompson. London: Carpenter, 1812.

Allcard, Edward C. *Single-Handed Passage.* New York: Norton, 1950.

Anderson, Rasmus B., Arthur Middleton Reeves, and North Ludlow Beamish. *The Flatey Book and Recently Discovered Vatican Manuscripts Concerning America as Early as the Tenth Century.* London: Noroena Society, 1906.

————, ed. *The Norse Discovery of America.* London: Noroena, 1911.

Annandale, Nelson. *The Faeroes and Iceland.* Oxford: Clarendon, 1905.

Arbolí y Fernando, Servando, and Simón de la Rosa y López. *Biblioteca Colombina: Catálogo de sus Libros Impresos*. Sevilla: Rasco, 1888.

"Archaeologists Confirm Antiquity of Prehistoric Canoes." *News from Indian Country*, 14: 24 (December 2000–January 2001): 15B.

Arciniegas, Germán. *America in Europe: A History of the New World in Reverse*. Translated by Gabriela Arciniegas and R. Victoria Arana. New York: Harcourt, Brace, Jovanovich, 1986.

Armstrong, Richard. *The Discoverers*. New York: Praeger, 1969.

"Artifact in Iceland Reveals its Ancient American Origins." *American Archaeology* 1:4 (1997): 6–7.

Ashe, Geoffrey, Thor Heyerdahl, Helge Ingstad, J. V. Luce, Betly J. Meggers, and Birgitta L. Wallace. *The Quest for America*. London: Pall Mall, 1971.

Avebury, Lord, Baron. See Lubbock, Sir John.

Bajot, Louis Marin. *Abrégé historique et chronologique des principaux voyages de découvertes par mer*. Paris: Imprimerie Royal, 1836.

Ballard, W. L. *The Yuchi Green Corn Ceremonial: Form and Meaning*. Los Angeles: UCLA American Indian Studies, 1978.

Bancroft, Hubert Howe. *The Native Races of the Pacific States*. San Francisco: History Company, 1886.

Barcía Carballido y Zuñiga, Andrés González de. *Ensayo Cronológico, para la Historia General de la Florida hasta el de 1722*. Madrid: Oficina Real, Franco, 1723.

Baring-Gould, S. *Curious Myths of the Middle Ages*. New York: Longmans, Green, 1897.

Barrau, Jacques, ed. *Plants and the Migrations of Pacific Peoples*. Honolulu: Bishop Museum Press, 1963.

Barrère, Pierre. *Nouvelle Relation de la France Equinoxiale*. Paris: Piget, Monneville, Durand, 1743.

Bassett, Fletcher S. *Legends and Superstitions of the Sea and of Sailors*. Chicago: Belford, Clarke, 1885.

Bates, H. W., ed. *Illustrated Travels*. London: Cassell, Petter and Galgin, n.d.

Beck, Horace. *The American Indian as a Sea-Fighter in Colonial Times*. Mystic, Conn.: Marine Historical Society, 1959.

———. *Folklore and the Sea*. Middletown, Conn.: Wesleyan University Press, 1973.

Beck, Peggy V., Anna Lee Walters, and Nia Francisco, *The Sacred Ways of Knowledge, Sources of Life*. Tsaile, Navajo Nation, Arizona: Navajo Community College Press, 1995.

Beckwith, Martha Warren. *Myths and Hunting Stories of the Mandan and Hidatsa Sioux*. Poughkeepsie, N.Y.: Vassar College, 1930.

Beddoe, John. *The Races of Great Britain*. Bristol: Arrowsmith, 1885, and London: Hutchinson, 1971.

Belt, Thomas. *The Naturalist in Nicaragua*. London: Dent, 1911.

Bembo, Pietro. *Opere del Cardinale Pietro Bembo*. 2 vols. Venezia: Hertzhauser, 1729.

Benson, Elizabeth, P., ed., *The Sea in the Pre-Columbian World*. Washington, D.C.: Dumbarton Oaks Research Library, Harvard University, 1977.

Benzoni, Geronimo. *La Historia del Mundo Nuevo*. Translated by Carlos Radicati Primeglio. Lima: University of San Marcos, 1967.

————. *History of the New World*. London: Hakluyt, 1857.

Bernaldez, Andrés. *Memorias del Reinado de los Reyes Católicos*. Madrid: Real Academia de la Historia, 1962.

Biard, Pierre. *Relation de la Nouvelle France,* in Reuben Gold Thwaites, ed. *The Jesuit Relations and Allied Documents: Travels and Explorations (1610–1791)*. Cleveland: Burrows, 1897.

Biggar, H. P. "The Voyages of the Cabots and of the Corte-Reals to North America and Greenland," *Revue Hispanique,* 10:35–36 (1903): 485–593.

Birket-Smith, Kaj. "The Earliest Eskimo Portraits," *Folk: Dansk Etnografisk Tidsskrift* 1 (1959): 5–13.

————. *Ethnography of the Egedesminde District*. København: Bianco Lunos, 1924.

Bisschop, Eric de. *Kaimiloa*. Paris: Plon, 1939.

Black, Robert F. "Geology and Ancient Aleuts, Amchatka and Unmak Islands, Aleutians," *Arctic Anthropology* 11:2 (1974): 126–40.

Boorstin, Daniel J. *The Discoverers*. New York: Random House, 1983.

Bourne, Julius E., and Edward Gaylord, eds. *The Northmen, Columbus and Cabot, 985–1503*. New York: Scribner's Sons, 1906.

Bourque, Bruce J. "Comments on the Late Archaic Populations of Maine: The View from the Turner Farm," *Arctic Anthropology* 12:2 (1975): 35–44.

Bowen, Emrys George. *Saints, Seaways and Settlements*. Cardiff: University of Wales Press, 1969.

Boxer, C. R. *The Portuguese Seaborne Empire, 1415–1825*. London: Hutchinson, 1969.

————. *Race Relations in the Portuguese Colonial Empire, 1415–1825*. Oxford: Clarendon, 1963.

Boyd, Julian P., ed. *Indian Treaties Printed by Benjamin Franklin, 1736–62*. Philadelphia: Historical Society of Pennsylvania, 1938.

Bradstreet, Theodore E., and Ronald B. Davis. "Mid-Post-Glacial Environments in New England with Emphasis on Maine," *Arctic Anthropology* 12:2 (1975): 18–19.

Brain, Jeffrey P. "The Great Mound Robbery," *Archaeology* 41:3 (May–June 1988): 18–25.

Brand, John. *A Brief Description of Orkney, Zetland, Pightland Firth, and Caithness*. Edinburgh: Mosman, 1701.

Brandon, William. *New Worlds for Old: Reports from the New World and their Effect on the Development of Social Thought in Europe, 1500–1800.* Athens: Ohio University Press, 1986.

Brasio, Antonio. *Os Pretos em Portugal.* Lisbon: Agencia das Colonias, 1944.

Bristol and Gloucestershire Archaeological Society. *A Gloucestershire and Bristol Atlas.* London: Percy, Lund, Humphries, 1961.

Brochado, Costa. *Descobrimento do Altantico.* Lisbon: Comissâo Executiva das Comemoracoes do Quinto Centenário da Morte de Infante D Henrique, 1958.

Brotherston, Gordon. *Book of the Fourth World: Reading the Native Americas through Their Literature.* Cambridge, U.K.: Cambridge University Press, 1992.

———. *Image of the New World: The American Continent Portrayed in Native Texts.* London: Thames and Hudson, 1979.

Bruce, Lesley J., David J. Anstee, Frances A. Spring, and Michael J. A. Tanner, "Band 3 Memphis Variant II," *Journal of Biological Chemistry* 269:23 (June 10, 1994): 16155–16158.

Burl, Aubrey. *The Stonehenge People.* London: Dent, 1987.

Bury, J. B., ed. *The Cambridge Medieval History.* Cambridge: Cambridge University Press, 1930.

Buve, R. Th. J. "Traffic of American Indians and Negroes to Holland During the 17th and 18th Centuries; its Social Impacts." *36 Congreso Internacional de Americanistas* 4, Sevilla, 1966.

Camden, William. *Britannia.* London: Bishop, 1594.

———. *Britannia.* Francofurti: Bringeri, 1616. A reprint of the 1594 edition.

———. *Britannia.* Translated by Richard Gough. London: Stockdale, 1806. A translation from the 1607 Latin edition.

Cantarella, Eva. *Pompei: I volti dell'Amore.* Milano: Mondadori, 1998.

Carew, Jan. *Fulcrums of Change.* Trenton, N.J.: Africa World Press, Inc., 1988.

Cary, M., and Warmington, E. H. *The Ancient Explorers.* Baltimore: Penguin, 1963.

Castellanos, Juan de. *Elegías de Varones ilustres de Indias.* Madrid: Rivadeneyra, 1857.

———. *Historia del Nuevo Reino de Granada,* edited by Antonio Paz y Mélia. Madrid: Pérez Dubrull, 1886.

Chambers, R.W. *Thomas More.* London: Cape, 1962.

Chen, Tiemei, Yang Quan, and Wu En. "Antiquity of Homo Sapiens in China," *Nature* 368:3 (March 1994): 55–56.

Chiappelli, Fredi, Michael J. B. Allen, and Robert L. Benson, *First Images of America: The Impact of the New World on the Old.* Berkeley: University of California Press, 1976.

Childrey, Joshua. *Britannia Baconia, or the Natural Rarities of England, Scotland, and Wales.* London: by the author, 1661.

Christiansen, Reidar Th. "Norwegian Research on the Language and Folklore of the Lapps," *Journal of the Royal Anthropological Institute of Great Britain and Ireland* 80, parts 1 and 2 (1950): 89–94.

Ciudad Real, Antonio de, and Alonso de San Juan, *Relación Breve y Verdadera de Algunas Cosas de las Muchas Que Sucedieron al Padro Fray Alonso Ponce.* Madrid: Calero, 1873.

Coe, Michael D. *Lords of the Underworld: Masterpieces of Classic Maya Ceramics.* Princeton, N.J.: Princeton University Press, 1978.

Cole, Robert. *Rental of All the Houses in Gloucester, AD 1455.* Gloucester: Bellows, 1890.

Colombo, Fernando. *Vita di Cristoforo Colombo.* Londres: Dulau, 1867.

Colón, Cristobal. *Textos y Documentos Completos, Relaciones y Viajes, Cartas y Memoriales,* edited by Consuelo Varela. Madrid: Alianza Universidad, 1982.

Colón, Ferdinand Hernando. *The Life of the Admiral Christopher Columbus.* Translated and edited by Benjamin Keen. New Brunswick: Rutgers, 1959.

Colón, Fernando. *Vida del Almirante, Don Cristóbal Colón,* edited by Ramon Iglesia. México: Fondo de Cultura Economica, 1947.

Columbus, Christopher. *The Diario of Christopher Columbus' First Voyage to America, 1492–1493,* abstracted by Bartolomé de las Casas, translated and edited by Oliver Dunn and James E. Kelley Jr. Norman: University of Oklahoma Press, 1989.

Cooper, Richard. "Eskimo Voyages to Europe: Evidence the Inuits Canoed the Atlantic," *Oceans* 17:5 (September–October 1984): 20–22.

Cordry, Donald. *Mexican Masks.* Austin: Texas, 1980.

Cornell, Jimmy. *World Cruising Routes.* Camden, Maine: International Marine Publishing, 1987.

Court de Gebelin, Antoine. *Monde Primitif.* Paris: Valleyre, 1781.

Crane, Werner W. "An Historical Note on the Westo Indians." *American Anthropologist,* n.s., 20 (1918): 332.

———. *The Southern Frontier, 1670–1732.* Ann Arbor: University of Michigan Press, 1956.

Crawford, Michael H. *The Origins of Native Americans.* Cambridge: Cambridge University Press, 1998.

Cremo, Michael A., and Richard L. Thompson, *Forbidden Archaeology: The Hidden History of the Human Race.* San Diego: Bhaktivedanta, 1993.

Crosby, Alfred W., Jr. *The Columbian Exchange: Biological and Cultural Consequences of 1492.* Westport, Conn.: Greenwood, 1972.

———. "The Early History of Syphilis: A Reappraisal." *American Anthropologist* 71:2 (April 1969): 218–27.

d'Agnese, Joseph. "Not Out of Africa." *Discover* 23:8 (August 2002): 54–56.

d'Ailly, Pierre. *Imago Mundi, with Annotations by Christopher Columbus.* Boston: Massachusetts Historical Society, 1927.

———. *Ymago Mundi,* edited by Edmond Buron. Paris: Maisonneuve Frères, 1930.

Dalgarno, James. "Donations to the Museum and Library," *Proceedings of the Society of Antiquaries of Scotland,* January 10, 1876, vol. 11, p. 407.

Dam-Mikkelsen, Bente, and Torben Lundbaek, *Etnografiske Genstande in Det Kongelige danske Kunstkammer 1650–1800.* Copenhagen: National museet, 1980.

Daniels, Geoff. *Human Blood Groups.* Oxford: Blackwell, 1995.

d'Arbois de Jubainville, H. *Les Premiers Habitants de L'Europe.* Paris: Dumoulin, 1877.

———. *Les Premiers Habitants de L'Europe.* Second edition, with G. Dottin. Paris: Thorin, 1889–94.

Darvill, Timothy. *Prehistoric Britain.* London: Batsford, 1987.

d'Ávezac-Macaya, Parm. *Notice des Découvertes Faites au Moyen-Age Dans L'Océan Atlantique.* Paris: Fain et Thunot, 1845.

Debes, Lucas Jacobson. *Faeroe; and Foeroa Reserata: That is, a Description of the Islands and Inhabitants of Faeroe.* Translated by John Sterpin. London: Iles, 1676.

Delpar, Helen, ed. *The Discoverers: An Encyclopedia of Explorers and Exploration.* New York: McGraw-Hill, 1980.

Dennison, W. Traill. "Orkney Folk-Lore: Sea Myths." *The Scottish Antiquary* 7, part 3 (1893): 112–20.

———. "Orkney Folk-Lore: Selkie Folk." *The Scottish Antiquary* 7, part 4 (1893): 171–77.

De Roo, P. *History of America Before Columbus.* Philadelphia: Lippincott, 1900.

De Vries, Jan. *Altnordisches Etymologisches Wörterbuch.* Leiden: Brill, 1961.

Díaz-Alejo, R., and Joaquin Gil, eds. *América y el Viejo Mundo.* Buenos Aires: Gil-Editor, 1942.

Díaz del Castillo, Bernal. *The Discovery and Conquest of México.* Translated by A. P. Maudslay, edited by Irving A. Leonard. New York: Grove, 1956.

———. *Historia Verdadera de la Conquista de la Nueva España.* México: Porrua, 1955.

Dickason, Olive Patricia. "The Traffic Was Two-Way: Amerindians in Europe," in *Ancient Travellers: Proceedings of the 27th Annual Conference of the Archaeological Association of the University of Calgary, 2002.*

Dillehay, Thomas D. *The Settlement of the Americas: A New Prehistory.* New York: Basic Books, 2000.

Dixon, E. James. *Quest for the Origins of the First Americans.* Albuquerque: University of New Mexico Press, 1993.

Domínguez Ortiz, Antonio. "La Esclavitud en Castilla durante la Edad Moderna." *Estudios de Historia Social de España.* Madrid: Instituto Balmes de Sociología, 1952.

Doran, Glen H., David N. Dickel, and Lee A. Newsom, "A 7,290 Year Old Bottle Gourd from the Windover Site, Florida," *American Antiquity* 55:2 (1990): 354–60.

Douglas, Francis. *A General Description of the East Coast of Scotland.* Paisley: Alexander Weir, 1782.

Douglass, William A., and John Bilbao. *Amerikanuak: Basques in the New World.* Reno: University of Nevada Press, 1975.

Dumond, Don E. *The Eskimos and Aleuts.* London: Thames and Hudson, 1987.

Du Tertre, Jean Baptiste. *Histoire General des Antilles.* Paris: Jolly, 1667–71.

Edwards, Clinton R. "Possibilities of Pre-Columbian Maritime Contacts among New World Civilizations," *Mesoamerican Studies* 4 (1969): 3–10.

Edwards-Moulds, J. N., and J. B. Alperin, "Studies of the Diego Blood Group among Mexican-Americans," *Transfusion* 26:3 (1986): 234–36.

Egede, Hans. *A Description of Greenland.* London: Allman, 1818.

Eusebius. *Chronicon, id est Teporu breviariu,* as added to by Joannes Multivallis and Henricum Stephanum. Paris: Henricum Stephanum, 1512.

Evans, E. Estyn. *The Personality of Ireland: Habitat, Heritage and History.* Belfast: Blackstaff, 1981.

———, and C. F. C. Hawkes. "An Eskimo Harpoon-head from Tara, Co. Down (?)." *Ulster Journal of Archaeology* 3:127–32.

Fabregas Valcarce, Ramon. "Dos Objetos de Origen Oriental: Una Revisión." *Pontevedra Arqueológica* 2 (1985–86): 83–90.

Feest, Christian, ed., *Indians and Europe.* Aachen: Alano, 1989.

Fernandez de Oviedo, Gonzalo. *De la Natural Historia de las Indias.* Madrid: Editorial Summa, 1942.

———. *Historia General y Natural de las Indias.* Madrid: Biblioteca de Autores Españoles, 1959.

Fernández-Armesto, Felipe. *Before Columbus: Exploration and Colonisation from the Mediterranean to the Atlantic, 1229–1492.* London: Macmillan, 1987.

———. *Columbus.* Oxford: Oxford University Press, 1991.

"The First Americans." *Discover* 22:1 (January 2001): 52.

"The First Americans, circa 20,000 BC" *Discover* 19:6 (June 1998): 24.

"The First Americans in Europe." *Atlantic Monthly,* 70:417 (July 1892): 140–42.

Fiske, John. *The Discovery of America.* Boston: Houghton-Mifflin, 1892.

———. *The Dutch and Quaker Colonies in America.* Boston: Houghton Mifflin, 1899.

Fite, Emerson D., and Archibald Freeman, *A Book of Old Maps Delineating American History.* New York: Dover, 1969.

Fitzhugh, William W. "A Maritime Archaic Sequence from Hamilton Inlet, Labrador, " *Arctic Anthropology* 12:2 (1975): 1–6, 117–32.

———, and Peter S. Allen, "Secrets of the Lost Red Paint People," review, *Archaeology* 40:6 (November–December 1987): 71, 84.

Forbes, Jack D. *Africans and Native Americans.* Urbana-Champaign: University of Illinois Press, 1993.

———. *Afro-Americans in the Far West.* Berkeley: Far West Laboratory, 1967.

———. *Apache, Navaho, and Spaniard.* Norman: University of Oklahoma Press, 1960.

———. *Apache, Navaho, and Spaniard.* Norman: University of Oklahoma Press, 1994.

———. *Atlas of Native History.* Davis: D-Q University Press, 1982.

———. *Columbus and Other Cannibals.* Brooklyn: Autonomedia, 1992.

———. *The Indian in America's Past.* Englewood Cliffs, N.J.: Prentice-Hall, 1964.

———. "Indigenous Americans: Spirituality and Ecos," *Daedalus* 130:4 (Fall 2001): 283–300.

———. *Native Americans of California and Nevada.* Healdsburg: Naturegraph, 1967, and Happy Camp: Naturegraph, 1982.

———. "Nature and Culture: Problematic Concepts for Native Americans," in John A. Grim, ed., *Indigenous Traditions and Ecology.* Cambridge: Harvard University Press, 2001.

———. "The Urban Tradition among Native Americans," in Susan Lobo and Kurt Peters, eds. *American Indians and the Urban Experience.* Walnut Creek, Calif.: Altamira, 2001.

——— et al., eds. *Handbook of Native American Studies and Chronology of Native American History.* Davis: Tecumseh Center, 1970.

Forde, C. Daryll. *Ancient Mariners: The Story of Ships and Sea Routes.* New York: Morrow, 1928.

Foreman, Carolyn Thomas. *Indians Abroad, 1493–1938.* Norman: University of Oklahoma Press, 1943.

Fournier, Père Georges. *Hydrographie, contenant la théorie et la pratique de toute les parties de la navigation.* Paris: DuPuis, 1643–67.

Friederici, Georg. *Der Charakter der Entdeckung und Eroberung Amerikas Durch die Europäer.* 3 vols. Osnabrück: Zeller, 1969.

———. *Die Schiffahrt der Indianer.* Stuttgart: Strecker and Schröder, 1907.

Fryer, Peter. *Staying Power: The History of Black People in Britain.* London: Pluto, 1984.

Gad, Finn. *The History of Greenland.* London: Hurst, 1970.

Gaffarel, Paul. *Étude sur les Rapports de l'Amerique et de L'Ancien Continent Avant Christophe Colomb.* Paris: Thorin, 1869.

———. *Histoire de la Découverte de L'Amérique Depuis les Origines Jusqu'à la Mort de Christophe Columb.* Paris: Rousseau, 1892.

Gallois, L. Review of Paul Gaffarel, *Histoire de la Découverte de l'Amerique Depuis les Origines Jusqu'à la Mort de Christophe Columb,* 1892 edition, in *Revue Historique* 50:1 (September–December 1892): 158.

Galvano, Antonie. *The Discoveries of the World.* Amsterdam: De Capo, 1969.

"The Game of Coman Played by the North American Indians." *The Dublin Penny Journal* 1, 1832–33.

Garcia, Gregorio. *Origen de los Indios del Nuevo Mundo.* México: Fondo de Cultura Economica, 1981.

Gaskell, T. F. *The Gulf Stream.* London: Cassell, 1972.

Gerbault, Alain. *The Fight of the "Firecrest."* New York: Appleton, 1926.

———. *The Gospel of the Sun.* London: Hodder and Stoughton, 1933

———. *Seul à travers l'Atlantique.* Paris: Grasset, 1924..

Girard, Raphael. *Esotericism of the Popol Vuh.* Translated by Blair A. Moffet. Pasadena, Calif.: Theosophical University Press, 1979.

Gjessing, Gutorm. "Circumpolar Stone Age," *Acta Arctica* 2 (1944): 1–70.

Glare, P. G. W., ed. *Oxford Latin Dictionary.* Oxford: Clarendon, 1982.

Glob, P. V. *The Bog People: Iron Age Man Preserved.* Translated by Rupert Bruce-Mitford. Ithaca, N.Y.: Cornell University Press, 1969. Also London: Faber and Faber, 1969.

Gonsalves de Mello, José Antonio. *Tempo dos Flamengos.* Sao Paulo: Olympio, 1947.

Goodman, Jeffrey. *American Genesis.* New York: Summit, 1981.

Gordon, Cyrus H. *Before Columbus: Links Between the Old World and Ancient America.* New York: Crown, 1971.

Gottesman, Jane. "French Rower Expected to Reach Land Today." *San Francisco Chronicle,* November 21, 1991, A8.

Graves, John. *The History of Cleveland.* Carlisle: Jollie, 1808.

Greenberg, Joseph H. "A *CA* Book Review," *Language in the Americas* in *Current Anthropology* 28:5 (December 1987): 647–67.

———, Christy G. Turner II, Stephen L. Zegura. "The Settlement of the Americas: A Comparison of the Linguistic, Dental, and Genetic Evidence," *Current Anthropology* 27:5 (December 1986): 477–97.

Greenman, E. F. "The Upper Palaeolithic and the New World," *Current Anthropology* 4:1 (February 1963): 41–91.

Grinnell, George B., ed. *Pawnee Hero Stories and Folk Tales.* Lincoln: Nebraska, 1961.

Guralnick, Eleanor, ed. *Vikings in the West.* Chicago: Archaeological Institute of America, 1982.

Hacquebord, Louwrens, and René de Bok, *Spitsbergen 79°N.B.* Amsterdam: Elsevier, 1981.

Haeser, Heinrich. *Lehrbuch der Geschichte der Medicin und der epidemischen Krankheiten.* Jena: Gustav Fischer, 1882.

Hardiman, James. *The History of the Town and County of Galway.* Dublin: Folds, 1820.

Harp, Elmer, Jr. *The Cultural Affinities of the Newfoundland Dorset Eskimo.* Ottawa: National Museum, 1964.

Harrisse, Henry. "Autographes de Christophe Colomb Récemment Découverts," *Revue Historique* 50:1 (January–April 1893): 59–64.

———, ed. *Christophe Colomb, Son Origine, Sa Vie, Ses Voyages, Sa Famille et Ses Descendants.* Paris: Leroux, 1884.

———. *Découverte et Evolution Cartographique de Terreneuve et des Pays Circonvoisins.* Paris: Welter, 1900.

———. *The Discovery of North America.* Amsterdam: Israel, 1961.

———. *Don Fernando Colón, Historiador de su Padre.* Sevilla: Sociedad de Bibliófilos Andaluces, 1871.

———. *Excerpta Columbiniana.* Paris: Welter, 1887.

———. *John Cabot, The Discoverer of North America and Sebastian Cabot his Son.* Chicago: Argosy-Antiquarian, 1968.

———. *Juan et Sebastian Cabot, leur Origine et leurs Voyages.* Amsterdam: Grünen, 1968.

———. *Notes on Columbus.* New York: Riverside Press, 1866.

Heaviside, John T. C. *American Antiquities, or, the New World the Old, the Old World the New.* London: Trübner, 1868.

Hemming, John. *Het Rode Goud.* Utrecht: Spectrum, 1980.

———. *Red Gold: The Conquest of the Brazilian Indians.* London: Macmillan, 1978.

Hennig, Richard. *Columbus und seine Tat: Eine kritische Studie über die Vorgeschichte der Fahrt von 1492.* Bremen: Arthur Geist, 1940.

———. *Terrae Incognitae.* Leiden: Brill, 1944.

———. *Von Rätselhaften Ländern.* München: Delphin Verlag, 1925.

Herrera y Tordesillas, Antonio de. *The General History of the Vast Continent and Islands of America* [Originally pub. 1740]. New York: AMS, 1973.

Herrmann, Paul. *Conquest by Man: The Saga of Early Exploration and Discovery.* Translated by Michael Bullock. New York: Harper & Brothers, 1954.

Heyerdahl, Thor. *Early Man and the Ocean.* London: Allen and Unwin, 1978.

———. "Feasible Ocean Routes to and from the Americas in Pre-Columbian Times." *American Antiquity* 28:4 (1963): 484–88.

Hoffman, Bernard G. *Cabot to Cartier: Sources for a Historical Ethnography of Northeastern North America, 1457–1550.* Toronto: University of Toronto Press, 1961.

Holden, Constance. "Tooling Around: Dates Show Early Siberian Settlement," *Science* 275 (February 28, 1997): 1268.

Honour, Hugh. *The New Golden Land: European Images of America from the Discoveries to the Present Time.* New York: Pantheon, 1975.

Horn, Georg. *De originibus americanis libri quatuor.* The Hague: Vlacq, 1652.

Hornell, James. "Sea-Trade in Early Times." *Antiquity* 15 (September 1941): 233–56.

————. *Water Transport: Origins and Early Evolution.* Cambridge: Cambridge University Press, 1946.

Hourani, George Fadlo. *Arab Seafaring.* Beirut: Khayats, 1963.

Howley, James P. *The Beothuks or Red Indians: The Aboriginal Inhabitants of Newfoundland.* Cambridge: Cambridge University Press, 1915.

Hristov, Romeo, and Santiago Genovés. "Mesoamerican Evidence of Pre-Columbian Transoceanic Contacts." *Ancient Mesoamerica* 10 (1999): 207–13.

Hulme, Peter. *Colonial Encounters: Europe and the Native Caribbean, 1492–1797.* London: Methuen, 1986.

————, and Ludmilla Jordanova, eds. *The Enlightenment and its Shadows.* London: Routledge, 1990.

————, and William H. Sherman, eds. *"The Tempest" and its Travels.* London: Reaktion Books, 2000.

————, and Neil L. Whitehead, eds. *Wild Majesty: Encounters with Caribs from Columbus to the Present Day.* Oxford: Clarendon, 1992.

Humboldt, Alexander de. *Examen Critique de L'Histoire de la Géographie de Nouveau Continent.* Paris: Gide, 1836.

————. *Views of Nature.* Translated by E. C. Otté and Henry G. Bohn. London: Bohn, 1950.

Hyde, Walter Woodburn. *Ancient Greek Mariners.* New York: Oxford University Press, 1947.

Ibarra Grosso, Dick Edgar. *Los Hombres Barbados en la América Precolombina.* Buenos Aires: Kier, 1997.

Ingstad, Helge. Translated by Eric J. Friis. *Westward to Vinland.* New York: St. Martin's Press, 1969.

Ireland, John de Courcy, and David C. Sheehy, eds. *Atlantic Visions.* Dublin: Boole, 1989.

————. *Ireland and the Irish in Maritime History.* Dublin: Glendale, 1986.

————. *Wreck and Rescue on the East Coast of Ireland.* Dublin: Glendale Press, 1983.

Ispizúa, Segundo de. *Historia de la Geografía y de la Cosmografía.* 2 vols. Madrid: Mateu, 1926.

————. *Historia de la Geografía y de la Cosmografía en las Edades Antigua y Media.* 2 vols. Madrid: Reunidas, 1922.

Jacobs, Melville. "Coos Narrative and Ethnologic Texts," *University of Washington Publications in Anthropology* 8:1 (April 1939): 45–51.

Jane, Cecil. *The Voyages of Christopher Columbus.* London: Argonaut, 1930.

Jenkins, J. T. *A History of the Whale Fisheries.* Port Washington: Kennikat, 1971.

Jennings, Jesse D. *Ancient North Americans.* San Francisco: Freeman, 1983.

———, and Norbeck, Edward, eds. *Prehistoric Man in the New World.* Chicago: University of Chicago Press, 1971.

Jett, Stephen C., "Nicotine and Cocaine in Egyptian Mummies and THC in Peruvian Mummies: A Review of the Evidence and of Scholarly Reaction," pre-print furnished by Stephen C. Jett, from *Precolumbiana: A Contacts Journal of Long Distance* 2:4.

———. "'Ye'iis Lying Down,' A Unique Navajo Sacred Place," in *Navajo Religion and Culture: Selected Studies,* edited by David M. Brugge. Santa Fe: Museum of New Mexico Publications in Anthropology, no. 17, 1981.

Jones, Gwyn. *The Norse Atlantic Saga.* Oxford: Oxford University Press, 1964.

Jorrin y Bromosio, Jose Silverio. *Los Autografos Ineditos del Primer Virez de las Indias.* Habana: Soler, Alvarez, 1888.

Joseph, E. L. *History of Trinidad.* Trinidad: Mills, 1938.

Kaalund, Bodil. *The Art of Greenland: Sculpture, Crafts, Painting.* Translated by Kenneth Tindall. Berkeley: University of California Press, 1983.

Kauffmann-Doig, Federico. *Ancestors of the Incas.* Translated by Eudogio Guzmán. Memphis: Wonders, 1998.

Komnoff, Manuel, ed. *Contemporaries of Marco Polo.* New York: Dorset, 1989.

Krishnamurthy, R. V., K. A. Syrup, M. Baskaran, A. Long, "Late Glacial Climate Record," *Science* 269:15 (September 1995): 1565.

Kunstmann, Friedrich. *Die Entdeckung Amerikas.* München: Asher, 1859.

———. *Die Kenntnis Indiens in Fünfzehnten Jahrhundert.* München: Weis, 1863.

Kunzig, Robert. "Erectus Afloat," *Discover* 20:1 (January 1999): 80.

LaFarga Lozano, Adolfo. *Los Vascos en el Descubrimiento y Colonización de America.* Bilbao: Gran Enciclopedia Vasca, 1973.

Lappenberg, J. M. *Hamburgische Chroniken in Niedersächsischer Sprache.* Wiesbaden: Sändig, 1971.

Las Casas, Bartolomé de. *Historia de las Indias.* México: Fondo de Cultura Economica, 1951.

Laughlin, W. S. "Comment" in *Current Anthropology* 4:1 (February 1963).

Lawson, John. *History of North Carolina.* Richmond, Va.: Garrett and Massie, 1952.

Leach, Douglas Edward. *Flintlock and Tomahawk.* New York: Norton, 1966.

Lechuga, Ruth D., and Chloë Sayer, *Mask Arts of Mexico.* London: Thames and Hudson, 1994.

Lee, Sidney. "The Call of the West: America and Elizabethan England," *Scribner's Magazine* 42:3 (September 1907).

Lefroy, J. Henry, ed. *The Historye of the Bermudaes or Summer Islands.* London: Hakluyt Society, 1882.

Leite, Serafim, ed. *Monumenta Brasiliae.* 4 vols. Rome: Society of Jesus, 1960.

———. *Novas Cartas Jesuíticas.* Sao Paulo: Editora Nacional, 1940.

Lewis, Charlton T., and Charles Short. *A Latin Dictionary.* Oxford: Clarendon, 1958.

Linderman, Frank B., ed. *Pretty Shield.* Lincoln: Nebraska, 1972.

Lindeström, Peter. *Geographica Americae,* ed. Amandus Johnson. Philadelphia: Swedish Colonial Society, 1925.

Lindroth, Carl H. *The Faunal Connections Between Europe and North America.* New York: Wiley, 1957.

Llop, Elena, and Francisco Rothhammer. "A Note on the Presence of Blood Groups A and B in Pre-Columbian South America," *American Journal of Physical Anthropology* 75 (1988): 107–11.

Lobo, Susan, and Kurt Peters, eds. *American Indians and the Urban Experience.* Walnut Creek, Calif.: Altamira, 2001.

Longpérier, Henri Adrien Prevost de. "Notice des Bronzes Antiques exposés dans les Galeries du Musée du Louvre," Paris, 1868. Cited in Shiern, F., *"Une Enigme Ethnographique."*

López de Gómara, Francisco. *Historia de la Conquista de México.* Caracas: Ayacucho, 1979.

———. *Historia General de las Indias.* Madrid: Calpe, 1922.

———. *Historia General de las Indias y vida de Hernan Cortes.* Caracas: Ayacucho, 1979.

Lorant, Stefan, ed. *The New World: The First Pictures of America.* New York: Dull, Sloan & Pearce, 1965.

Loven, Sven. *Origins of the Tainan Culture.* Goteborg: Elanders, 1935.

Lubbock, Sir John, Lord Avebury. *Pre-Historic Times. As Illustrated by Ancient Remains and Manners and Customs of Modern Savages.* New York: J. A. Hill, 1904.

Lutz, Hartmut. "German Indianthusiasm," in Colin G. Calloway, Gerd Gemünden, and Suzanne Zomtop, eds. *Germans and Indians: Fantasies, Encounters, Projections.* Lincoln: University of Nebraska Press, 2002, 167–83.

———. "'Okay, I'll Be Their Annual Indian for Next Year': Thoughts on the Marketing of a Canadian Indian Icon in Germany," in Helmbrecht Breinig, ed., *Imaginary (Re-) Locations.* Tübingen: Stauffenburg Verlag, 2003, 217–45.

Lyschander, Claudius Christopherson. *Gronlandske Chronica.* Kobenhavn; Laurent, 1608.

MacLeish, William H. *The Gulf Stream: Encounter with the Blue God.* Boston: Houghton Mifflin, 1989.

MacRitchie, David. *Fians, Fairies, and Picts.* London: Kegan Paul, Trench, Trübner, 1893.

———. "Der Kajak im nördlichen Europa." *Petermanns Geographische Mitteilungen* 51:1911, nos. 1 and 2, pp. 284–86.

―――. "The Kayak in North-Western Europe," *Journal of the Royal Anthropological Institute* 42 (1912): 493–510.

―――. "Kayaks of the North Sea." *The Scottish Geographical Magazine,* 28 (1912): 126–33.

―――. *The Testimony of Tradition.* London: Kegan Paul, Trench, Trübner, 1890.

Magnus, Olaf. *De Gentibus Septentrionalibus Historia.* Ambergae: Forsteriano, 1599.

Magnusson, Magnus, and Hermann Pálsson, trans. and ed. *The Vinland Sagas: The Norse Discovery of America.* Hammondsworth: Penguin, 1965.

Mallet, Paul Henry. *Northern Antiquities.* London: Carnan, 1847.

Marshall, Ingeborg Constanze Luise. *Beothuk Bark Canoes: An Analysis and Comparative Study.* Ottawa: Canadian Ethnology Service, 1985.

―――. *A History and Ethnography of the Beothuk.* Montreal: McGill-Queen's University Press, 1996.

Mártir de Anglería, Pedro. *Decadas del Nuevo Mundo.* 2 vols. Mexico: Porrua, 1965.

―――. *Opera.* Graz: Akademische Druk, 1966.

―――. *Opus Epistolarum.* Amsterdam: Elsevier, 1670.

Marwick, Ernest W. *The Folklore of Orkney and Shetland.* London: Batsford, 1975.

Mason, Peter. "The Ethnography of the Old World Mind: Indians and Europe," *Anthropos* 84 (1989): 549–54.

Maurer, Konrad. *Island von Seiner Ersten Entdecking bis zum Untergange des Freistaats.* München: Kaiser, 1874.

Maxwell, Moreau S. *Prehistory of the Eastern Arctic.* Orlando: Academic, 1985.

McKillop, Heather. *In Search of Maya Sea Traders.* College Station: Texas A&M University Press, 2005.

McKusick, Marshall B. "Aboriginal Canoes in the West Indies," *Yale University Publications in Anthropology* 63 (1960): 2–11.

Mela, Pomponius. *The Work of Pomponius Mela, Cosmographer, Concerning the Situation of the World.* Translated by Arthur Golding. London: T. Hackett, 1585.

Meldgaard, Jørgen. "The Prehistoric Cultures in Greenland: Discontinuities in a Marginal Area," in *Continuity and Discontinuity in the Inuit Culture of Greenland.* Groningen: Arctic Centre, University of Groningen, November 1976.

Menon, Shanti. "More than a Pointy Rock." *Discover* 18:1 (January 1997): 10.

―――. "The Earthmovers." *Discover* 19:2 (February 1998): 30.

Merrien, Jean, a.k.a René Marie de la Poix de Fréminville. *Christophe Colomb.* Paris: Denoël, 1955.

―――. *Christopher Columbus: The Mariner and the Man.* Translated by Maurice Michael. London: Odhams, 1958.

―――. *Dictionnaire de la Mer.* Paris: Laffont, 1958.

―――. *Les Drames de la Mer.* Paris: Hachette, 1961.

———. *Les Mémoires d'un Yacht.* Paris: Denöel, 1953.

———. *Lonely Voyagers.* Translated by J. H. Watkins. London: Hutchinson, 1954.

———. *Les Navigateurs Solitaires.* Paris: Denöel, 1953.

———. *Possession de la Mer.* Paris: Denöel, 1956.

———. *La Vie Quotidienne des Marins au Moyen Age: Des Vikings aux Galères.* Paris: Hachette, 1969.

———. *La Vie Quotidienne des Marins au Temps du Roi Soleil.* Paris: Hachette, 1964.

Metzer, David J. "Pleistocene Peopling of the Americas." *Evolutionary Anthropology* 5 (1993): 157–61.

Mewhinney, H. *A Manual for Neanderthals.* Austin: University of Texas Press, 1972.

Mikkelsen, Ejnar. "Kajakmanden Fra Aberdeen," *Grønland* (Kryolitselskabet øresund Aktieselskab), February 1954, no. 2.

Mitchell, R. J. *The Laurels and the Tiara, Pope Pius II, 1458–1464.* London: Harvill, 1962.

Mithun, Marianne. "Studies of North American Indian Languages." *Annual Review of Anthropology* (1990): 309–25.

Morales Padrón, Francisco. *Canarias y America.* Madrid: Gela-Espasa-Calpe-Argantonio, 1988.

———. *Jamaica Española.* Sevilla: Escuela de Estudios Hispano-Americanos, 1952.

Morison, Samuel Eliot. *Admiral of the Ocean Sea: A Life of Christopher Columbus,* 2 vols. Boston: Little, Brown, 1942.

———. *The European Discovery of America, The Northern Voyages* A.D. *500–1600.* New York: Oxford, 1971.

———. *Journals and Other Documents on the Life and Voyages of Christopher Columbus.* New York: Heritage Press, 1963.

———. *Portuguese Voyages to America in the Fifteenth Century.* Cambridge, Mass.: Harvard University Press, 1940, and New York: Octagon, 1965 and 1973.

Morrison, David. "Dating Thule Culture," *Arctic Anthropology* 26:2: 48–77.

Mourant, A. E., Ada C. Kopec, and Kazimiera Domaniewska-Sobczak. *The Distribution of Human Blood Groups.* London: Oxford, 1976.

Müller, Werner. *America, the New World or the Old?* Translated by Anne Heritage and Paul Kremmel. Frankfurt: Lang, 1989.

Muñoz, Juan Bautista. *Historia del Nuevo Mundo.* Madrid: Ibarra, 1793.

Murphy, Henry C. *The Voyage of Verrazano.* Albany: Munsell, 1875–76, and Freeport, New York: Books for Libraries Press, 1970.

Nadaillac, Marquis de. *Prehistoric America.* Translated by N. d'Anvers. London: Murray, 1885.

Nansen, Fridtjof. *In Northern Mists, Arctic Exploration in Early Times.* Translated by

Arthur G. Chater, Westport: Greenwood, 1970, originally pub. as *In Northern Mists.* New York: Stokes, 1911. These editions have the same pagination.

———. *Pa Ski Over Grønland-Eskimoliv.* Oslo: Aschehoug, 1942.

Nelson, E. Charles. "Exotic Drift Fruits and Seeds from the Coasts of Britain and Adjacent Islands,"*Journal of the Royal Institution of Cornwall,* n.s., 10:2 (1988): 147–86.

———. "Models for the Moment—Pre-Norman and Medieval," *English Heritage, Book of Tintagel, Arthur and Archaeology* (London: B. T. Batsford, 1993.

Nelson, J. G. "Geography of the Balsa," *The American Neptune* 21:3 (July 1961): 157–95.

Nicholson, Henry B. *Topiltzin Quetzalcoatl, the Once and Future Lord of the Toltecs.* Boulder: University Press of Colorado, 2001.

Nitecki, Matthew H., and Doris V. Nitecki, eds. *Origins of Anatomically Modern Humans.* New York: Plenum, 1994.

Nooter, Gert. *Old Kayaks in the Netherlands.* Leiden: Brill, 1971.

Nordby, Will. "Sea Kayaks," *Oceans* 17:5 (September–October 1984): 8–19.

Norman, Charles. *Discoverers of America.* New York: Thomas Y. Crowell, 1968.

O'Brien, Bernard. "Memorial Autobiográfico de Bernardo O'Brien," edited by Thomas G. Mathews. *Caribbean Studies* 10:1 (April 1970): 89–106.

"Ohio Artifacts Contradict 'Land Bridge' Theory of Migration." *News from Indian Country* 15:2 (January 2001): 14A.

Olearius, Adam. *Vermehrte Newe Beschreibung Der Muscowitischen und Persischen Reyse.* Tübingen: Niemeyer, 1971.

Olson, Julius E., and Edward Gaylord Bourne, eds. *The Northmen, Columbus and Cabot, 985–1503.* New York: Scribner, 1906.

Ostermann, H., ed. *Knud Rasmussen's Posthumous Notes on the Life and Doings of the East Greenlanders in Olden Times.* København: Reitzels, 1938.

O'Sullivan, M. D. *Old Galway: The History of a Norman Colony in Ireland.* Cambridge: Heffer, 1942.

Parival, I. de, *Las Délices de la Hollande.* Paris: Librairies du Palais, 1665.

Park, Robert W. "The Dorset-Thule Succession in Arctic North America: Assessing Claims for Culture Contact." *American Antiquity* 58 :2 (1993): 203–34.

Parker, John. *Discovery: Developing Views of the Earth.* New York: Scribner, 1972.

Parks, Douglas R., A. Wesley Jones, and Robert C. Hollow, eds., *Earth Lodge Tales from the Upper Missouri.* Bismarck: Mary College, n.d.

Parry, J. H., ed. *The European Reconnaissance, Selected Documents.* New York: Walker, 1968.

Patterson, Thomas C. *America's Past: A New World Archaeology.* Glenview, Ill.: Foresman, 1973.

Pausanias, *Description of Greece.* Translated by W. H. S. Jones. Vol. 1. London: Heinemann 1959.

Payne, Edward John. *History of the New World Called America.* 2 vols. Oxford: Clarendon, 1899.

Penhallwick, R. D. *Turtles off Cornwall, the Isles of Scilly, and Devonshire.* Truro: Dyllansow Pengwella, 1990.

Pennick, Nigel. *Lost Lands and Sunken Cities.* London: Fortean Tomes, 1987.

Peyrère, Isaac de la. "Histoire du Groenland," in *A Collection of Documents on Spitsbergen and Greenland.* London: Hakluyt, 1855.

———. *Relation de l'Islande.* Paris: Billaine, 1663.

———. *Relation du Groenland.* Paris: Courbe, 1647.

Piccolomini, Aeneas Sylvius. See Sylvius, Aeneas.

Pidgeon, Harry. *Around the World Single-Handed: The Cruise of the "Islander."* London: Hart-Davis, 1954.

Pigafetta, Antonio. *Primer Viaje en Torno del Globo.* Translated by Carlos Amoretti. Buenos Aires: Espasa Colpe, 1954.

Piggott, Stuart. *Ancient Europe.* Edinburgh: Edinburgh University Press, 1965.

———. *The Neolithic Cultures of the British Isles.* Cambridge: Cambridge University Press, 1954.

Pinkerton, John, ed. *A General Collection of the Best and Most Interesting Voyages and Travels in all Parts of the World.* London: Longman, 1812.

Pires de Lima, J. A. *Mouros, Judeus e Negros na História de Portugal.* Oporto: Livraria Civilizaçao, 1940.

Pliny. *Natural History.* Translated by H. Rackham. London: Heinemann, 1938.

Plischke, Hans. "Eine Verschlagung von Eskimo nach Holland aus dem Jahre 1577," *Petermanns Geographische Mitteilungen* 67 (1921): 125.

———. "Verschlagung von Bewohnern Amerikas nach Europa im Altertum und Mittelalter," *Petermanns Geographische Mitteilungen* 62 (1916): 93–95.

Pohl, Frederick Julius. *Atlantic Crossings Before Columbus.* New York: Norton, 1961.

Poix de Fréminville, René Marie de la. See Merrien, Jean.

Pontanus, John Isaac. *Rerum Danicarium Historia.* Amsterdam: Hondii, 1631.

Pontoppidan, Erich. *The Natural History of Norway.* London: Linde, 1755.

Posnansky, Arthur. *Las Americas son un nuevo mundo.* La Paz: Instituto Tiahuanacu, 1943.

———. *Precursores de Colon, Las Perlas Agri.* Buenos Aires: Sociedad de Historia Argentina, 1933.

———. *Tiahuanacu: The Cradle of American Man.* New York: Agustin, 1945–58.

Pringle, Heather. "Hints of Frequent Pre-Columbian Contacts," *Science* 288:5 (May 2000): 783–85.

———. "New Respect for Metal's Role in Ancient Arctic Cultures," *Science* 277:8 (August 1997): 766–67.

Prins, Harald E. L. "To the Land of the Mistogoches: American Indians Traveling to Europe in the Age of Exploration." *American Indian Culture and Research Journal* 17:1 (1993): 175–95.

Proceedings of the Cotteswold Naturalist's Field Club 11, 1895.

Proceedings of the Society of Antiquaries of Scotland 11, 1876.

Purchas, Samuel, ed. *Hakluytus Posthumus, or Purchas His Pilgrimes.* 20 vols. Glasgow: MacLehose, 1906.

———. *Purchas His Pilgrimage, or Relations of the World and the Religions Observed in All Ages.* 4 vols. London: Stansby, 1613.

Quinn, Bob. *Atlantean: Ireland's North African and Maritime Heritage.* London: Quartet, 1986.

Quinn, David Beers. *England and the Discovery of America.* New York: Knopf, 1974.

Ramusio, Giovanni Battista. *Navigationi e Viaggi.* 3 vols. Venetia: De Giunti, 1565, and *Navigazioni e Viaggi.* 6 vols. Torino: Einaudi, 1979.

Reese, T. R. "A Red Indian Visit to 18th-Century England," *History Today* 4:5 (May 1954): 334–37.

Reid, R. W. *Illustrated Catalogue of the Anthropological Museum, University of Aberdeen.* Aberdeen: University Press, 1912.

Reinaga, Fausto. *América India y Occidente.* La Paz: Ediciones Partido Indio de Bolivia, 1974.

"Réunion du 16. Mars 1859." *Bulletin de la Société des Antiquaries de France,* 1859.

Riley, Carroll L., J. Charles Kelley, Campbell W. Pennington, and Robert L. Rands, eds. *Man Across the Sea: Problems of Precolumbian Contacts.* Austin: University of Texas Press, 1971.

Rink, Henry. *The Eskimo Tribes.* Copenhagen: Reitzel, 1887–91 and New York: AMS Press, 1975.

Rivière, Peter. *Christopher Columbus.* Stroud, England: Sutton Publishing, 1999.

Robinson, Tim. *Stones of Aran: Pilgrimage.* Dublin: Lilliput and Wolfhound, 1986.

Robinson, William Albert. *10,000 Leagues Over the Sea.* New York: Harcourt Brace, 1932.

Roncière, Charles de la. *Histoire de la Marine Française Avant Christophe Colomb.* Paris: Plon, Nourrit, 1899, 1909.

Rochefort, Charles de (Cesar de). *Histoire Naturelle et Morale des Antilles de l'Amérique.* Rótterdam: Leers, 1658.

———. *The History of the Caribby-Islands.* Translated by John Davies. London: Dring and Starkey, 1666. (Also published as *The History of Barbados, St. Christophers, Nevis, St. Vincents . . . and the Rest of the Caribby-Islands.*)

Rose, J. Holland, A. P. Newton and E. A. Benians, eds. *Cambridge History of the British Empire.* Cambridge: Cambridge Cambridge University Press, 1930.

Ruiz de Montoya, Antonio. *"Tesoro" de la Lengua Guarani.* Madrid: Sanchez, 1639.

Rumeu de Armas, Antonio. *Libro Copiador de Cristóbal Colón.* Pittsburg: Latin American Literary Review Press, 1991.

Saco, José Antonio. *Historia de la Esclavitud de los Indios en el Nuevo Mundo.* Havana: Cultural, 1932.

———. *Historia de la Esclavitud desde los Tiempos mas Remotos Hasta Nuestros Dias.* Vol. 1: Paris: LaHure, 1875; Vol. 2: Paris: Kugelmann, 1875; Vol. 3: Barcelona: Jepús, 1877.

Sanderson, Ivan T. *Follow the Whale.* Boston: Little, Brown, 1956.

Sanger, David. "Culture Change as an Adaptive Process in the Maine-Maritimes Region," *Arctic Anthropology* 12:2 (1975): 60–75.

Sanz, Carlos. *La Geographia de Ptolomeo.* Madrid: Libraria General, 1959.

Saunders, A. C. de C. M. *A Social History of Black Slaves in Britain, 1441–1555.* Cambridge: Cambridge University Press, 1982.

Schele, Linda, and David Freidel. *A Forest of Kings: the Untold Story of the Ancient Maya.* New York: Morrow, 1990.

Schiern, F. *"Une Enigme Ethnographique de L'antiquité."* Translated by L. Morillot, in *Mémoires de la Société Royale des Antiquaries du Nord.* Copenhagen, n.s., 1878–83. 245–88.

Scholes, France V., and Ralph L. Roys. *The Maya Chontal Indians of Acalan-Tixchel: A Contribution to the History and Ethnography of the Yucatan Peninsula.* Norman: University of Oklahoma Press, 1968.

Schultz-Lorentzen, Christian. *Dictionary of the West Greenland Eskimo Language.* Copenhagen: Reitzels, 1927.

Scott, Lindsey. "Drift Timber in the West," *Antiquity* 25:99 (September 1951): 151–53.

Sébillot, Paul. *Légendes, Croyances, and Superstitions de la Mer.* Paris: Charpentier, 1886.

———. *Légendes Locales de la Haute-Bretagne.* Nantes: Sociètè des Bibliophiles Bretons, 1899.

———. *Traditions et Superstitions de la Haute-Bretagne.* Paris: Maisonneuve, 1881.

Severin, Timothy. "The Voyage of Brendan," *National Geographic* 152:6 (December 1977): 768–97.

Shutler, Richard, Jr., ed. *Early Man in the New World.* Beverly Hills: Sage, 1983.

Shyllon, Folarin. *Black People in Britain, 1555–1833.* London: Institute of Race Relations, 1977.

Simmons, R. T., J. A. Albrey, J. A. G. Morgan, and A. J. Smith. "The Diego Blood Group: Anti-Dia and the Di(a+) Blood Group Antigen Found in Caucasians," *Medical Journal of Australia,* 55:1 (March 9, 1968): 406–7.

Slocum, Victor. *Captain Joshua Slocum: The Life and Voyages of America's Best Known Sailor.* New York: Sheridan House, 1950.

———. *Sailing Alone Around the World.* New York: Blue Ribbon Books, 1900.

Smith, James F. "Heir to Columbus," *Modern Maturity,* 35:1 (February–March 1992).

Snow, Dean R. "The Passadumkeag Sequence," *Arctic Anthropology* 12:2 (1975): 46–59.

Sorensen, John L., and Martin H. Raish, *Pre-Columbian Contact with the Americas across the Oceans, an Annotated Bibliography.* Provo, Utah: Research Press, 1990. 2 vols.

Souter, William Clark. *The Story of Our Kayak and Some Others.* Aberdeen: University Press, 1934.

Southey, Robert. *History of Brazil.* London: Longman, 1822.

Staden, Hans. *The True History of His Captivity.* Translated and edited by Malcom Letts. London: Routledge, 1928.

Staden, Juan (Hans). *Vera Historia y Descripción de un País de los Salvages . . . en el Nuevo Mundo América.* Translated and edited by Edmundo Wernicke. Buenos Aires: Editorial Coni, 1944.

Steck, Max. *Dürer and his World.* Translated by J. Maxwell Brownjohn. London: Thames and Hudson, 1964.

Stedman, John Gabriel. *Narrative of a Five Years' Expedition.* Barre, Mass.: Imprint Society, 1971.

Stengel, Marc K. "The Diffusionists Have Landed," in *Atlantic Monthly* 235:1 (January 2000): 35–48.

Stephen, Leslie, and Sidney Lee, eds. *Dictionary of National Biography.* London: Oxford University Press, 1921–22.

Stöcklein, H. "Naturgeschichtl. Raritäten d. 16 Jahrhrdts. In d. Münchener Staats=Sammlgn.," *Das Bayerland,* 1911.

Stommel, Henry. *The Gulf Stream: A Physical and Dynamical Description.* Berkeley: University of California Press, 1965.

Stone, Richard. "Testing New Theory of Mammoth Extinction in the Cold Zone," *Discover* 22:2 (February 2001): 63.

Strabo, *The Geography of Strabo.* Translated by Horace Leonard Jones. London: Heinemann, 1917.

Stringer, Christopher B. "The Emergence of Modern Humans," *Scientific American* 263:6 (December 1990): 98–104.

Stuart, Anthony J. *Life in the Ice Age.* Aylesbury: Shire, 1988.

Sturlason, Snorre. *Heimskringla, or the Lives of the Norse Kings.* Edited by Erling Monsen and A. H. Smith. Cambridge: Heffer, 1932.

Sturtevant, William C. "The Significance of Ethnological Similarities Between

Southeastern North America and the Antilles," *Yale University Publications in Anthropology* 64 (1960): 3–58.

Svitil, Kathy A. "The Greenland Viking Mystery." *Discover* 18 (July 1997): 29.

Sylvius, Aeneas. *Asiae Europae Que Elegantissima Descriptio.* Paris: Chearallonium, 1534.

———. *Historia Rerum Ubique Gestarum Cum Locorum Descriptione Non Finita Asia Minor Incipit.* Brixiae: Britannicum, 1498.

———. *Opera Geographica et Historica.* Helmstadii: Sustermanni, 1699.

Tedlock, Dennis, trans. and ed. *Popol Vuh.* New York: Simon and Schuster, 1985.

Thalbitzer, William. *A Phonetical Study of The Eskimo Language.* New York: AMS, 1976.

Thompson, J. Eric S. "Canoes and Navigation of the Mayas and their Neighbors." *Journal of the Royal Anthropological Institute,* 79:1–2 (1949–50): 69–77.

———. *Maya History and Religion.* Norman: University of Oklahoma Press, 1970.

Thompson, Lucy. *To the American Indian.* Berkeley: Heyday, 1991.

Thomson, David. *The People of the Sea.* London: Granada, 1980.

Thorne, Alan G., and Milford H. Wolpoff. "The Multiregional Evolution of Humans." *Scientific American* 266:4 (April 1992): 76–83.

Tickell, Crispin. "Climate and History," *Oxford Today,* Hilary 8:2 (1996).

Tills, D., Ada C. Kopec, and Rosemary E. Tills, *The Distribution of the Human Blood Group and Other Polymorphisms,* Supplement 1. Oxford: Oxford University Press, 1983.

Todd, Michael. *The Northern Barbarians, 100 BC-AD 300.* Oxford: Blackwell, 1987.

Torfaeus, Thormod. *Ancient History of Orkney, Caithness, and the North.* Translated by Alexander Pope. Wick: P. Reid, 1866.

———. *The History of Ancient Vinland.* Translated by Charles G. Herkermann. New York: Shea, 1891.

Toscanelli, Paolo, and Henry Vignaud. *Toscanelli and Columbus.* London: Sands, 1902.

Tuck, James A. "The Northeastern Maritime Continuum: 8,000 Years of Cultural Development in the Far Northeast," *Arctic Anthropology* 12:2 (1975): 139–47.

———, and Robert McGhee. "Arctic Cultures in the Strait of the Belle Isle Region, Labrador," *Arctic Anthropology* 12:2 (1975): 76–91.

Turk, Jon. "Ocean Chaos." *Kayak Touring 2003* (special issue).

Ugurgieri della Beardenga, C. *Pio II Piccolomini.* Firenze: Olschki, 1973.

Ure, John. *Prince Henry the Navigator.* London: Constable, 1977.

Vázquez de Espinosa, Antonio. *Compendium and Description of the West Indies.* Translated by Charles Upson Clark. Washington: Smithsonian Institution, 1942.

Verlinden, Charles. *L'Esclavage dans l'Europe Médiévale*. Bruges: De Tempel, 1955.

Veyrin, Philippe. *Les Basques*. Bayonne: Musee Básque, 1947.

Volney, Constantin François de. *Oeuvres Completes*. Paris: Didot, 1837.

Wagner, Andreas Johann. *Geschichte der Urwelt*. Leipzig: L. Voss, 1845.

Wagner, Henry R., trans. and ed. *The Discovery of New Spain in 1518 by Juan de Grijalva*. Berkeley: Cortes Society, 1942.

Wallace, James. *A Description of the Isles of Orkney*. Edinburgh: Reid, 1693.

Waters, Michael R., Steven L. Forman, and James M. Pierson. "Diring Yuriakh: A Lower Paleolithic Site in Central Siberia," *Science* 275:28 (February 1997): 1281–83.

Wells, H. G. *The Outline of History*. New York: Macmillan, 1921.

Werner Encyclopaedia. Akron: Werner, 1908.

West, Frederick H. "Migrations and New World Origins," *The Review of Archaeology* 10:1 (Spring 1989): 158–66.

Westropp, Thomas Johnson. "Brasil and the Legendary Islands of the North Atlantic: Their History and Fable. A Contribution to the 'Atlantis' Problem," *Proceedings of the Royal Irish Academy*, 30, sec. 3 (1912–13): 223–40.

———. "Early Italian Maps of Ireland from 1300 to 1600, with Notes on Foreign Settlers and Trade," *Proceedings of the Royal Irish Academy*, 30, sec. 3 (1912–13): 373–76.

Whitaker, Ian. "The Scottish Kayaks and the 'Finn-men,'" *Antiquity*, 28:110 (June 1954).

———. "The Scottish Kayaks Reconsidered," *Antiquity*, 51:201 (March 1977).

Williams, Roger. *A Key Into the Language of America*. Merston, U.K.: Scholar Press, 1971.

Wilson, Allan C., and Rebecca L. Cann. "The Recent African Genesis of Humans," *Scientific American* 266:4 (April 1992): 68–73.

Winsor, Justin. *Christopher Columbus and How He Received and Imputed the Spirit of Discovery*. Boston: Houghton Mifflin, 1892.

———, ed. *Narrative and Critical History of America*. New York: Houghton, Mifflin, 1889.

Wright, Karen. "First Americans," *Discover* 20:2 (February 1999): 53–54.

Wuthenau, Alexander von. *The Art of Terracotta Pottery in Pre-Columbian Central and South America*. New York: Crown, 1965.

Wytfliet, Cornille. *Histoire Universelle des Indes, Orientales et Occidentales*. Douay: Fabri, 1604.

Young, George. *A History of Whitby and Streoneshalh Abbey*. Whitby: Clark and Medd, 1817.

Index

Page numbers for illustrations and maps are in italics.

JACK D. FORBES is professor emeritus of Native American Studies and Anthropology at the University of California, Davis. A historian and ethnohistorian, he has been a Guggenheim Fellow; a Fulbright Scholar at the University of Warwick; Tinbergen Chair at the Erasmus University of Rotterdam; a Lifetime Achievement Award recipient of the Before Columbus Foundation; a visiting scholar at Oxford University (Institute of Social Anthropology and Linacre College); visiting professor in Ethnic Studies at University of California, Berkeley; and visiting professor in literature at Essex University. He is the author of numerous books and other works, including *Apache, Navajo, and Spaniard* (1960), which helped to launch the field known as "the new American Indian history." Other books include *Africans and Native Americans; Columbus and Other Cannibals; Native Americans of California and Nevada; Aztecas del Norte: The Chicanos of Aztlan; Warriors of the Colorado; Native Americans and Nixon; The Indian in America's Past;* and *Nevada Indians Speak*. He is of Powhatan-Renàpe, Delaware-Lenàpe, and other Native American ancestry, as well as being of part European background.

The University of Illinois Press
is a founding member of the
Association of American University Presses.

———————————————————

Composed in 10.5/13 Hoefler Text
with Historical Fell Type display
at the University of Illinois Press
Designed by Dennis Roberts
Manufactured by Thomson-Shore, Inc.

University of Illinois Press
1325 South Oak Street
Champaign, IL 61820-6903
www.press.uillinois.edu